LOCOMOTIVES OF THE L.N.E.R. I

Class AI No. 4476 *Royal Lancer*

LOCOMOTIVES OF THE L.N.E.R. I

Part I

PRELIMINARY SURVEY

THE RAILWAY CORRESPONDENCE AND TRAVEL SOCIETY

First Impression 1963
Second Impression 1976
Third Impression 1997

ISBN 0 901115 11 8

**Published by The Railway Correspondence and Travel Society
11 Suffield Close, Long Stratton, Norfolk NR15 2JL, England**

Printed by Cave Printing, Leicester

CONTENTS

PREAMBLE TO THIRD IMPRESSION

The last section of this book presents additional information and revisions that have come to light over the three decades since first publication.

Many correspondents have provided additional information, confirmation and revisions. The Society would like to take this opportunity to express thanks to our L.N.E.R. series production team, for their efforts over many years which have produced the expert work on L.N.E.R. locomotives. The Society pays tribute to their labours of love.

PREFACE

The London & North Eastern Railway was the second largest of the four British railway systems formed under the Railways Act 1921 and its territory embraced most of the east of Great Britain from the Thames to the Moray Firth, in addition to large areas in the centre and north-west of both England and Scotland, with even a penetration into Wales at Wrexham.

The locomotives inherited by the L.N.E.R. from the seven major constituent companies, as well as several smaller lines, were naturally a varied collection. Many of the practices of these companies continued to flourish under the new regime but the policy of one company, the Great Northern Railway, became dominant due largely to the fact that Sir (then Mr.) Nigel Gresley, the Locomotive Engineer of the G.N.R., was called upon to take charge of locomotive design on the newly formed L.N.E.R., a position he held for just over eighteen years.

Within the compass of ten volumes an attempt will be made to describe in detail the history of the 10,000 or so locomotives owned at one time or another by the L.N.E.R. and the work they have done.

Before going further, a few words must be written concerning the origins of this project by members of the Railway Correspondence & Travel Society. In 1941 the Society produced a work entitled THE LOCOMOTIVES OF THE L.N.E.R. 1923-1937 written by K. Risdon Prentice and Peter Proud, much of the information therein having previously appeared in a series of articles in the Society's magazine, *The Railway Observer*, by the same authors. This book became a classic work of reference and after the War consideration was given to issuing a revised edition and information was collated and written for this purpose by the original authors and others. Permission was sought and granted for official railway records not previously available to be examined with a view to the checking of data. During the examination of these records an *embarras de richesse* was discovered and as a result the whole concept of the project underwent radical alteration. In 1951 the Society had commenced publication of a series on Great Western Railway locomotives based on information contributed by a team of Society members backed up by generous assistance given by the G.W.R. and the Western Region of British Railways in permitting access to official records. With this project as an example, though with a somewhat different approach, those concerned with the production of the revised L.N.E.R. work decided to expand considerably the scope of their efforts.

Additional authors, all knowledgeable in their chosen field, were empanelled and charged with the production of detailed locomotive class articles. Division of work among the team approximated to the pre-Grouping constituent companies that formed the L.N.E.R., but much collaboration took place and advice and assistance were sought and freely given by many other members of the Society. Those mainly responsible for the preparation of the locomotive class articles have been Dr. I. C. Allen, Messrs. M. G. Boddy, W. A. Brown, A. G. Dunbar, E. V. Fry, W. Hennigan, K. Hoole, the late R. Justin, R. G. Lucas, F. Manners, R. Miller, E. Neve, P. Proud, T. E. Rounthwaite, W. D. Spencer, V. R. Webster, and W. B. Yeadon.

The Preliminary Survey has, in the main, been compiled by Messrs. M. G. Boddy, E. V. Fry, W. Hennigan, P. Proud and W. B. Yeadon. The whole project is under the general editorship of Mr. E. V. Fry, with advice and help from Messrs. D. R. Pollock, P. Proud and D. E. White.

The authors wish to express their deep debt of gratitude to the authorities in the Eastern, North Eastern, Scottish and London Midland Regions of British Railways for the generous facilities granted for the examination of official records without which their work would have been impossible. Especial thanks must go to the staffs at Doncaster, Darlington, Gorton, Stratford, Cowlairs and Inverurie locomotive works, the offices of the Chief Mechanical & Electrical Engineers at Doncaster and St. Rollox, the officials at Hamilton House, London and those at Parliamentary Road, Glasgow for their assistance in tracing old records, also the Chief Civil Engineer's staff at King's Cross for assistance with the Preliminary Survey.

In addition grateful acknowledgment must be made to the Archives Department of British Railways in London, York and Edinburgh, the Historical Model Railway Society,

I

and the following private locomotive building firms :—

Armstrong Whitworth (Metal Industries) Ltd. ;
Beyer, Peacock & Co. Ltd. ;
Hudswell, Clarke & Co. Ltd. ;
Hunslet Engine Co. Ltd. ;
Motor Rail Ltd. ;
North British Locomotive Co. Ltd. ;
Sentinel (Shrewsbury) Ltd. ;
Robert Stephenson & Hawthorns Ltd. ;
Vulcan Foundry Ltd. ;
Yorkshire Engine Co. Ltd.

Thanks are also due to those who so kindly consented to read and criticise the proofs, especially to Messrs. H. S. Steel of British Railways, Doncaster and F. E. Wilson of British Railways, Hamilton House.

The map at the back of this book was kindly drawn by Mr. D. Swale. Finally, a general acknowledgement and thanks to the Society members and others who so generously responded to the appeal for suitable photographs to serve as illustrations ; individual acknowledgement is made elsewhere.

INTRODUCTION

It is intended to cover in this series the history of all locomotives taken over on 1st January 1923 by the L.N.E.R., together with subsequent additions to stock by purchase, absorption and new construction. As mentioned in the Preface, the subject will be dealt with in ten Parts ; the authors chose to delay publication of this, the first Part, until the bulk of their research work had been completed, thus a fairly rapid rate of publication of the remaining Parts should be achieved.

The present Part forms the introduction to the series and as such is mainly intended to give the basis upon which the history of the L.N.E.R. locomotive classes may be told in later Parts. By giving full details of, for instance, classification systems and renumbering schemes, much needless repetition will be avoided in later Parts and readers will be able to comprehend such systems and schemes in their entirety rather than piecemeal. As far as possible the photographs in this Part have been chosen to illustrate points dealt with in the text, but in addition many typical scenes in L.N.E.R. days have been included.

Parts 2 to 9 will be devoted to the individual locomotive classes. Tender and tank engines will be segregated and the order of the L.N.E.R. classification system will be adhered to, rather than division into pre-Grouping ownership. The pattern follows that adopted by the various departments of the L.N.E.R., who based all their records and statistics on this classification system. Part 10 will include full details of service locomotives, railcars, diesel, petrol and electric locomotives as well as statistical material and a complete numerical index : it is also hoped to include a chapter on proposed designs of locomotives.

The Parts will not necessarily be produced in order, nevertheless they will be arranged so as to permit binding into larger volumes at a later date, if desired.

The articles on individual locomotive classes will be on a uniform basis covering the full history of all engines ever owned by the L.N.E.R. including those constructed to its designs after nationalisation. Difficulties faced the authors as to what information should be included, bearing in mind that their terms of reference were to produce a history of L.N.E.R. locomotives from the Grouping to the present day. Nevertheless, they have felt able to go back to the time each engine was built, where this was before Grouping, in order to give a balanced picture of each class. Full details will be given of the origins, leading dimensions, dates of construction, rebuilding and withdrawal of each engine, together with sections covering detail variations, classification, engine diagrams and allocation and work. In general, photographs will show engines as running in L.N.E.R. days.

Certain information in the present work will be found to differ from previously published material, and in such cases every effort has been made to ensure the accuracy of the data now given. Generally speaking official records have been accepted unless clear proof to the contrary has been established. Where any doubt exists this will be indicated in the text.

It is hoped that this, the most ambitious locomotive history ever attempted by any group of amateurs, will give as much pleasure to those who read it as to those who wrote it, and if this is achieved, then the authors will have been well rewarded for their efforts.

2

HISTORY OF THE L.N.E.R.

The London & North Eastern Railway owed its formal existence to the Railways Act 1921. Following the 1914-18 War, during which the railways had been under Government control, proposals were laid before Parliament for the amalgamation of the many railway systems of Great Britain into larger units in the interests of economy and efficiency of working. In their final form these proposals were embodied in the Railways Act 1921 which received the Royal Assent on 19th August of that year. The Act provided for the railways of Great Britain to be formed into four groups of "constituent" and "subsidiary" companies as set out in the First Schedule to the Act. The effective date for the amalgamations was 1st January 1923, but constituent companies could submit amalgamation schemes prior to that date (as happened in the case of the North Eastern and Hull & Barnsley Railways) and in some cases (as with certain of the subsidiary companies of the L.N.E.R.) absorption did not take place until a slightly later date.

In the First Schedule to the Railways Act 1921, the L.N.E.R. was the last of the four groups. It was termed "North Eastern, Eastern and East Scottish Group." There had been discussions on proposals for a separate Scottish group but these had not materialised on account of financial considerations. The constituent companies of the group which formed the London & North Eastern Railway were as follows :—

Great Northern Railway
Great Central Railway
Great Eastern Railway
North Eastern Railway
Hull & Barnsley Railway
North British Railway
Great North of Scotland Railway.

The order in which the constituent companies are here listed is not that of size nor that in the Act, but, as part of an account of the locomotives of the L.N.E.R., the order followed as elsewhere in this publication is that used for the L.N.E.R.'s locomotive classification.

Before dealing with the subsidiary companies and also the important joint lines with which the L.N.E.R. was concerned, some brief notes will be given of the constituent companies as at the amalagamation.

The GREAT NORTHERN RAILWAY had at Grouping a total route mileage (including lines leased and share of lines worked or leased jointly) of 1051 with, on 31st December 1922, a total of 1359 locomotives in capital stock. It had been incorporated in 1846 and its principal route had become that from King's Cross to Doncaster, operating thence to Leeds. York was reached by running

powers over the North Eastern Railway, so forming the southern section of the East Coast main line from London to Edinburgh and Aberdeen. It also had extensive systems of lines in Lincolnshire, Nottinghamshire and the West Riding of Yorkshire, and from the latter two systems considerable coal traffic originated, but the G.N.R. was the only one of the constituent companies that had no appreciable traffic through a port. In the London area it served the "Northern Heights" and had important suburban traffic, part of which, by an agreement with the North London Railway, it avoided having to work itself.

The GREAT CENTRAL RAILWAY had a total of 855 route miles with 1358 locomotives. Originally incorporated in 1837 as the Sheffield, Ashton-under-Lyne & Manchester Railway, the Company had after various amalgamations been re-incorporated as the Manchester Sheffield & Lincolnshire Railway by an Act of 1849. That name gave an indication of the general area of operation in its earlier days but following an extension southwards from Annesley through Nottingham and Leicester to London, the title was changed to Great Central Railway on 1st August 1897. The Railway, however, was still often termed the "Sheffield" and its stocks were so known on the London Stock Exchange right up to Grouping. The Railway's traffic was largely freight (including extensive coal traffic) and in addition to participation in other joint lines, basic locomotive power for the Cheshire Lines Committee was supplied by it. Lines taken over by the Great Central Railway whose locomotives survived Grouping were the Wrexham Mold & Connah's Quay Railway (absorbed 1st January 1905) and the Lancashire Derbyshire & East Coast Railway (absorbed 1st January 1907).

The GREAT EASTERN RAILWAY had 1191 total route miles with 1336 locomotives in capital stock. It was an amalgamation of a number of railways with the Eastern Counties Railway (incorporated 1836) which was constituted as the Great Eastern Railway in 1862. Apart from a very extensive and highly developed London suburban service, it principally served agricultural districts. It also however worked a large volume of coal traffic through Peterborough and March, principally to London, and had developed a considerable passenger traffic to East Anglian coast resorts and an excellent continental service through the port of Harwich. The G.E.R. had through working arrangements to the Nottingham coalfield and to York.

Plans for the amalgamation prior to the 1914-18 War of the G.N.R., G.C.R. and G.E.R. had not come to fruition. There was,

3

however, a measure of association between the Companies; for example road delivery services in London were jointly operated.

The NORTH EASTERN RAILWAY was the oldest and largest of the constituent companies of the L.N.E.R. It had a total route mileage of 1866 at 31st December 1922 (including the Hull & Barnsley Railway) and 2156 locomotives in capital stock, of which 138 came from the H. & B.R. The Railway was incorporated in 1854 as an amalgamation of the York Newcastle & Berwick Railway, the York & North Midland Railway and the Leeds Northern Railway. There had been important subsequent additions, one of the most noteworthy being that of the famous Stockton & Darlington Railway (incorporated 1821 and opened on 27th September 1825) which was amalgamated with the N.E.R. in 1863. With its main line from York to Berwick and running powers thence to Edinburgh, the N.E.R. was a very active partner with the G.N.R. in the development and working of the services of the East Coast main line. Its principal traffic, however, was coal and other minerals and the N.E.R. had a larger tonnage of such traffic than any other railway in the United Kingdom. It also had extensive steam and electric suburban services around Newcastle, and owned many docks on the North East Coast.

The HULL & BARNSLEY RAILWAY was amalgamated with the North Eastern Railway as from 1st April 1922 under the provisions of the Railways Act 1921 which allowed such a scheme. At 31st December 1921 it had a route mileage of 106 and a total of 181 locomotives, of which 43 were withdrawn before the formation of the L.N.E.R. It had been incorporated as the Hull Barnsley & West Riding Junction Railway & Dock Company in 1880 (with the strong support of Hull to break the North Eastern Railway monopoly) and assumed the name of Hull & Barnsley Railway in 1905. It owned docks and lines in Hull with a main line to Hull from Cudworth (just outside Barnsley) and several branches. Its principal traffic was, of course, freight.

The NORTH BRITISH RAILWAY had a total of 1378 route miles with 1075 locomotives. It was originally incorporated in 1844 for a line from Edinburgh to Berwick. Other important railways were amalgamated with it, including the Edinburgh Perth & Dundee and the Edinburgh & Glasgow Railways. Although basically an East Coast line, it served practically all the principal industrial districts and coal fields of Scotland and was thus larger than its rival, the Caledonian Railway; it had very extensive freight services. On its passenger services it worked closely in connection with the G.N.R. and N.E.R. in the operation of the East Coast services but at the same time it maintained the closest connections also with the Midland Railway through Carlisle. It also

provided many cross-country and branch services in sparsely populated areas of Scotland and the North of England, where it owned a significant mileage of track and exercised running powers over the North Eastern from Hexham to Newcastle.

THE GREAT NORTH OF SCOTLAND RAILWAY was a small line with a total of 334 route miles and 122 locomotives. It was incorporated in 1846 for a railway from Aberdeen to Inverness, which only reached Elgin and terminated there on account of the action of Inverness interests building a line of their own. It served principally an agricultural district of Northern Scotland but also had an extensive fish traffic. On the L.N.E.R. map it appeared detached from the remainder of the system; the link with the N.B.R. at Aberdeen was only achieved by the latter's running powers over 38 miles of the Caledonian Railway from Kinnaber Junction to Aberdeen.

JOINT LINES AND SUBSIDIARY COMPANIES. —Before referring to the subsidiary companies of the L.N.E.R., mention should be made of the principal joint lines. Two of the largest of these which became wholly part of the L.N.E.R. were the Great Northern & Great Eastern Joint Line (123 miles), running from Huntingdon via St. Ives and March to Doncaster, and the West Riding & Grimsby Joint Line (31½ miles), belonging to the G.N.R. and G.C.R. which gave the former its main line into Leeds. Also akin to joint lines were joint services, the most famous of which were those which produced the E.C.J.S. (East Coast Joint Stock), a separate organisation of rolling stock jointly owned by the G.N.R., N.E.R. and N.B.R.

Other principal joint lines, which remained joint after Grouping, included the Cheshire Lines Committee, which had a route mileage of 143 equally owned by the G.N., G.C. and Midland Railways, and so after Grouping became two-thirds L.N.E.R. and one-third L.M.S.R. By an award dated 30th May 1882 of John Ramsbottom as arbitrator, it was decided that locomotives for purely C.L.C. requirements should be provided by the M.S. & L.R. and the L.N.E.R. inherited this privilege. The C.L.C. had its own carriages and wagons, though of M.S. & L.R. and, later, mainly G.C.R. and L.N.E.R. designs; hence the Sentinel Cammell steam railcars for the C.L.C. were the property of the Committee. The Midland & Great Northern Joint Railway was equally owned by the G.N. and the Midland Railways. It had a route mileage of 183 and furthermore had not only separate carriages and wagons but a separate stock of locomotives with 101 engines in 1922. It had its own works at Melton Constable. As from 1st October 1936, operation of the line including its 85 locomotives then in capital stock, was taken over by the

4

L.N.E.R. The motive power thereafter was supplied and managed by the L.N.E.R. Although repainting of M. & G.N. locomotives in L.N.E.R. livery commenced in October 1936, the 85 engines in capital stock and the one M. & G.N. service locomotive were not immediately added to L.N.E.R. stock. During 1936-37, 26 including the service locomotive were condemned leaving only 60 M. & G.N. engines to appear in the L.N.E.R. stock figures for 31st December 1937.

Three other independently operated joint lines were (i) the East London Railway, in which the L.N.E.R. had a one-sixth share as successor to the G.E.R.; it was managed by the Metropolitan Railway, which operated the passenger service whilst the freight service was worked by the G.E.R. and later the L.N.E.R.; (ii) the Manchester South Junction & Altrincham Joint Railway, equally owned by the London & North Western Railway and the G.C.R., whose trains were worked for alternate periods by the owning Companies until, upon electrification in 1931, separate electric rolling stock for the joint railway was provided; (iii) the Axholme Joint Railway opened in 1902, jointly owned by the N.E.R. and Lancashire & Yorkshire Railway. For some years it possessed its own Sentinel steam railcar, but this was eventually transferred from joint L.N.E.R./L.M.S. to L.N.E.R. stock.

There were many other joint lines, including the Metropolitan & Great Central, and the Great Western & Great Central, which gave the G.C.R. its two approaches to London, and the Forth Bridge Railway Company, whose shareholding was G.N.R. 18¾%, N.E.R. 18¾%, N.B.R. 30% and Midland Rly. 32½%, but which was wholly leased to the N.B.R. and later the L.N.E.R.

The subsidiary companies included even the old London & Blackwall Railway but it will be sufficient to mention those which had locomotives. These were :—

East & West Yorkshire Union Rlys.—opened 1891; taken over on 1st July 1923 (6 locomotives).

Colne Valley & Halstead Rly.—opened 1860; taken over on 1st July 1923 (5 locomotives).

Mid-Suffolk Light Rly.—opened 1904; taken over on 1st July 1924 (3 locomotives).

Finally, for completeness, it should be mentioned that as from 1st November 1937, the L.N.E.R. assumed responsibility for the steam services of the former Metropolitan Railway, which had been taken over by the London Passenger Transport Board on 1st July 1933. The eighteen modern Metropolitan Line engines were taken into L.N.E.R. stock.

LONDON AND NORTH EASTERN RAILWAY. —On the formation of the L.N.E.R., with a

vast system extending from London to Lossiemouth and varying practices of management and operation, many problems arose.

Mr. William Whitelaw (fig. 1), former Chairman of the North British Railway, became Chairman of the new Board of Directors of the L.N.E.R. He was succeeded in 1938 by Sir Ronald Matthews who held office until nationalisation.

The Headquarters of the new group were established at Marylebone, the London terminus of the G.C.R., but from the start a policy of decentralisation was adopted. Mr. R. L. Wedgwood (fig. 2), who received a knighthood in the birthday Honours of 1924, was appointed Chief General Manager; he had joined the N.E.R. in 1896 and became General Manager of that line in 1922. He held office as Chief General Manager of the L.N.E.R. until 1939. As soon as he had taken office, he announced the policy of operating the L.N.E.R. in three areas. The "Three Greats" as one area and the North Eastern as another would have separate Divisional General Managers and there would be a General Manager for Scotland. For a period there was a Northern Scottish Area for certain purposes covering the lines of the former G.N.S.R., but basically the L.N.E.R., throughout its existence, was operated in three Areas—Southern, North Eastern and Scottish. In the Southern Area, the G.N. and G.C. sections on the one hand and the G.E. section on the other remained distinct for varying purposes for part or the whole of the period of the L.N.E.R.; they were referred to as the Western and Eastern Sections respectively. A relatively small General Headquarters sufficed. Certain departments, e.g. that of the Chief Mechanical Engineer, embraced the entire railway, but on traffic and operational matters the three Areas were truly distinct. From the point of view of the story of the locomotives of the L.N.E.R., the relative autonomy of the three Areas is important; only rarely were locomotives transferred from one Area to another and, once transferred, they often so remained for years after the initial reason for the transfer had passed.

Upon his retirement in 1939, Sir Ralph Wedgwood was succeeded by Mr. C. H. Newton who had come from the Great Western Railway to the G.E.R. in 1916 and had been its Chief Accountant at the time of the Grouping; latterly he had been Divisional General Manager of the Southern Area of the L.N.E.R. He received the honour of knighthood in 1943 and upon his retirement in June 1947, Sir Charles Newton was appointed a Director. For the period until the end of 1947, Mr. Miles Beevor, Chief Legal Adviser of the L.N.E.R., was appointed Acting Chief General Manager. During the greater part of its existence, the L.N.E.R. suffered particularly severely from the financial stringency of the hard times which followed the General Strike of 1926. It served areas that were hard hit by the depressions of industry and it lacked the financial resources needed for many desired improvements. Despite these difficulties, however, the L.N.E.R. succeeded in keeping itself to the forefront in express passenger operation, also in other fields such as fast goods services and signalling developments.

By an Order of 1st September 1939, the L.N.E.R., in common with other British railway systems, came under Government control through the Railway Executive Committee, of which Sir Ralph Wedgwood was the first Chairman. Valiant feats of haulage and operation were performed during the war years. After the war, the L.N.E.R. had a programme for repairing the ravages of six years of war service, but its Five Year Plan was never fully implemented and a Memorandum of the Board dated October 1946, giving an alternative to nationalisation, went unheeded. On 1st January 1948 the L.N.E.R. was vested in the British Transport Commission. The Southern Area became the Eastern Region of British Railways and the North Eastern Area formed the North Eastern Region. In Scotland former L.M.S. and L.N.E.R. lines were merged to form the Scottish Region.

The last General Meeting of the Proprietors of the L.N.E.R. was held on 5th March 1948 and the Company was liquidated shortly afterwards. At the final meeting a resolution to pay the Directors compensation for loss of office was defeated on a show of hands and the final dividend on the five per cent. Preferred Ordinary Stock was accordingly 19s. 2d. per cent., leaving an undistributed balance of £224 to be paid to the British Transport Commission.

THE COAT OF ARMS

In 1924, the L.N.E.R. obtained its coat of arms. Its official heraldic description was :—

Argent on a Cross Gules between in the first and fourth quarters a Griffin segreant Sable in the second a Rose of the second leaved and slipped proper and in the third quarter a Thistle also leaved and slipped proper the Castle of Edinburgh proper between four Lions passant guardant Or And for the Crest On a Wreath of the Colours Issuant from Clouds of Steam the figure of Mercury proper.

At the foot was the L.N.E.R. motto " Forward " taken from the design of the G.C.R. The L.N.E.R. Coat of Arms appears on the title page of this publication and is still perpetuated in Dutch tiles on the s.s. *Arnhem*, the last steamer for the Harwich to Hook of Holland service completed by the L.N.E.R.

Regrettably the Coat of Arms was not displayed as part of the standard livery of locomotives and carriages. It appeared on the cab side of No. 4472 *Flying Scotsman* (fig. 9) whilst on display at the Wembley Exhibitions of 1924 and 1925, but was removed in 1926. The only other L.N.E.R. engine to be similarly embellished was the Ivatt 4-4-0 specially set aside in 1944 as No. 2000 for hauling Directors and Officers Specials (fig. 8).

The old G.N.R. coat of arms had appeared on Atlantic No. 1442 which was the Royal engine of that railway ; it continued to appear on that engine as L.N.E.R. 4442, even after wartime black livery was adopted and was still perpetuated until the engine was scrapped as 2872 in 1947. A coat of arms from this engine is preserved in York Railway Museum.

THE LOCOMOTIVE ENGINEERS

The term " Locomotive Engineer " is used in this chapter as being the generic description of the man responsible for locomotive design and normally in earlier days for operation of the locomotives. It would be overloading detail to no good purpose if undue stress were placed on exact titles. Let it suffice at this stage to mention that on the seven constituent companies of the L.N.E.R., the appointment carried at the time of Grouping the title of Chief Mechanical Engineer on all except the G.N.R. and G.N.S.R. where the title of Locomotive Superintendent or Engineer was still used, although carriage and wagon

stock was under the same superintendence. After Grouping the L.N.E.R. adopted the title of Chief Mechanical Engineer.

This publication is a history of the locomotives of the L.N.E.R. : its constituent and subsidiary companies and their predecessors are, however, extensively mentioned Quite apart from locomotives extant at Grouping, earlier types will require to be mentioned in certain cases from the historical point of view of then current designs. In dealing with the Locomotive Engineers, it is not necessary in every case to start from the initial incorporation of the constituent companies and their predecessors, but it may be mentioned in passing that George Stephenson himself was the first Engineer of the Stockton & Darlington Railway, appointed in 1822. It is, however, proposed to give a short reference to every locomotive engineer whose designs survived Grouping or whose designs though extinct by then will be referred to historically or as influencing subsequent designs.

GREAT NORTHERN RAILWAY

1850-1866   ARCHIBALD STURROCK
1866-1895   PATRICK STIRLING
1896-1911   HENRY ALFRED IVATT
1911-1922   HERBERT NIGEL GRESLEY

Prior to 1850, the G.N.R. had no full-time locomotive superintendent. In that year ARCHIBALD STURROCK was appointed Locomotive Engineer. After apprenticeship at Dundee, his early experience had been on the Great Western Railway in its earliest days and in 1843 Gooch had appointed him as the first Manager of the then new Swindon Works. The G.W.R. was, of course, then a broad gauge railway but Sturrock set out on the G.N.R. to provide locomotives with like qualities as to speed and power on the standard gauge. He certainly succeeded and his engines played their part when the young G.N.R. was fighting its way to the front line of trunk railways by sheer merit. During Sturrock's time all G.N. locomotives were still built by outside contractors, but the foundations of the great importance of Doncaster in G.N.R. and L.N.E.R. locomotive history were laid by him; it was under his superintendence that Doncaster Works was built in 1853, replacing the earlier establishment at Boston. After his retirement in 1866, Sturrock lived the life of a country gentleman, hunting with the hounds until long after the age of 70 and dying on 1st January 1909 in his 93rd year.

Sturrock's successor was very little younger than himself. He was PATRICK STIRLING, born at Kilmarnock in 1820. He also had served an apprenticeship at Dundee; after various employments he had, prior to coming to the G.N.R., been locomotive superintendent of the Glasgow & South Western Railway since 1853 and his early designs on that railway are clearly predecessors of the engines he designed for the G.N.R. Upon his arrival at Doncaster, he immediately instituted the policy of constructing locomotives there and thereafter orders for new locomotives were only placed with private firms when the works were otherwise fully employed. A very considerable degree of standardisation was introduced; with very few exceptions, a design, once instituted by Stirling, was continued throughout his tenure of office with merely modifica-

tions of detail as the years passed. It was under Stirling that the familiar lines of the Doncaster locomotive were evolved, though his cabs with short roofs and boilers without domes were not perpetuated by his successors. Undoubtedly his most famous design was his eight-foot 4-2-2, which even figured on the postage stamps of a South American state. His other standard designs, though in many cases no larger than their Sturrock predecessors, also did good work for many years and often were multiplied with varying modifications by his successors. For example, despite their large side tanks in place of saddle tanks, the L.N.E.R. class J50 0-6-0T's still being built in 1939, were the direct descendants of a Stirling design of 1874. Stirling died in office, after a short illness, on 11th November 1895.

The successor to Stirling, appointed in March 1896, was HENRY ALFRED IVATT. Trained at Crewe under John Ramsbottom and F. W. Webb, he had joined the Great Southern & Western Railway of Ireland. Since 1886 he had been chief of the locomotive department of that railway and so came to Doncaster from Inchicore. Some of his early designs followed Stirling practice but steam domes were introduced and the cab roof extended. On passenger engines he introduced bogies, eschewed by Stirling for tender engines except on his famous 4-2-2's where they had been unavoidable with the large eight-foot driving wheels and outside cylinders. For express passenger work with increasing loads and heavier rolling stock, the famous Atlantic design was evolved which in its 1902 development with large boiler put the seal on the G.N.R. tradition of the " big engine." Ivatt retired in the autumn of 1911 and died on 25th October 1923 at the age of 72. H. G. Ivatt, the last C.M.E. of the L.M.S. was his son, whilst O. V. S. Bulleid, later C.M.E. of the Southern Railway, who was for many year's Gresley's principal assistant, was his son-in-law.

As successor to Ivatt, the Directors of the Great Northern Railway appointed HERBERT NIGEL GRESLEY. Born in 1876, in Edinburgh of English parents, he had served his apprenticeship at Crewe under F. W. Webb, and in 1905, after appointments on the Lancashire & Yorkshire Railway, had been given the post of Carriage & Wagon Superintendent of the G.N.R. Gresley was not slow to put new ideas into locomotive design. Certain traditional G.N.R. features were retained but the two-cylinder 2-6-0 Mogul of 1912 foreshadowed many changes and this was followed in the succeeding year by a two-cylinder 2-8-0. The War years of 1914-18 impeded development, of course, but the first three-cylinder design appeared in 1918 to be followed by the large-boilered three-cylinder 2-6-0 in 1920. Finally, in 1922 the first of the famous Gresley Pacifics was completed. With these designs built and on the rails, Gresley was well fitted to assume in 1923 the post of Chief Mechanical Engineer of the newly formed L.N.E.R. and to hold that office for eighteen years as recounted below.

GREAT CENTRAL RAILWAY

1841-1854	RICHARD PEACOCK
1854-1859	WILLIAM GRINDLEY CRAIG
1859-1886	CHARLES REBOUL SACRE
1886-1893	THOMAS PARKER
1894-1900	HARRY POLLITT
1900-1922	JOHN GEORGE ROBINSON

The first Chief Locomotive Superintendent of the Manchester Sheffield & Lincolnshire Railway was Richard Peacock who came to its predecessor the Sheffield Ashton-under-Lyne & Manchester Railway in October 1841 at the age of twenty-one, having previously been Locomotive Superintendent of the Leeds & Selby Railway. He resigned in 1854 to found the firm of Beyer, Peacock & Co., locomotive manufacturers, at Gorton. Following this early association with that firm, coupled with the proximity of its works to those of the Railway, a close relationship with these makers was maintained.

WILLIAM GRINDLEY CRAIG had been Locomotive Superintendent of the Monmouthshire Railway & Canal Co. from 1849 to 1854 and was previously with the Neath Abbey Iron Works, one of the earliest locomotive builders in Wales. He succeeded Peacock in May 1854 but his contract was not renewed when it expired after five years. He built the first four engines constructed at Gorton.

CHARLES REBOUL SACRE, born in 1839, and who had been apprenticed to Sturrock, was appointed Engineer and Superintendent of the Locomotive and Stores Department in April 1859 at the age of twenty ! He held office until April 1886 and his locomotives were solidly and soundly built ; this tradition of solidity of construction and durability was followed by his successors. As will appear from the description of individual locomotive classes, a considerable number of Sacré's engines survived until after Grouping. A feature of Sacré's designs was the use of double frames on the engines designed for the heaviest type of work. S. W. Johnson, mentioned later in connection with the Great Eastern and North British Railways and ultimately the famous locomotive engineer of the Midland Railway, was Sacré's principal assistant at Gorton from 1859 to 1864. Sacré eventually also took over the steamship, dock and canal engineering of the M.S. & L.R. After retirement, he committed suicide in 1889.

Sacré's successor at Gorton in 1886 was THOMAS PARKER. He had served his apprenticeship with Robert Sinclair (later of the G.E.R.) at the Greenock Works of the Caledonian Railway and had been Carriage & Wagon Superintendent of the M.S. & L.R. since 1858. After initial designs, which were transitional from those of Sacré, basic designs with inside frames were introduced which set the lines which were followed with enlargement and development throughout the remainder of the history of the Company. The first Belpaire firebox constructed in Great Britain had been on Beyer, Peacock & Co.'s engines of 1872 for the Malines-Terneuzen Railway, a Belgian company, but it was under Parker that the first instance occurred of the use of Belpaire fireboxes in this country ; they appeared on his 0-6-2T's in 1891 and thereafter became a standard feature of the Company's locomotives.

Upon Parker's retirement at the end of 1893, his son Thomas Parker Junior succeeded him as Carriage & Wagon Superintendent but his successor as Locomotive Engineer was HARRY POLLITT who had been trained on the M.S. & L.R. Under his superintendence, construction in the main was of standard Parker designs with, for the opening of the London extension, enlarged 4-4-0's. Pollitt, however, designed the handsome 7ft. 9in. 4-2-2 Singles which were of note also as being the only single-driver express tender engines to survive to form part of the L.N.E.R. stock. Pollitt, who resigned in 1900, was son of Mr. (later Sir) William Pollitt who from 1886 to 1903 was General Manager of the Company.

In June 1900, JOHN GEORGE ROBINSON was appointed Locomotive Engineer of the G.C.R. In 1902 the carriage and wagon departments were also placed under his charge and the title of his office changed to Chief Mechanical Engineer. Born in 1856, he had served his apprenticeship under J. Armstrong and William Dean on the G.W.R. at Swindon, but had joined the Waterford Limerick & Western Railway of Ireland at Limerick in 1884 and from 1888 to 1900 he had been in charge of the Locomotive Carriage & Wagon Department of that railway. He arrived on the G.C.R. at a time of expanding traffic and increasing loads. He produced a wide variety of designs, following the symmetrical outlines of his predecessors but with enlarged cylinder capacities and boilers. Apart from his actual locomotives handed down to the L.N.E.R., two other important contributions made by Robinson must be mentioned. His experiments with superheating led to the well known superheater which bears his name, whilst during the War of 1914-18, it was his design of 2-8-0 which was adopted by the Ministry of Munitions for construction for war

8

service ; with purchases of many such locomotives by the L.N.E.R. in 1924-29, the number of modern locomotives of Great Central design on the L.N.E.R. was increased out of proportion to the size of the original locomotive stock of the G.C.R. Upon the formation of the L.N.E.R., Robinson was the first choice of the directors for the post of Chief Mechanical Engineer of the large grouped system. He was then, however, 66 years old and he declined the appointment in favour of Gresley who was a much younger man. Robinson continued in office for a period with the L.N.E.R. in a consultative capacity and also became a director of Beyer, Peacock & Co. He died in retirement on 7th December 1943 at the age of 87.

In connection with the Great Central, mention should be made of ROBERT A. THOM. Born at Aberdeen in 1873, he had been apprenticed at Kittybrewster on the G.N.S.R. and, after intervening appointments, had in October 1902 been appointed Locomotive Carriage & Wagon Superintendent of the Lancashire Derbyshire & East Coast Railway. During his superintendence at Tuxford the L.D. & E.C.R. 0-6-4T's, which became class M1 on the L.N.E.R., were designed. On the absorption of the L.D. & E.C.R. by the Great Central Railway in 1907, he went to Gorton and, continuing in the service of the Great Central Railway and the L.N.E.R., and was the latter's Scottish Area Mechanical Engineer until appointed Mechanical Engineer at Doncaster in 1927. He retired in 1938 and died in 1955.

GREAT EASTERN RAILWAY

1856-1865	ROBERT SINCLAIR
1866-1873	SAMUEL WAITE JOHNSON
1873-1878	WILLIAM ADAMS
1878-1881	MASSEY BROMLEY
1882-1885	THOMAS WILLIAM WORSDELL
1885-1907	JAMES HOLDEN
1908-1912	STEPHEN DEWAR HOLDEN
1912-1922	ALFRED JOHN HILL

ROBERT SINCLAIR, born in 1817, had come to the then Eastern Counties Railway as Locomotive Carriage & Wagon Superintendent in 1856 after having been Locomotive Superintendent and also General Manager of the Caledonian Railway. From 1857 he was also Engineer-in-Chief. He was largely responsible for the early development of Stratford Works and introduced a considerable measure of standardisation in his designs, including the stovepipe chimneys perpetuated by Adams and his successors. He resigned at the end of 1865, set up in private practice and died in 1898.

His successor as Locomotive Carriage & Wagon Superintendent of the G.E.R. was

SAMUEL WAITE JOHNSON. Born at Leeds, he had been in the service of the G.N.R. and M.S. & L.R. before becoming Locomotive Superintendent of the Edinburgh & Glasgow Railway. He took office on the G.E.R. in July 1866 but resigned in June 1873 to take up the appointment of Locomotive Superintendent of the Midland Railway, an office he held until December 1903. He died in January 1912.

WILLIAM ADAMS succeeded Johnson at Stratford in July 1873. Born in 1823, he had initially been a marine engineer, and in 1848-52 had an important post as engineer in the newly formed Royal Sardinian Navy. In 1855 he had become the first Locomotive Superintendent of the North London Railway. He resigned from the G.E.R. in 1878 to take a similar appointment on the London & South Western Railway, which office he held until resigning in 1895 ; he died in 1904.

With the exception of three 0-6-0T's on the departmental list, originally built to Johnson's design, and two standard Neilson 0-4-0ST's built during Adams' terms of office, no G.E.R. locomotives of the Johnson and Adams periods survived the Grouping, though remains of a Johnson 0-6-0 lingered at Stratford into the 1930's. In many cases however the Johnson and Adams features of design had their influence on certain later G.E.R. classes and the G.E.R. designs were also the forerunners of better known later engines on the Midland Railway and the L.S.W.R.

MASSEY BROMLEY held office for the short period from February 1878 to August 1881. It was during this time that the policy of meeting requirements of new construction principally at Stratford Works was adopted. This policy was pursued with such effect by Bromley's successors that all new construction after 1882 was at Stratford except for nineteen engines in 1884 and twenty locomotives built in 1920-21 after the war years of 1914-18 had caused arrears of construction. Bromley was killed in the Penistone accident on the M.S. & L.R. in 1884. None of his locomotive designs for the G.E.R. survived Grouping, though some of his tenders were still in service.

THOMAS WILLIAM WORSDELL took office at Stratford in February 1882. He was born in 1838 and was the eldest son of Nathaniel Worsdell, who had been Carriage Superintendent of the Grand Junction Railway and who with his father Thomas Clarke Worsdell (1788-1862) had been entrusted with the construction of the first passenger coaches for the Liverpool & Manchester Railway. After initial experience at Crewe, T. W. Worsdell had in 1865 gone to the United States of America and entered the service of the Pennsylvania Railroad where he soon became Master Mechanic at the Altoona Works. He returned to England in 1871 and for ten years was Works Manager at Crewe under F. W. Webb. On the G.E.R. his term of office was short as in 1885 he was offered, and accepted, the vacant post of Locomotive Superintendent of the North Eastern Railway. His passenger tender engines for the G.E.R., which included two-cylinder compounds, were not particularly successful. However, his 0-6-0 tender and 2-4-2T designs laid down standards which, with his austereness of external fittings, became the basic outline of many G.E.R. and N.E.R. locomotives for several decades.

JAMES HOLDEN, who succeeded T. W. Worsdell in July 1885, had started his railway career at Gateshead. Born in 1837 he had been apprenticed to his uncle Edward Fletcher on the then York Newcastle & Berwick Railway. In 1865 he had joined the Carriage & Wagon Department of the Great Western Railway and prior to his appointment to the G.E.R. had become chief assistant at Swindon to William Dean. His term of office on the G.E.R. was the longest of any of its locomotive superintendents. It was a period of expanding traffic. Developing from Worsdell's designs, a great measure of standardisation and interchangeability of parts characterised Holden's engines. In the later years of his office, the designs were dependent greatly on the work of Frederick V. Russell, who, having joined the G.E.R. as Holden's apprentice in 1886 had been attached to Stratford Drawing Office in 1893 and finally became chief of the locomotive designing section before passing on to other duties, culminating in being the Superintendent of Operation and Special Assistant to General Manager under Sir Henry Thornton in the last days of the G.E.R. Most of the engines built during James Holden's superintendency survived Grouping. Provision had to be made not only for the express passenger and freight services but also for the colossal steam-operated suburban service. James Holden resigned at the end of December 1907 and died on 26th May 1925 at the age of 87.

The successor to James Holden was his son STEPHEN DEWAR HOLDEN. He was born in 1870 and apprenticed to his father in 1886. He had subsequently served in the Locomotive Department of the G.E.R., but after his appointment in 1908, he only held office until 1912.

The last Locomotive Superintendent of the G.E.R. was ALFRED JOHN HILL. Born in 1862, he had been apprenticed at Stratford in 1877. After having held office as Assistant Works Manager, he had in 1899 become Manager of the Locomotive Carriage & Wagon Works. He became Locomotive Superintendent in November 1912 and the title of the office was in April 1915 changed to Chief Mechanical Engineer. He retired at Grouping and died on 14th March 1927. The greatest locomotive contribution of Hill was undoubtedly the N7 class 0-6-2T, but his term of office also saw the

adoption of the Robinson superheater on the G.E.R. and the construction of the most powerful 0-6-0 tender engines in the British Isles prior to Bulleid's Q1 class on the Southern Railway more than twenty years later.

NORTH EASTERN RAILWAY

1854-1882	EDWARD FLETCHER
1882-1884	ALEXANDER MCDONNELL
1885-1890	THOMAS WILLIAM WORSDELL
1890-1910	WILSON WORSDELL
1910-1922	VINCENT LITCHFIELD RAVEN

EDWARD FLETCHER was born in 1809. He served his apprenticeship with George Stephenson and was on the footplate with him when the *Rocket* underwent trials at Killingworth Colliery before being sent to Rainhill for the famous competition in October 1829. After that he was with the Canterbury & Whitstable Railway from its opening in 1830 for two years ; he thereafter joined the staff of the York & North Midland Railway and in 1845 became Locomotive Superintendent at Gateshead of the Newcastle & Darlington Junction Railway, later a part of the York Newcastle & Berwick. In 1853, in anticipation of the North Eastern Railway Incorporation Act of 1854, he was appointed acting locomotive superintendent of the three companies concerned, with works at Gateshead, York and Leeds, but Gateshead always remained his headquarters. On the N.E.R., Fletcher showed that like his contemporaries on the G.N.R. he was an apostle of the " big engine " policy which continued down to the end of the L.N.E.R.'s existence. Fletcher's designs were ahead of their time in size and general conception ; however, within the broad lines of the designs many variations in detail occurred. Possibly it was only inability to incorporate the variants on one L.N.E.R. engine diagram that led to his tender engines which survived Grouping getting no L.N.E.R. classifications. Fletcher retired in 1882 and died in 1889.

Mention has been made of three locomotive works of the N.E.R. The fourth, Darlington, came under N.E.R. control on the amalgamation with the Stockton & Darlington Railway in July 1863. The S. & D. system continued however to be managed separately by a specially constituted Darlington Committee for ten years. WILLIAM BOUCH, brother of the designer of the first Tay Bridge, who had been in charge, first at Shildon and then at Darlington, continued in office until the end of 1875, but Fletcher influence began to appear before then. During the ten year period of separate management, S. & D. locomotive stock remained quite distinct and it was not until after 1873 that they were renumbered in the N.E.R. lists by addition of 1000 to their original numbers. One S. & D. engine of Bouch's design survived Grouping and has since withdrawal been in York Museum. Only after Bouch's retirement did Darlington effectively come under Fletcher's control for all purposes.

ALEXANDER MCDONNELL was appointed successor to Fletcher at Gateshead as from 1st November 1882. He had been Locomotive Superintendent of the Great Southern & Western Railway of Ireland at Inchicore since 1864. There he had been responsible for producing a considerable degree of standardisation and for laying the foundations of efficient workshop practice. Good though Fletcher's engines were, there was need for standardisation and reorganisation in the locomotive building department. McDonnell's method of attempting reforms was, however, unpopular and his locomotive designs were received with opposition. Suffice it to say that in the autumn of 1884 he resigned.

In 1885, when new express locomotives were urgently needed on the inception of non-stop running from Newcastle to Edinburgh, the N.E.R. had no locomotive superintendent. The General Manager, Henry Tennant, then had a most successful class of 2-4-0 (L.N.E.R. class E5), designed by a committee of officials of the mechanical engineering department.

Later in 1885 THOMAS WILLIAM WORSDELL, the elder brother of Wilson Worsdell (mentioned below), was appointed to the vacant office. With his excellent administrative abilities, evidenced by his career already recounted in connection with the G.E.R. and with his brother (twelve years younger) already in office as his assistant, he was able to provide the necessary standardisation and ordered progress that was required. His term of office on the N.E.R. was short but during it the basic Worsdell designs, both compound and non-compound, rapidly replaced some of the more heterogeneous of the oldest engines. T. W. Worsdell had to retire in 1890 on account of ill health but he lived in retirement until his death in 1916 at the age of 78.

T. W. Worsdell was succeeded by his brother WILSON WORSDELL, who was born in 1850. After a short period at Crewe he had gone out to the U.S.A. in 1867 to join his brother and become a pupil at the Altoona Works of the Pennsylvania Railroad. He returned to England in 1871 and held appointments on the L.N.W.R. until 1883 when he was appointed an assistant locomotive superintendent of the N.E.R. He held this office till he succeeded his brother in 1890 as Locomotive Superintendent, the title being changed to Chief Mechanical Engineer in 1902. During Wilson Worsdell's period of office great progress in locomotive design took place. One of his characteristics was ability to delegate.

Thus considerable contribution was made by Walter M. Smith who, born in 1842, had, after association with S. W. Johnson both on the Edinburgh & Glasgow Railway and the G.E.R. and service with the Imperial Government Railways of Japan, joined the N.E.R. in 1883. Smith was Chief Draughtsman at Gateshead for many years and was responsible for the introduction of piston valves on the N.E.R. in 1888. His well known three-cylinder compound design was represented on the N.E.R. by one engine (No. 1619 as rebuilt in 1898, fig. 33) but it was the predecessor of famous Midland compounds and also the compound Atlantics of the G.C.R. He also designed the two N.E.R. four-cylinder compound Atlantics of 1906, in which year he died at the early age of 64. As to general locomotive design the " big engine " policy was carried a stage further under Wilson Worsdell. Following a visit of senior officers of the N.E.R. to the U.S.A. in 1901, boilers of 5ft. 6in. diameter became features of many classes and, on Wilson Worsdell's retirement in 1910, the N.E.R. was well equipped with locomotive power for a railway then one of the most prosperous in Great Britain. Wilson Worsdell died in 1920.

VINCENT LITCHFIELD RAVEN succeeded Wilson Worsdell. He was born in 1859 and spent his entire railway career on the N.E.R., starting as a pupil of Fletcher, and since December 1893 he had been Assistant Mechanical Engineer. Designs during his period of office followed the N.E.R. traditions, although there was no conservatism in ideas. The Shildon to Newport electrification was carried out and extensive further electrification was in contemplation, whilst he also developed a successful and widely applied system of cab signalling. In 1915 Raven became Superintendent of the Royal Arsenal, Woolwich and the honour of K.B.E. was conferred on him in 1917. On the formation of the L.N.E.R., Sir Vincent Raven was appointed Technical Adviser to the new Company and A. C. Stamer who had been Assistant Chief Mechanical Engineer at Darlington and in charge during Sir Vincent's absence at Woolwich became Chief Assistant Mechanical Engineer of the L.N.E.R. under Gresley. Sir Vincent Raven resigned his office of Technical Adviser in 1924 and died in 1934. Edward Thompson, later C.M.E. of the L.N.E.R., was his son-in-law.

HULL & BARNSLEY RAILWAY

1885-1922 MATTHEW STIRLING

The initial locomotives of this railway were to the designs of William Kirtley, then Locomotive Superintendent of the London Chatham & Dover Railway, who acted as consultant. None of these survived to come into L.N.E.R. stock, though some were still running at the time of the amalgamation with the N.E.R. in April 1922.

Shortly before the railway was opened to traffic, a Locomotive Superintendent was appointed. He was MATTHEW STIRLING. Born at Kilmarnock in 1856, he was the son of Patrick Stirling of the G.N.R. He served his apprenticeship at Doncaster and, after subsequent appointments on the G.N.R., took office at Hull in May 1885. Stirling retained command until the end of the separate existence of the H. & B.R. and died at Hull on 5th October 1931.

Stirling's engines followed the family tradition. Domeless boilers and plain cabs were universal features. Possibly it was proximity to the N.E.R. that encouraged enlargement of boilers, but apart from that, Stirling traditions continued to the end.

NORTH BRITISH RAILWAY

1867-1874   THOMAS WHEATLEY
1875-1882   DUGALD DRUMMOND
1882-1903   MATTHEW HOLMES
1903-1919   WILLIAM PATON REID
1920-1922   WALTER CHALMERS

Mention has already been made of S. W. Johnson having been Locomotive Superintendent of the Edinburgh & Glasgow Railway. He had continued in charge of the Western Division of the North British Railway after amalgamation and the N.B.R. Locomotive Superintendent, William Hurst, had done little in the way of reorganisation to meet the needs of the amalgamated company.

However, in 1867, a locomotive superintendent of the enlarged system as a whole was appointed and the choice fell upon THOMAS WHEATLEY. Born at Micklefield near Leeds in 1821 he took charge on 1st February 1867. He had been apprenticed on the Leeds & Selby Railway, then worked on the Midland and Manchester Sheffield & Lincolnshire Railways before spending five years as the Locomotive Superintendent of the L. & N.W.R. (Southern Division). During his term of office on the N.B.R., Wheatley concentrated on producing more powerful standard designs and also set about the modernisation of existing heterogeneous types. He also developed Cowlairs Works as the main workshops for the integrated system. A few of his locomotives survived at Grouping, but none of his most notable achievement, the first orthodox British inside cylinder 4-4-0's. His appointment was terminated in October 1874 and he then took a lease of the Wigtownshire Railway which he operated on his own account until his death at Wigtown on 13th March 1883.

Wheatley's successor was DUGALD DRUMMOND, whose father had been a permanent way inspector for the Company. Born at Ardrossan in 1840, he had served his apprenticeship in Glasgow. Next he worked under William Stroudley at Cowlairs, then went with him to the Highland Railway and later to the London Brighton & South Coast Railway. It was from Brighton that in February 1875 he returned to Cowlairs as Locomotive Superintendent. His earlier basic designs followed those of Stroudley but he departed entirely from Stroudley traditions in his inside cylinder 4-4-0's of 1876, basing these on the foundations laid by Wheatley. His locomotives set the pattern of N.B.R. locomotive practice for many years and the similarity of many of the designs of his successors to later Drummond designs for other railways can be noted. Drummond resigned from the N.B.R. in June 1882 on accepting the post of Locomotive Superintendent of the Caledonian Railway, where he held office until July 1890. His final appointment after a period in private business was on the London & South Western Railway in 1895 ; he died, after an accident at Eastleigh Works, in November 1912.

Drummond's successor on the N.B.R. was MATTHEW HOLMES, who had joined the Edinburgh & Glasgow Railway in 1859 in the days of William Paton and subsequently served in successive appointments on the N.B.R. His term of office of twenty-one years was the longest of any N.B.R. locomotive superintendent. Except in some details, the general Drummond tradition of design continued, though in some cases with enlarged boilers and increased boiler pressures. Methodical rebuilding of older engines to current standards was a policy of Holmes which was continued by his successor. Holmes retired in June 1903 and died on 3rd July 1903.

The next N.B.R. locomotive superintendent was likewise an N.B.R. man, WILLIAM PATON REID. He had been apprenticed at Cowlairs in 1879 and had served in various appointments on the N.B.R., ultimately as Holmes' second-in-command. His father had been Carriage & Wagon Superintendent on the N.B.R. Reid continued the well-established N.B.R. traditions, but the Directors forced his hand in the production of much larger and more powerful types of engine in 1906. Once this revolution was accomplished, the new standards were accepted and improved by Reid, particularly on the introduction of superheating. Reid continued the Holmes practice of rebuilding and modernising older engines in systematic batches and retired at the end of 1919, dying on 2nd February 1932 aged 77.

The last locomotive engineer of the N.B.R. was WALTER CHALMERS who took office on 1st January 1920. He also was an N.B.R. man ; his father had forty-three years service on the railway and was latterly Assistant Locomotive Superintendent under Reid. Chalmers himself had served his apprenticeship at Cowlairs and been in the service of the N.B.R. all his life, ultimately as Chief Draughtsman since 1904. On assuming charge of the locomotive department Chalmers became Chief Mechanical Engineer, but the functions of Locomotive Running Superintendent were transferred to a newly formed department with a separate organisation. His term of office was short and as the N.B.R. directors had ruled out new development so as not to prejudice the early production of group standard designs on the passing of the Railways Act 1921, he had little scope; however, one notable new design did reach the drawing-board, that of a three-cylinder 2-8-0 for mineral work. Chalmers retired in June 1924, after which R. A. Thom, mentioned above, became Mechanical Engineer for the whole of the Scottish Area of the L.N.E.R.

GREAT NORTH OF SCOTLAND RAILWAY

1857-1883	WILLIAM COWAN
1883-1890	JAMES MANSON
1890-1894	JAMES JOHNSON
1894-1914	WILLIAM PICKERSGILL
1914-1922	THOMAS EDWARD HEYWOOD

The first locomotive superintendent of the G.N.S.R., appointed in 1853, was the famous engineer D. K. Clark; his assistant at Aberdeen, J. F. Ruthven succeeded him in 1855. In August 1857 WILLIAM COWAN was appointed. He introduced outside cylinder 4-4-0's, giving greater boiler power than earlier designs, but sufficiently flexible for the winding nature of the G.N.S.R. lines. Some of these engines survived the Grouping. On his resignation in 1883 he found employment with the German firm of Krupps as a salesman for steel tyres in Britain and U.S.A.

JAMES MANSON, Cowan's successor, came from the Glasgow & South Western Railway. He had been born at Saltcoats in 1845. He completely revolutionised locomotive design on the G.N.S.R.; all old features such as brass domes, copper-capped chimneys and open splashers were swept away and inside cylinders became standard. Whilst on the G.N.S.R. he invented the tablet exchange apparatus which bears his name; he refused to patent it so that it could be freely adopted by all in the interests of safety. Manson's term of office was relatively short but during it two new locomotives were even built at Kittybrewster. Manson resigned in August 1890 on his appointment as Locomotive Superintendent of his old line, the G. & S.W.R., where he held office until retiring in November 1911; he died on 5th June 1935 aged 89.

His successor JAMES JOHNSON came to the G.N.S.R. from Derby; he was a son of S.W. Johnson. He was only on the G.N.S.R. for four years, but during that period he adopted as standard the 4-4-0 design with 6ft. 1in. coupled wheels which was to be followed for the rest of the Company's existence and also introduced the useful 0-4-4T's (L.N.E.R. class G10).

WILLIAM PICKERSGILL was born at Crewe in 1861, but had served his apprenticeship with the G.E.R., and subsequently worked on that railway prior to his appointment to the G.N.S.R. in May 1894. During his superintendency the new locomotive works at Inverurie were planned and built. Whilst he made no radical changes in design, he left the G.N.S.R. with a very adequate locomotive stock in first class condition when he departed for the Caledonian Railway in March 1914. Pickersgill continued after Grouping as Mechanical Engineer of the Northern Division of the L.M.S. until retirement in 1925; he died on 2nd May 1928.

THOMAS EDWARD HEYWOOD came to the G.N.S.R. from the Taff Vale Railway. He had been a pupil there and eventually chief assistant to T. Hurry Riches, and he had served also in Burma. Heywood was responsible for the extension of superheating on the G.N.S.R. After the Grouping he continued as Mechanical Engineer & Superintendent of the Northern Scottish Area of the L.N.E.R., then in August 1924 he went to Gorton, returning to Scotland in 1927 and retiring in June 1942. He died in November 1953 at Aberdeen.

MIDLAND & GREAT NORTHERN JOINT RAILWAY

Although its locomotives did not come under L.N.E.R. control until 1936, it is convenient to interpolate here a note on the locomotive engineers of this, the largest post-Grouping addition to L.N.E.R. locomotive stock.

On the formation of the Joint Committee, primary responsibility for locomotive power was undertaken by the Midland Railway. The majority of the new locomotives supplied in 1894 and succeeding years were accordingly to the designs of S. W. Johnson, though exceptionally in 1900 twelve 0-6-0's of a G.N.R. order to H. A. Ivatt's design were delivered to the M. & G.N.J.R.

Like Highbridge on the Somerset & Dorset Joint Railway (where also the Midland Railway was responsible for locomotive design) the Melton Constable works of the M. & G.N. were a long way from Derby. For this reason and because of locomotives inherited from its predecessors, there was an individuality about M. & G.N. locomotive design, although boilers nearly always adhered to the standards of Derby.

Amongst the locomotive engineers of the M. & G.N., special mention must be made of WILLIAM MARRIOTT. He had been apprenticed with Ransomes & Rapier at Ipswich and subsequently became Engineer and Contractor's Agent on the construction of various sections of the Yarmouth & North Norfolk Railway and Yarmouth Union Railways. In 1883 he was appointed Engineer to the Eastern & Midlands Railway and retained the appointment on the purchase of that line in 1893 by the Midland Railway and G.N.R. In 1919 he became also Traffic Manager. He retired in 1924. It was during Marriott's term of office that various tank engines were designed at Melton Constable and built or rebuilt there. He was also responsible for rebuilding existing tender engine designs.

Marriott's successors as Resident Mechanical Engineer were W. E. Newman and A. H. Nash. As no new tender engines had been supplied to the M. & G.N.J.R. since the nineteenth century a good job had been done with increasing weights of trains in maintaining a serviceable locomotive stock right up to its coming under L.N.E.R. control on 1st October 1936.

LONDON & NORTH EASTERN RAILWAY

1923-1941 HERBERT NIGEL GRESLEY
1941-1946 EDWARD THOMPSON
1946-1947 ARTHUR HENRY PEPPERCORN

As already mentioned it was HERBERT NIGEL GRESLEY of the Great Northern Railway whom the directors of the newly formed L.N.E.R. appointed to hold the office of Chief Mechanical Engineer (fig. 3). Gresley's larger G.N.R. designs and their developments were well suited for the services of the East Coast main line and its ancillary routes. For lesser services Gresley relied to a large extent on well tried designs of the constituent companies and where these did not suffice, his practice in the earlier years was to lay down merely the general principle leaving the detailed designing to be completed elsewhere as with the J38, J39, D49 and B17 classes. Gresley himself was a brilliant locomotive designer but he concentrated on the perfection of the steam engine and his outstanding designs rather than the general run of the locomotive stock as a whole. Where existing engines could perform their work satisfactorily, he saw no cause for their replacement particularly as the L.N.E.R.'s financial resources were limited.

Gresley's achievements as a locomotive engineer have already been extensively described in various works. It is not proposed to enlarge on these in this introduction but all

will be recounted in detail in the description of the individual classes constructed or modified by him.

Reorganisation of the locomotive works led to concentration of new construction principally at Doncaster and Darlington, also occasionally at Gorton, and for a number of years the separate Drawing Offices at Doncaster and Darlington continued to function, with consequent variations of practice and detailed design.

During Gresley's period of office, scope for construction was always limited by financial considerations ; the odd numbers of engines in later years in the various batches, construction of engines without tenders and the like bear witness to this. Despite all these difficulties, however, there is no doubt that with the continuance of the " big engine " policy Gresley kept the L.N.E.R. well to the fore in British locomotive design, culminating in his Green Arrows, A4 Pacifics, and finally in *Bantam Cock*, which, with the demise of Gresley and the advent of war, never had a fair chance of being multiplied.

Gresley was awarded a knighthood in the King's Birthday Honours of 1936 and died in office on 5th April 1941.

EDWARD THOMPSON (fig. 4) was Gresley's successor. He had served with Beyer, Peacock and the Midland Railway but had left the latter in 1905 to join the staff of the Royal Arsenal, Woolwich. In the following year he had gone to the N.E.R. In 1912 he had become Carriage & Wagon Superintendent of the G.N.R., but returned to the N.E.R. in 1920. Subsequently under the L.N.E.R. he had held office as Assistant Mechanical Engineer at Stratford, Darlington and Doncaster. Thompson has been much criticised for the changes of policy he introduced on taking office as C.M.E., but he was very fully cognisant of the conditions of wartime and the post-war period as regards maintenance which particularly affected the Gresley three-cylinder designs ; their conjugated valve gear required a higher standard of care and attention than was then available. He, therefore, sought simplification of design in the interests of easier and cheaper maintenance and also to provide adequate locomotives of the medium-powered size, which field Gresley had largely neglected. Thompson also sought greater standardisation of parts, carrying this at times to excess as was apparent when the tractive effort of his K1 and L1 classes is related to their adhesive weight and boiler capacity. But his basic designs were still true to L.N.E.R. traditions as a whole, though not necessarily those of Doncaster. Thompson retired in June 1946 at the age of 65 and died in July 1954.

For the short period until nationalisation ARTHUR HENRY PEPPERCORN (fig. 5) held

14

office as C.M.E. He had been a Doncaster pupil having been apprenticed in 1905 and held appointments thereafter on the G.N.R. and L.N.E.R., culminating with that of Assistant Chief Mechanical Engineer in 1941. His principal feature of design was that in his A1 and A2 class Pacifics he broke away from the Thompson insistence upon identical length of connecting rods with three-cylinder engines. He produced a modernised Pacific which, whilst having separate valve motion for each cylinder, had a wheelbase and overall length of comparable proportions to Gresley's designs. Peppercorn's A1 class Pacifics proved to be amongst the most free-running engines ever constructed. He retired from the position of C.M.E. Eastern and North Eastern Regions on 31st December 1949 and died in March 1951 aged 62.

LOCOMOTIVE POLICY AND CONSTRUCTION

The system adopted in this publication is to present the history of each class of locomotive in the order of its L.N.E.R. classification (details of which appear in a later chapter) with one modification : the tender engines are dealt with as a whole, under their respective wheel arrangements, the tank engines following. The use of this method facilitates reference but precludes to a large extent an historical sequence. So far as the constituent companies are concerned this is not so important, as the general trends of pre-Grouping design will appear from the class articles, but when considering the locomotives of the L.N.E.R. itself, a chronological approach is also required to appreciate the development of the various classes, and of L.N.E.R. locomotive construction and design.

In the first year of the L.N.E.R., new construction merely perpetuated the policies of the constituent Companies, including completion of orders already commenced or authorized. Consequently the 126 engines built in 1923 were of a wide variety of types :—

G.N.R.	4-6-2	A1	10
,,	2-8-0	O2	8
G.C.R.	4-6-0	B7	8
,,	4-6-2T	A5	10
G.E.R.	4-4-0	D16	10
,,	0-6-0T	J68	10
,,	0-6-2T	N7	3
N.E.R.	4-6-0	B16	30
,,	0-6-0	J27	10
,,	0-4-0T	Y7	5
N.B.R.	0-6-2T	N15	22

In 1924, the first new engines to purely L.N.E.R. orders were built. They were to existing pre-Grouping designs of the G.N.R. and G.C.R., modified to fit the all-line loading gauge of the new system (see pp. 78/9). The 1924 programme consisted of orders for 40 Gresley Pacifics, 24 Robinson Director class 4-4-0's and 50 Gresley K3 2-6-0's, and part of this programme had to be entrusted to outside contractors. The balance of certain orders for pre-Grouping designs were also completed in this year, namely :—

G.N.R.	2-8-0	O2	7
,,	0-6-0T	J50	10
G.C.R.	4-6-0	B7	2
G.E.R.	0-6-2T	N7	7
N.E.R.	4-6-2	A2	3
,,	4-6-0	B16	2
,,	0-8-0	Q7	10
N.B.R.	0-6-2T	N15	8

Of the 1924 L.N.E.R. programme, the following entered service in that year :—

4-6-2	A1	32
4-4-0	D11	24
2-6-0	K3	27

Altogether, new locomotives put into traffic in 1924 totalled 132, but the need for additional power had become urgent, particularly on the N.B.R. where many old engines were due for early withdrawal, and in 1924-25 to meet this requirement ten O4 2-8-0's and twenty-five J9 0-6-0's from the G.C., fourteen K2 2-6-0's and all fifteen D1 4-4-0's from the G.N. (the last mentioned nominally to replace D31's transferred to the G.N.S. Section), and twelve J24 0-6-0's from the N.E. were transferred to the N.B. Section. This policy continued, and in later years quite a number of engines from the G.N., G.E. and N.E. Sections found their way to the N.B. Section.

The year 1925 saw the celebration at Darlington of the Railway Centenary to mark the one hundredth anniversary of the opening of the Stockton & Darlington Railway. Two new Gresley designs were completed in time to take part in the celebrations, the freight engine version of the Pacific in the shape of the P1 class 2-8-2 Mikado and the Garratt for banking on the Worsborough incline of the G.C. Section. Other new construction followed existing designs of the four principal English constituent companies. The G.C. Robinson 4-6-2T type was adopted to enable an immediate order to be placed to meet a need for large passenger tank engines for the N.E. Section. The

G.N.R. design of 0-6-2T was built for service in Scotland but the G.E.R. design was built for London suburban services on the G.N. and G.E. Sections. Two existing N.E.R. shunting tank designs were also multiplied. An additional ten K3's were ordered. Inclusive of completion of the 1924 orders, a total of 114 engines was built in 1925, namely :—

4-6-2	A1	8
2-6-0	K3	33
2-8-2	P1	2
4-6-2T	A5	9
0-6-0T	J72	10
0-6-2T	N2	18
0-6-2T	N7	28
4-8-0T	T1	5
2-8-0+0-8-2	U1	1

It will be observed that apart from the two Mikados no eight-coupled freight tender engines were built. This position obtained for many years as during 1924-29 the L.N.E.R. took delivery from the Government of no less than 273 Robinson 2-8-0's of class O4 which had been built for the Railway Operating Division in 1917-19 and had been on the R.O.D. stock list. The practice of naming the principal express engines of L.N.E.R. construction (see p. 50) was adopted in 1925, mainly in the interests of publicity ; with the exception of the N.B.R. and to a lesser extent the G.C.R. the constituent companies of the L.N.E.R. had been sparing in the practice of naming locomotives.

In 1926 only 104 new locomotives were constructed. Two new designs of 0-6-0 appeared, both the product of Darlington drawing office, though of course with Gresley features. The first of these new designs comprised the J38 class 0-6-0 with 4ft. 8in. coupled wheels for mineral service in Scotland, the entire class being constructed in 1926. The other new design was the J39 class with coupled wheels six inches larger for general goods traffic ; construction of this class continued in every subsequent year until 1938, and with eighteen more engines built in 1941 it became numerically the largest class on the L.N.E.R., apart from the Robinson 2-8-0, though with completion after nationalisation of the orders for Thompson B1 class 4-6-0's its total was considerably surpassed. Other construction in 1926 was of tank engines in continuation of existing orders and a new order for Gresley J50 0-6-0T's, now adopted as a standard design for heavy shunting work after trials at Ardsley in October 1925 of J77 No. 1313 and J83 No. 9806. The 104 engines built in 1926 were :—

0-6-0	J38	35
0-6-0	J39	17
4-6-2T	A5	4
0-6-0T	J50	27
0-6-2T	N7	21

In 1927 two new designs were evolved. The most important was not yet the subject of new construction but resulted from the rebuilding of two Gresley Pacifics with higher boiler pressure and long-travel valve gear as class A3. While this rebuilding was being dealt with at Doncaster, Darlington completed a new three-cylinder 4-4-0 design, the D49 Shire class, carrying the same boiler as the J39 class 0-6-0. In the same year Sentinel shunting engines first appear as additions to the running stock, although the first had been delivered in 1925 on the Departmental Stock list. Following the General Strike of 1926 and its economic consequences, new construction in 1927 totalled only 81 engines :—

4-4-0	D49	7
0-6-0	J39	27
0-6-0T	J50	5
0-6-2T	N7	38
Sentinel	Y1	2
Sentinel	Y3	2

The year 1928 saw the first construction at Doncaster of new engines of the A3 class Pacific design, for which an order for ten was placed, and in addition three further conversions from A1 to A3 were carried out at Darlington. At the same time the famous corridor tenders were built in connection with non-stop running between London and Edinburgh ; most of these ten tenders were in fact fitted to earlier Pacifics (see page 64). For the G.E. Section the need for new locomotive power had become a matter of urgent concern. Projected designs belong to another part of this publication ; suffice it here to say that the first Gresley essays for a 4-6-0 for the G.E. Section did not satisfy the stringent limitations of weight and length at that time operative, whilst a design for a large tank engine prepared at Stratford was abandoned. As a matter of urgency, therefore, ten additional G.E.-type 4-6-0's of the B12 class were built by outside contractors, though at the end of the year an order for ten three-cylinder 4-6-0's of a new design, the B17 Sandringham class, was delivered, the product of collaboration between the Darlington drawing office and the North British Locomotive Company who were the builders. For suburban tank engines, the G.E. design continued to be built, and for the G.N. Section and for Scotland more engines of the G.N. design were constructed. In 1928 a total of 116 new engines appeared :—

4-6-2	A3	6
4-6-0	B12	10
4-6-0	B17	10
4-4-0	D49	19
0-6-0	J39	30
0-6-2T	N2	16
0-6-2T	N7	25

The year 1929 saw the last 0-6-2T's built and also, with lean times ahead, was the last in which new construction exceeded 100 except for 1935, until the post-war years of 1946 and 1947. The total of 106 engines built in 1929 consisted of :—

4-6-2	A3	4
4-4-0	D49	10
0-6-0	J39	40
2-6-0	K3	20
0-6-2T	N2	13
Sentinel	Y1	13
Sentinel	Y3	6

The major new design of 1930 was Gresley's experimental " Hush-hush " 4-6-4 No. 10000 with its Yarrow water-tube boiler. Also in that year, more Pacifics were needed and an order was placed for eight, bringing the total up to 75 ; it was not until 1933 that the first Pacific for the West Coast route was built by the L.M.S. After teething troubles, the Sandringham 4-6-0 design was accepted as successful and further orders for the class were placed. At last the design of a Gresley three-cylinder passenger tank engine went into production with the V1 class 2-6-2T, and two special Sentinels for tramway work on the G.E. Section were built. Total new construction in 1930 was only 74 engines :—

4-6-2	A3	8
4-6-0	B17	12
0-6-0	J39	9
2-6-0	K3	9
4-6-4	W1	1
0-6-0T	J50	6
2-6-2T	V1	9
Sentinel	Y3	18
Sentinel	Y10	2

New construction in 1931 included further orders for existing designs and it will be noted that the K3 class continued to be multiplied. In all 69 engines were built :—

4-6-0	B17	15
0-6-0	J39	9
2-6-0	K3	20
2-6-2T	V1	19
Sentinel	Y3	6

In 1932 a series of modified D49 class 4-4-0's, the Hunts, was constructed, the last design from the Darlington drawing office. The financial crisis of 1931 and the ensuing depression had its effect on the L.N.E.R. Only 34 engines were built, but it is of interest that construction was at last required of eight-coupled tender engines, and for this the Gresley three-cylinder G.N. 2-8-0 design was adopted. For additional hump-shunting engines, two more were built of a class that had been introduced by Robinson in 1908, though the 1932 engines were similar in most details to a 1932 rebuild of the original design and were equipped with boosters. The 34 engines built in 1932 were :—

4-4-0	D49	10
0-6-0	J39	14
2-8-0	O2	8
0-8-4T	S1	2

In 1933 there was an order for six Sandringhams and eight more 2-8-0's. Only 17 engines were completed :—

4-6-0	B17	6
4-4-0	D49	5
0-6-0	J39	2
2-8-0	O2	4

Such limited new locomotive construction could not continue for more than a short period and the year 1934 saw several new orders placed, including one for the last nine A3 Pacifics and two orders with contractors for a total of twenty K3 class 2-6-0's, the forerunners of succeeding orders for 54 more engines of the class, 30 with contractors and 24 at Darlington, which were completed in the following three years. The first of a new order for V1 2-6-2T's was also constructed. What is of importance, however, is that 1934 began the final seven years of Gresley's long term of office at Doncaster ; the P2 class 2-8-2 *Cock o' the North* for express passenger service in Scotland was the first of the series of new designs, representing the final developments of his principles, which appeared during those seven years. Total new construction rose to 60 engines during the year :—

4-6-2	A3	8
4-4-0	D49	20
0-6-0	J39	12
2-6-0	K3	13
2-8-0	O2	4
2-8-2	P2	2
2-6-2T	V1	1

The year 1935 marked King George V's silver jubilee, and the outstanding feature of the year on the L.N.E.R. was the high-speed " Silver Jubilee " express, with the specially designed streamlined A4 Pacifics built to work it. Also during 1935 a Government-assisted loan scheme enabled new construction to be stepped up for that and the succeeding year, 22 engines ordered in the Company's shops being charged to this account in addition to ten K3 class 2-6-0's built by Armstrong, Whitworth & Co. in 1936. Generally withdrawal policy had hitherto been on a sectional basis, older engines being broken up as replacements became available, but the Government loan scheme enabled the withdrawal as a class of the small Ivatt Atlantics of class C2. Locomotive construction in 1935 rose to 102 engines, including a large order for J39 class 0-6-0's ; details are :—

4-6-2	A3	1
4-6-2	A4	4
4-6-0	B17	5
4-4-0	D49	5
0-6-0	J39	39
2-6-0	K3	27
2-6-2T	V1	21

In 1936 the streamlined version of the P2 class appeared, but more important was the

17

construction of the first of the mixed-traffic class V2 2-6-2 Green Arrows which were to play so large a part in assisting the Pacifics with the heavy traffic of the 1939-45 war. The original order for class V2 was for five engines. On completion during the following year of existing orders, no more class K3 2-6-0's were built, but two orders for fourteen and eleven Sandringhams respectively were in the 1936 and 1937 construction programmes. The success of the A4 class Pacifics led to the placing of an order for seventeen more, to be followed in 1937 by an order for an additional fourteen, bringing the total of the class up to thirty-five engines on completion of the latter order in 1938. Total construction in 1936 was of 88 engines :—

4-6-2	A4	2
4-6-0	B17	14
0-6-0	J39	25
2-6-0	K3	26
2-8-2	P2	4
2-6-2	V2	5
2-6-2T	V1	12

In 1937 Doncaster Plant was fully occupied building A4 class 4-6-2's and construction of an order for 28 further V2 class 2-6-2's was undertaken at Darlington. In this year another new Gresley design appeared, the K4 class 2-6-0, "tailor made" for the special problems of the West Highland line, and the prototype was the first of an order for six engines. Total construction in 1937 was of 69 engines :—

4-6-2	A4	19
4-6-0	B17	11
0-6-0	J39	10
2-6-0	K3	8
2-6-0	K4	1
2-6-2	V2	20

The 1938 programme underwent a significant change ; an order for 32 Sandringhams was cancelled in favour of 28 more Green Arrows, making a total of 39, to be completed in 1938-39. An order for J39 class 0-6-0's announced as for 38 engines, was reduced to 37, possibly on account of rising costs of construction. Two new tank engine orders were begun, one for twenty V1 class 2-6-2T's and the other for fourteen J50 class 0-6-0T's. New construction in 1938 totalled 91 engines :—

4-6-2	A4	10
0-6-0	J39	37
2-6-0	K4	5
2-6-2	V2	19
0-6-0T	J50	5
2-6-2T	V1	15

The year 1939 saw the outbreak of war. A new class introduced was the V3 class 2-6-2T, a modification of the earlier V1 design employing a higher boiler pressure ; an order for ten engines was placed. The main feature of locomotive construction for the year was the steady multiplication of the V2 class. During the year 62 engines were built :—

2-6-2	V2	42
0-6-0T	J50	9
2-6-2T	V1	5
2-6-2T	V3	6

In 1940 construction was limited to 36 engines consisting mainly of Green Arrows, whilst the order for V3 class 2-6-2T's was completed. The 36 engines were :—

2-6-2	V2	32
2-6-2T	V3	4

During the year 1941 the sudden death of Sir Nigel Gresley occurred. Just prior to this, his last new design of steam locomotive to be constructed had appeared, namely the V4 class 2-6-2 *Bantam Cock*. A further series of J39 class 0-6-0's was built, bringing the total of the class up to 289 engines, also the prototype 1500-volt 0-4-4-0 locomotive for the Manchester-Sheffield electrification was completed. Total construction in the year was 37 locomotives :—

0-6-0	J39	18
2-6-2	V2	16
2-6-2	V4	2
0-4-4-0	Electric	1

During Gresley's term of office and taking the figures to the end of 1941, a total of 1518 locomotives was constructed for the L.N.E.R. Of these, 1153 (to which a further 75 were added in 1942-44) were of designs initiated by Gresley, the remainder being designs of the constituent companies (other than G.N.R.) or the manufacturers in the case of Sentinel locomotives. Locomotive policy during Gresley's period of office was undoubtedly affected to a considerable extent by the depressed state of industry in a large part of the country served by the L.N.E.R. and the financial consequences to the railway. The L.M.S. under Sir Henry Fowler was able to implement a policy of wholesale scrapping of pre-Grouping engines and their replacement by standard types, mostly of Midland origin, a policy continued by Sir William Stanier with his own designs. The G.W.R. had completely eliminated the four-coupled express engine by 1933, and could cheerfully undertake the replacement of its entire stock of 0-6-0T's, over 1200 of them, by a similar number of modern engines of the same wheel arrangement. On the L.N.E.R., on the other hand, while new construction was sufficient to allow Gresley to persevere with the development of his specialised designs and to pursue the "big engine" policies of his predecessors, standardisation had perforce to be largely confined to such things as engine and boiler fittings, which were made interchangeable as far as possible. Gresley was fortunate in having taken over a reasonably efficient stud of locomotives from the constituent companies and judicious rebuilding enabled them to keep

Fig. 1
William Whitelaw, Esq.,
Chairman of the L.N.E.R., 1923-38

Fig. 2
Sir Ralph Wedgwood, Chief General
Manager of the L.N.E.R., 1923-39

Fig. 3   Sir Nigel Gresley (left), Chief Mechanical Engineer of the L.N.E.R.,
1923-41, with the Hon. Vincent Massey at the naming ceremony of class A4
No. 4489 Dominion of Canada at King's Cross, 15th June 1937. Stainless
steel Gill Sans lettering on cabside

Class A1 No. 4476 Royal Lancer

Fig. 4   Edward Thompson, Esq.,
Chief Mechanical Engineer of
the L.N.E.R., 1941-46

Fig. 5   Arthur H. Peppercorn, Esq.,
Chief Mechanical Engineer of the
L.N.E.R., 1946-47

Fig. 6

Fig. 7

End views of Gresley eight-wheeled corridor tender

Fig. 8

Class D3 No. 2000 at Doncaster Works, 1947.
With side window cab, green livery and Gill Sans lettering.
L.N.E.R. coat of arms on the tender

Fig. 9

Class A1 No. 4472 *Flying Scotsman* at Doncaster Works, 1924. With L.N.E.R. coat of arms
on cab for the Wembley Exhibition. G.N.-type eight-wheel tender

Fig. 10   Class A4 No. 4498 *Sir Nigel Gresley* heading
north through Potters Bar, about 1938

Fig. 11   Class P2 No. 2001 *Cock o'the North* on trial passing Brookmans Park, 1934

Fig. 12   Class A1 No. 2543 *Melton* on the 1-30 p.m. down from King's Cross to
Edinburgh passing Wood Green, May 1926

Fig. 13   Class K3 No. 17 pausing at Ripon on the " Northern Belle " touring train, 1934

Fig. 14   The 4-0 p.m. " Coronation " and Leeds expresses leaving King's Cross hauled by class A4 No. 4467 *Wild Swan* and A3 No. 4480 *Enterprise*, about 1938

Fig. 15   Class A4 No. 4491 *Commonwealth of Australia* climbing Cockburnspath bank with the up "Coronation," 1937

Fig. 16   Class V2 No. 4798 on a down Newcastle express at New Southgate, 1937

Fig. 17   L.N.E.R. shaded numerals
on class A4 No. 2509
Silver Link. Normally
these were gilt or
yellow but several
A4's had silver as
shown

Fig. 18   Class A2 No. 2005
Thane of Fife showing
post-1943 method of
indicating classification
on bufferbeam, also
shed allocation

Fig. 19   Class K3 No. 3818 and V2 No. 4792 at Doncaster shed, about 1938.
Showing pre-1943 method of indicating classification on bufferbeam

abreast of requirements. This rebuilding did not aim at providing the prototypes for new standard designs, as in the case of Gresley's successor, but in the main at improving existing designs. Rebuilding was also carried out in some cases for experimental reasons, as for example with the four N.E. class C7 Atlantics. The principal new designs resulting from rebuilding under Gresley were:—

4-6-2	A3	1927
4-6-2T	A8	1931
4-4-2	C9	1931
4-6-0	B12/3	1932
2-8-0	O4/5	1932
4-4-0	D16/3	1933
0-6-0	J19/2	1934
4-6-0	B16/2	1937
2-8-0	O4/7	1939

In addition, in reviewing motive power during Gresley's term of office, it should be mentioned that in the years 1925 to 1932 no less than 91 steam railcars were put into service, with a further three diesel-electric railcars and a diesel railbus in 1931-34.

The Thompson era began in 1942, and he was at once faced with the problem of wartime conditions of maintenance, combined with a large stud of pre-Grouping engines, now twenty years older than when Gresley had become Chief Mechanical Engineer of the L.N.E.R.

In 1942, with the exception of one engine, all construction was to Gresley designs. The loss of 92 Robinson 2-8-0's to the War Department in Autumn, 1941 had accentuated the need for eight-coupled tender engines and an order for 25 Gresley O2 class 2-8-0's without new tenders was put in hand at Doncaster (see page 67). Production of the V2 class also continued. The first Thompson engine, the two-cylinder " General Service " 4-6-0, was completed at Darlington in December. In July Thompson's first rebuild had appeared, the 0-8-0T of class Q1 rebuilt from a G.C. Q4 class 0-8-0 tender engine, followed in August by D49 Hunt class No. 365 *The Morpeth* rebuilt with two inside cylinders. Reference is made in another chapter to temporary classifications ; to avoid confusion, ultimate L.N.E.R. classifications are used in describing Thompson's engines. The total of 53 locomotives built in 1942 comprised :—

4-6-0	B1	1
2-8-0	O2	23
2-6-2	V2	29

In 1943 construction of the V2 class continued, together with further engines of class B1. In January reconstruction of P2 class No. 2005 *Thane of Fife* as a 4-6-2 of class A2/2 provided the prototype for the Thompson Pacifics. Another rebuilding was of G.C. J11 class 0-6-0's with new motion and piston valves ; if the standardisation scheme

mentioned later had been fully implemented, new boilers of L.N.E.R. pattern would probably have replaced those with Belpaire fireboxes on these engines. The year 1943 also saw large orders for the Stanier-type 2-8-0 engines placed at various railway workshops. The first of these constructed by the L.N.E.R. was completed at Doncaster in June, being No. 8510 on the L.M.S. stock lists, the first engine with a Belpaire firebox to be built at Doncaster. Total new L.N.E.R. locomotive construction in 1943 was of 22 engines :—

4-6-0	B1	4
2-8-0	O2	2
2-6-2	V2	16

The year 1944 saw the last Green Arrows built, bringing the total of this very useful class to 184 engines ; four further engines on order were modified by Thompson and turned out as 4-6-2's of class A2/1, following the lines of the class A2/2 rebuild of the previous year, though smaller in certain dimensions. During the year, Stanier-type 2-8-0's first appeared in the L.N.E.R. stock list as class O6, 25 engines being built at the Brighton works of the Southern Railway ; construction of similar engines at L.N.E.R. works continued but the engines so built were on the L.M.S. stock list though remaining on the L.N.E.R. on loan. Success of diesel-electric shunting locomotives on other lines led to the first L.N.E.R. construction of this type. By rebuilding Robinson O4 class 2-8-0's with B1-type boilers, cylinders and motion, the Thompson standard mineral engine design of class O1 was produced, as also was class O4/8, a similar rebuild but retaining the original cylinders and valve gear. Rebuilding of Raven 4-6-0's as class B16/3 with three independent sets of Walschaerts valve gear also began : Gresley had started this process back in 1937 but used his derived valve gear for the middle cylinder. Total new L.N.E.R. locomotives in 1944 comprised 41 engines :—

4-6-2	A2/1	3
4-6-0	B1	5
2-8-0	O6	25
2-6-2	V2	5
0-6-0	Diesel	3

In addition 30 Stanier 2-8-0's for L.M.S. stock were built at Doncaster and Darlington.

In 1945, new construction included the prototype general service L1 class 2-6-4T engine. The rebuilding of K4 class 2-6-0 No. 3445 provided the prototype for the class K1 2-6-0's. Another new class was the B2 class 4-6-0, a two-cylinder rebuild of the B17 Sandringham class and very similar to the B3/3 class rebuilding of No. 6166 *Earl Haig* in October 1943. Also during 1945 a K3 class 2-6-0 was rebuilt with two cylinders and higher boiler pressure to become class K5. On

19

completion of the remaining 29 of the order for 60 Stanier 2-8-0's for L.M.S. stock, further engines of the same type for L.N.E.R. stock were built at Doncaster and Darlington. Only 21 new L.N.E.R. engines were built during the year :—

4-6-2	A2/1	1
2-8-0	O6	18
2-6-4T	L1	1
0-6-0	Diesel	1

With the cessation of hostilities, considerable additions to stock were made in 1946. In June, Thompson retired. Many of his locomotives were constructed after his retirement in the initial stages of the L.N.E.R.'s never-to-be completed "Five Year Plan," under which 1000 new locomotives were to have been built. Under Thompson's standardisation policy in its final form as laid down in 1945 and as published officially by the L.N.E.R., there were to be ten standard types :—

A1	4-6-2	Express Passenger
A2	4-6-2	Heavy Passenger and Freight
B1	4-6-0	General Utility
K1	2-6-0	Mixed Traffic
O1	2-8-0	Mineral
J11	0-6-0	Freight
L1	2-6-4T	Mixed Traffic Tank
Q1	0-8-0T	Heavy Shunting Tank
J50	0-6-0T	Medium Shunting Tank

Light Shunting Tank (to be designed).

The only other existing types which were to be reboilered and maintained were :—

A3	4-6-2	with further rebuilds from original series
A4	4-6-2	as built by Gresley
B2	4-6-0	as rebuilt from B17
B16	4-6-0	as rebuilt
D49	4-4-0	as rebuilt
K5	2-6-0	as rebuilt from K3
V2	2-6-2	as built by Gresley
V1	2-6-2T	as built by Gresley
V3	2-6-2T	as built by Gresley

All other classes were to be withdrawn as boilers wore out. Of the above standard designs the first of the new A1 class Pacifics was provided in September 1945 by completely rebuilding No. 4470 *Great Northern*, whilst the A2 class were new engines, following in general features Thompson's class A2/2 rebuilds. During 1946, in addition to new construction, the purchase was arranged of 275 locomotives from the Ministry of Supply ; 190 " Austerity " 2-8-0's were added to stock as class O7 in 1946 and 10 more in 1947, whilst 70 0-6-0ST's were acquired in 1946 as class J94, the remaining engine being delivered in 1947. Certain of these J94 class engines were in fact delivered direct from makers. These purchases obviated the construction of further eight-coupled tender engines and class J50

0-6-0T's which otherwise would doubtless have been ordered. Total new construction in 1946 was 112 engines, of which the B1 class engines were the first of a large order :—

4-6-2	A2/3	9
4-6-0	B1	78
2-8-0	O6	25

In 1947, during the last year of the L.N.E.R.'s existence, the first of Peppercorn's Pacifics was completed and the B1 class 4-6-0's were rapidly multiplied to bring the total up to 274, only fifteen behind the J39 class 0-6-0 total on 31st December 1947. Compared with the Gresley period, different financial considerations now obtained : the major problem was that of material and facilities for getting engines built rather than ruthless pruning of expenditure. In 1947 a total of 193 new engines were constructed, which brought the total new engines built in the twenty-five years, 1923-47, up to 1,960. The new engines of 1947 were :—

4-6-2	A2	1
4-6-2	A2/3	6
4-6-0	B1	186

But even while the L.N.E.R. still existed, the steam engine was doomed ; in 1947 the L.N.E.R. announced that 25 diesel-electric locomotives of 1600 h.p. would be built, intended for working in tandem on the principal Anglo-Scottish expresses. It was also planned to purchase 176 diesel-electric shunters of 350 h.p. to replace 217 steam engines.

Although covering a period after the L.N.E.R. was taken over by the British Transport Commission, mention must be made of further construction to L.N.E.R. design which took place in the next five years. Certain orders placed prior to nationalisation were fulfilled and in addition new construction to existing designs proceeded pending the formulation of British Railways standard locomotive designs.

In 1948 the first of Peppercorn's A1 class Pacifics were completed ; these engines were destined to play their part equally with the Gresley engines on the East Coast main line in succeeding years. A large number of an order for Thompson's 2-6-4T's also entered service. The total of new engines for the year was 162, made up as under :—

4-6-2	A1	21
4-6-2	A2	14
4-6-0	B1	68
2-6-4T	L1	59

Construction of standard designs continued in 1949. Delivery was taken of the majority of an order for 70 K1 class 2-6-0's. With no new design of light shunting engine (cf. Thompson's standardisation scheme mentioned above), reversion was made to Wilson Worsdell's N.E.R. 0-6-0T design of 1898. A total of 137 engines of L.N.E.R. design was delivered :—

4-6-2	A1	28
4-6-0	B1	18
2-6-0	K1	61
0-6-0T	J72	15
2-6-4T	L1	15

The year 1950 saw Doncaster and Darlington building . L.M.S.-type 2-6-0 engines to British Railways orders, and also completion of all orders for L.N.E.R.-designed engines except the B1 class. The 63 engines of L.N.E.R. design built during the year were :—

4-6-0	B1	24
2-6-0	K1	9
0-6-0T	J72	5
2-6-4T	L1	25

The order for J72 0-6-0T's was completed by the building of eight engines in 1951, whilst the final B1 class 4-6-0 engines were nineteen built in 1951 and seven in 1952.

LOCOMOTIVE CLASSIFICATION

POSITION AT GROUPING

All the constituent companies of the L.N.E.R. used some form of identification for their different classes of engines at the time of Grouping, but not one of them had gone so far as to do the job systematically. In use were letters only, numbers only, a letter followed by a number (or numbers) and a number (or numbers) preceding a letter, but in no case was there any real attempt at providing significant information.

Great Northern Railway

On the G.N.R. two systems had been in use. One was more correctly an order identification and was a very complicated series in which, for example, the 4-4-2T's were either T, X or X2. This is the classification used in G. F. Bird's *Locomotives of the G. N. R.*, but it does not seem to have been continued after Gresley succeeded Ivatt in October 1911. The other system, which was in wider use, appears to date from June 1900, and is of particular importance because the same basis was used by the L.N.E.R. The method was to allocate a class letter to each wheel arrangement, and to follow the letter by a number for each broad division, although this was not taken very far. The class letters in the original list were selected in ascending number of driving axles, but in descending number of leading carrying axles ; this worked out as :— A 4-2-2, B 2-2-2, C 4-4-2, D 4-4-0, E 2-4-0, F 0-4-2, G 0-4-4, H 2-6-0, J 0-6-0, and to these were added K 0-8-0 (in 1901), L 0-8-2 (in 1903), M 0-4-0 rail motors (in 1905), N 0-6-2 (in 1907), and O 2-8-0 (in 1913).

As mentioned, the numbers following the class letters did not extend very far. All the Atlantic-type tender engines, whether small or large boilered, saturated or superheated, simple or compound began, and remained, combined as class C1 and the 4-4-2T's were C2. This was over-simplification, and a more realistic approach was shown in the 0-6-0 type where, for example, engines with 4ft. 8in. diameter boilers became J4 and those with 4ft. 5in. diameter became J5. With only two minor exceptions, however, individual designs of the same wheel arrangement were arranged in descending order of driving wheel diameter.

Before Grouping, wheel types 4-2-2, 2-2-2 and 0-4-2 had disappeared but by then the first two 4-6-2 engines had been built and the vacant A1 classification allocated to them.

Great Central Railway

The G.C.R. was using a system begun by Sacré in 1859 and some engines which became L.N.E.R. property were still known by the class designations given to them in the 1870's. This method used a number for each class, in some cases with suffix letters, and examples of Sacré's original classification still in use at Grouping were classes 4 (from 1876), 6B (from 1877), 6C (from 1880), 7 (from 1885) and 12A (from 1875). Parker, Pollitt and Robinson all continued to use the same basis and, as the older engines were scrapped and their class numbers became vacant, these gaps were filled by more modern engines. No effort was made to increase the range of class numbers, indeed this tended to contract, but a multiplicity of suffix letters was allocated so that class 8 had thirteen of them and class 9 had them from A to Q inclusive. Their only basis seems to have been what was available when a new class designation was required, and they were quite uninformative. They gave no indication as to age, power, wheel type or even to the use of the same type of boiler. For example, classes 1 and 1A were both 4-6-0 types but class 1B were 2-6-4T's using quite a different boiler, whilst classes 9L and 9P had little more in common than the same livery ! The former was a 4-4-2T design with two inside cylinders and 5ft. 7in. coupled wheels built in 1907, the latter a four-

21

cylinder 4-6-0 type with 6ft. 9in. coupled wheels built from 1917 with a boiler having more than twice the heating surface of that on the tank engine. Some of the suffixes were however abbreviations, examples being classes 9A ALT (9A with *altered* bunker), 18 CONV (18 *converted* to tank engine), 12AT (a *Tank* engine version of 12A), 12AM (12AT fitted for *Motor* working), 6AI (an *improved* version of 6A), and 6DB (a *Bogie* version of 6D). Class 4 covered miscellaneous contractors-type tank engines of different designs and even wheel arrangements. The G.C.R. stock at Grouping still contained one engine peculiar to the Wrexham Mold & Connah's Quay Railway and this was without classification other than "W.M. & C.Q.," but the four classes taken over in 1907 from the Lancashire Derbyshire & East Coast Railway still retained that company's classification of A, B, C and D.

Great Eastern Railway

The G.E.R. method of engine classification was even older, dating back possibly to 1856 when Sinclair was the locomotive engineer. It was based on order numbers placed in Stratford Works and invariably used a letter followed by a number. This same system applied equally to the ordering of boilers, tenders and other items and so there was no continuity about the engine classification (for further details see p. 95). It was the custom to refer to the class by the number of the first order placed for it, so that the smallest of the 0-6-0T's were known as class E22, this being the order number of the first batch of ten built in 1889. The other batch of ten of this type were built in 1893 to order B32 but this designation was never used for the classification, all twenty engines being known as class E22 and this applied generally to the other classes. At Grouping there were still examples of two classes which were outside this system and these were known as classes " 204 " and " 209 " from the running numbers of the first engines built in these classes. The class " 204 " 0-6-0 crane tanks dated from 1868 and the class " 209 " 0-4-0T's from 1874 and both were bought from private locomotive firms so that Stratford Works order numbers could presumably not be used. Another engine of class " 209 " was obtained in 1876, but in 1897 and again in 1903 Stratford themselves built two identical engines and whilst these received order numbers (G40 and R55), they were never used for classification purposes.

North Eastern Railway

On the N.E.R. there were four different types of classification in use but each provided at least one item of information about the class concerned. Engines built prior to 1886 usually took the running number of one of the engines as their class designation and examples

which came into the L.N.E.R. were " 901 " (first built in 1872) and " 1463 " (built in 1885). There was one notable exception to this method—the Fletcher 0-4-4T's of 1874— these were always known in North Eastern circles as class BTP, which simply indicated " Bogie Tank Passenger." In 1886 T. W. Worsdell became locomotive superintendent and he introduced an alphabetical classification which was still in use at Grouping. His first new design was class A and succeeding designs took the next available letter, but where new engines were an improvement of, or a modification to, an existing class, a numerical suffix was used. Thus the piston valve 0-8-0's first built in 1901 were classified T and when a slide valve version appeared in 1902 it became class T1. In 1913 a bigger and superheated version appeared and took class T2, while the still more powerful three-cylinder development of 1919 became class T3. Even so, all twenty-six letters of the alphabet had been allocated when the class Z Atlantics were built in 1911, but with the rebuilding to 4-4-0 class F1 of two experimental compound 2-4-0's which had been class D, this letter provided a vacancy which was taken up by the 4-4-4T design of 1913. When Raven's Pacifics appeared late in 1922 this example could have been followed, as both classes I and J had recently become vacant by the scrapping of the 4-2-2 engines. Instead, the Pacifics were made class " 4.6.2 ".

The fourth North Eastern system of classifying their engines was their most descriptive, but covered only two classes comprising a total of three engines. These were 3CC for the three-cylinder compound 4-4-0 of 1898 and 4CC for the two four-cylinder compound Atlantics of 1906 and these descriptions were still in use at Grouping. Indeed engine 1619 retained " Class 3CC " on its front buffer beam to the end of its days in October 1930.

Hull & Barnsley Railway

On 31st March 1922 the Hull & Barnsley Railway ceased its independent existence and was absorbed by the North Eastern Railway. The H. & B.R. was already using a single letter classification, in some classes with a suffix which was usually a figure, but there was one case, the five superheated goods engines of 1915, where the suffix was another letter—they were class LS, which was short for " L Superheated ". The N.E.R. continued to use this classification and simply added " (HB) " to each designation to avoid confusion with their own use of the same letters. Thus class A were N.E.R. 2-4-2T's but A (HB) were 0-8-0 tender engines. By Grouping H. & B.R. class letters C, D, E, H and K had already gone out of use due to the engines in them having been either rebuilt, scrapped or sold.

22

North British Railway

From 1st September 1913 the N.B.R. endeavoured to give some indication of the power capabilities of its engines by its classification in connection with the introduction on that date of Train Control similar to the Midland pattern. Single letters only were used, A to G for goods and shunting engines, and H to R (with O and Q vacant) for passenger engines, generally on the basis of the earlier the letter, the higher the power, but the Scotts and Glens were out of step at J and K respectively. Quite a number of differing types could therefore have the same class letter, for instance class M included 4-4-0 tender as well as 4-4-2 and 0-4-4 tank engines. Of the engines which became L.N.E.R. stock only one did not have an N.B.R. class allocated to it—this was No. 1011 (L.N.E.R. class Y10). The principal defect of this scheme, not inherent in the system itself, was that no provision had been made for future developments in the original allocation of letters (for fuller details see under "Load and Power Classification," pages 88/9.

Great North of Scotland Railway

On the G.N.S.R. a single letter classification was also used which had been initiated by Wm. Cowan in either 1879 or 1880. This utilised the letters A to M (with the possible exception of I) in order of date of appearance of the first of each class, working upwards from the most elderly. It was also the practice to fill gaps as they became available and by 1885 classes A, C, D, E and G were all in use for the second time. The series then continued with class N in 1887 and proceeded with regularity (except that class U was never used) to class Y in 1915. There was a reversion to the practice of the early 1880's with the last G.N.S.R. class to be built, in that the eight superheated engines of 1920-21 took class F which had become vacant in 1916.

L.N.E.R. CLASSIFICATION

When Gresley was appointed Chief Mechanical Engineer of the L.N.E.R. in February 1923 he moved his headquarters from Doncaster to offices at King's Cross, but it seemed natural that the work of taking stock of what was now group motive power should be done by his old staff. Thus the Chief Draughtsman at Doncaster was made responsible for devising a classification of locomotives, but the actual work was done by one of his assistants, Edward Windle. Gorton, Stratford, Darlington and Cowlairs (acting also for Inverurie) were requested to submit the relevant information, and dealing with their engines in that sequence, a scheme was drawn up which Gresley approved on 3rd September 1923. This was essentially a revised version of the G.N.R. scheme in that a letter represented a wheel arrangement combined with a number indicating the variant within it. In every wheel arrangement but two (probably due to a change from the original intention) tender engines were dealt with first, followed by tank engines, whilst the numbers for the individual locomotive classes, with one exception, took the sequence G.N., G.C., G.E., N.E., N.B. and G.N.S. Railways. The selection of wheel arrangement this time took the form six-coupled passenger, four-coupled passenger, six-coupled goods, eight-coupled goods and small miscellaneous, as follows :— A 4-6-2, B 4-6-0, C 4-4-2, D 4-4-0, E 2-4-0, F 2-4-2, G 0-4-4, H 4-4-4, I not used, J 0-6-0, K 2-6-0, L 2-6-4, M 0-6-4, N 0-6-2, O 2-8-0, P 2-8-2, Q 0-8-0, R 0-8-2, S 0-8-4, T 4-8-0, X 2-2-4 and 4-2-2, Y 0-4-0, Z 0-4-2 and miscellaneous.

Although there were no engines of the 2-8-2 wheel arrangement in existence before June 1925, the P1 design was currently being prepared at Doncaster Drawing Office and the actual order for the two engines of this class was placed in November 1923. The letters U, V and W were left vacant but were subsequently utilised for the 2-8-0 + 0-8-2, 2-6-2 and 4-6-4 wheel arrangements respectively. The exceptions to the general rule were in wheel arrangements of only minor importance and where early clearance was probable. One was the X group where the three varieties of N.E. 2-2-4T came first followed by the G.C.R. 4-2-2 tender engines in the scheme as published. It could well be that the original intention was for the 4-2-2 wheel arrangement to have been W. The other exception was in the Y group, where tank engines again preceded the single 0-4-0 tender engine, which had come from the N.B.R. This became Y10, but possibly the original intention was for it to take Y1, a class which did not figure in the original list, and indeed did not appear in records until the end of 1927. It has been suggested that the engine portion (which was, in effect a 0-4-0T) of the G.N.R. rail motors was originally intended to be Y1, but on enquiry being made, Mr. Windle stated he had no recollection that the G.N. steam railcars ever came into the L.N.E.R. locomotive classification.

The sequence of class numbers by company in each wheel arrangement has already been mentioned. With very few exceptions each constituent's group of numbers was arranged in order of coupled wheel diameter, the largest diameter coming first. In the G.C.R. classes only D8, J11 and J13 broke this rule, by an inch in the case of J11 and by only half an inch in the other two. All the others (thirteen of them) which were out of step were former

N.E.R. or H. & B.R. classes, these being B14, C8, D18, D24, G6, J28, J72, J76, J80, N11, X2, X3 and Y8. In the case of Y8 there was certainly the excuse that the wheel diameter did not even appear on the first engine diagram sent by Darlington.

Having prepared the classification scheme and obtained the C.M.E.'s approval of it in September 1923, Doncaster issued it to the drawing offices at the other four main works and called on them to provide a line diagram for each class drawn to a scale of three-sixteenths-inch to a foot and tabulating (in standard sequence) all the main internal dimensions, together with weights and ratios (see chapter on Locomotive Diagrams). These diagrams arrived at Doncaster during January and February 1924 and an outside firm made lithographic copies which were put into binders, one set dealing with tender engines and the other with tank engines. These diagram folders were widely circulated during May 1924 and it was from then that the locomotive classification began to be generally used.

The classes which were in the original list, together with their corresponding pre-Grouping equivalents, will be found in the table opposite.

It may be observed that when Darlington submitted its diagrams in January 1924, the class M engines were shown as L.N.E.R. class D16 and only class Q were in L.N.E.R. class D17. To allow the G.E.R. " Super-Clauds " to take their appropriate place, class M was altered to D17 Part 1 and class Q to D17 Part 2. This splitting into ' Parts ' became a very common practice and varied widely in its application. It is detailed fully in the chapter on Locomotive Diagrams.

Omissions from Original List

In the early years of Grouping, there existed a considerable number of engines to which no L.N.E.R. classification was applied, or even allocated in some cases. The G.N.R. had two Service locomotives which did yard shunting, one at Boston and the other at Doncaster Works. The former (No. 470A) was a small 0-6-0ST (actually running as a 0-4-2) which remained in use until April 1927, and the other (later known as " L.N.E.R. Service Stock No. 3 ") a 0-4-4WT fitted with a crane which lasted until November 1928. It is probable that Z1 and Z2 were intended for these, but if so there is no record to show they were ever applied. On the G.C.R. the last remnant from the Wrexham Mold & Connah's Quay Railway, a curious 0-8-0T numbered 400B, received no L.N.E.R. classification and, in any event, was withdrawn in August 1923. Two 0-6-0T's of G.C. class 7 appear to

have had J64 allocated to them in the preliminary list but both had been withdrawn by July 1923, whilst the sole surviving 2-4-0 of G.C. class 12A could have had E3 in the first list, but was withdrawn in June 1923. No L.N.E.R. record recognises either of these two G.C.R. classes as J64 or E3.

It was on the N.E.R. that the most peculiar situation arose. For a reason which has never been established, Darlington made no claim for L.N.E.R. classifications for ten class " 901 " and nine class " 1440 " 2-4-0's, five class " 44 " 0-6-0T's and no less than eighty-six 0-6-0's of class " 398 " ! Admittedly all of these classes were on the withdrawal programme, but when Darlington submitted its engine diagrams in January 1924 there were still on its books seven class " 901 ", six class " 1440 ", five class " 44 " and seventy class " 398 " of which the last was not withdrawn until March 1928. Yet not one of these gained any L.N.E.R. recognition either in class or diagram, and there is no foundation in fact for attributing E6 to class " 901 " although it would have fitted there conveniently. In addition at Grouping there was still one of McDonnell's 4-4-0's of class " 38 " and one of the long boilered 0-6-0's of class " 1001 " (a Stockton & Darlington design), but as both were withdrawn in February 1923 neither appeared in the N.E.R. stock return to Doncaster.

Only one other class, the three G.N.S.R. engines of class K built in 1866, was not taken into account in the first L.N.E.R. classification list, but at the end of December 1924 they were allocated Part 2 of class D47.

To allow some degree of flexibility for probable future building, certain classes were left vacant in the original list. These were A3, A4, B10, B11, C3, C9, D37, D49, J29, J30, J38 to J49 inclusive, J87, J89, N3, O3, Q8, Q9, Y1 and Y3, and of these B10, B11, C3, D37, J29, J30, J42 to J44, J46 to J49, J87, J89, N3, Q8 and Q9 were never used. It is possible that J87 may have been intended for the 1904-05 and 1909 batches of engines of N.B.R. class F, and J88 for the 1912 and 1919 batches of the same class. The earlier engines were more than two tons lighter than the later ones and the N.B.R. had separate diagrams for them. However, the L.N.E.R. put them all together in J88, and J87 remained vacant.

No provision was made in the classification for other than steam engines and although there were both electric and petrol driven locomotives in stock, these were ignored.

Additions from Later Absorbed Companies

On 1st July 1923 two small companies were taken over, contributing in one case five, and in the other six, tank engines none of which had carried any previous classification. From

24

L.N.E.R. LOCOMOTIVE CLASSIFICATION—1923

L.N.E.R.	Pre-Group	L.N.E.R.	Pre-Group	L.N.E.R.	Pre-Group	L.N.E.R.	Pre-Group
A1	GN A1	D26	NB K	J11	GC 9J & 9M	J83	NB D
A2	NE 4.6.2	D27	NB M	J12	GC 6C	J84	NB E
A5	GC 9N	D28	NB M	J13	GC 9	J85	NB E
A6	NE W	D29	NB J	J14	GE N31	J86	NB E
A7	NE Y	D30	NB J	J15	GE Y14	J88	NB F
B1	GC 8C	D31	NB M	J16	GE F48	J90	GNS D
B2	GC 1	D32	NB K	J17	GE G58	J91	GNS E
B3	GC 9P	D33	NB K	J18	GE E72	K1	GN H2
B4	GC 8F	D34	NB K	J19	GE T77	K2	GN H3
B5	GC 8	D35	NB N	J20	GE D81	K3	GN H4
B6	GC 8N	D36	NB L	J21	NE C	L1	GC 1B
B7	GC 9Q	D38	GNS Q	J22	NE 59	M1	GC D
B8	GC 1A	D39	GNS C	J23	H & B B	N1	GN N1
B9	GC 8G	D40	GNS V & F	J24	NE P	N2	GN N2
B12	GE S69	D41	GNS S & T	J25	NE P1	N4	GC 9A & 9A
B13	NE S	D42	GNS O	J26	NE P2		alt
B14	NE S1	D43	GNS P	J27	NE P3	N5	GC 9C, 9F
B15	NE S2	D44	GNS A	J28	H & B L, L1		& 9O
B16	NE S3	D45	GNS M		& LS	N6	GC A
C1	GN C1	D46	GNS N	J31	NB E	N7	GE L77
C2	GN C1	D47	GNS L	J32	NB C	N8	NE B
C4	GC 8B & 8J	D48	GNS G	J33	NB D	N9	NE N
C5	GC 8D & 8E	D50	NB P	J34	NB D	N10	NE U
C6	NE V, V1	D51	NB R	J35	NB B	N11	H & B F1
C7	NE Z	E1	GN E1	J36	NB C	N12	H & B F2
C8	NE 4CC	E2	GC 6D	J37	NB B & S	N13	H & B F3
C10	NB I	E4	GE T26	J50	GN J23	N14	NB A
C11	NB H	E5	NE 1463	J51	GN J23	N15	NB A
C12	GN C2	E7	NB P	J52	GN J13	O1	GN O1
C13	GC 9K	E8	GC 12AM	J53	GN J14	O2	GN O2
C14	GC 9L	F1	GC 3 & 3 alt	J54	GN J15	O4	GC 8K
C15	NB M	F2	GC 9G	J55	GN J16	O5	GC 8M
C16	NB L	F3	GE C32	J56	GN J17	Q1	GN K1
D1	GN D1	F4	GE M15	J57	GN J18	Q2	GN K1
D2	GN D1	F5	GE M15 Rbt	J58	GC 18 conv	Q3	GN K2
D3	GN D3	F6	GE G69	J59	GC 18T	Q4	GC 8A
D4	GN D2	F7	GE Y65	J60	GC B	Q5	NE T & T1
D5	GC 11	F8	NE A	J61	GC 4	Q6	NE T2
D6	GC 11A	G1	GN G1	J62	GC 5	Q7	NE T3
D7	GC 2 & 2A	G2	GN G3	J63	GC 5A	Q10	H & B A
D8	GC 6DB	G3	GC C	J65	GE E22	R1	GN L1
D9	GC 11B, 11C	G4	GE S44	J66	GE T18	S1	GC 8H
	& 11D	G5	NE O	J67	GE R24	T1	NE X
D10	GC 11E	G6	NE BTP	J68	GE C72	X1	NE 66
D11	GC 11F	G7	NB P	J69	GE R24 Rbt	X2	NE 957
D12	GC 6B	G8	NB P		& S56	X3	NE 190
D13	GE T19 Rbt	G9	NB M	J70	GE C53	X4	GC 13
D14	GE S46	G10	GNS R	J71	NE E	Y2	GC 4
D15	GE D56	H1	NE D	J72	NE E1	Y4	GE B74
D16	GE H88	J1	GN J21	J73	NE L	Y5	GE 209
D17	NE M & Q	J2	GN J21	J74	NE 8	Y6	GE G15
D18	NE Q1	J3	GN J4	J75	H & B G3	Y7	NE H
D19	NE 3CC	J4	GN J5	J76	NE 124	Y8	NE K
D20	NE R	J5	GN J22	J77	NE 290	Y9	NB G
D21	NE R1	J6	GN J22	J78	NE H1	Y10	NB —
D22	NE F	J7	GN J9	J79	NE H2	Z4	GE 204
D23	NE G	J8	GC 6A1	J80	H & B G2	Z5	GNS X & Y
D24	H & B J	J9	GC 9B & 9E	J81	NB E		
D25	NB N	J10	GC 9D & 9H	J82	NB R		

the Colne Valley & Halstead Railway came three 2-4-2T's, one 0-6-2T and one 0-4-2T. Before the end of September the 0-4-2T and one of the 2-4-2T's had been condemned, but the survivors were added to the end of the list already prepared and given classes F9 and N18. N16 and N17 were left vacant. The East & West Yorkshire Union Railways contributed four 0-6-0ST's and two 0-6-2ST's, but one of each wheel type was withdrawn almost immediately. Class N19 was allocated to the remaining 0-6-2ST, but either some duplication, or some delay, in classifying the 0-6-0ST's took place. They were allocated J84 and J85 which, in the original list, had been occupied by some N.B.R. tanks, but these had all been withdrawn by September 1924 thus rendering their class numbers vacant. Even so, the selection is curious because both J87 and J89 had never been used and could well have been taken by the Yorkshire engines almost immediately they became L.N.E.R. stock.

Twelve months later, on 1st July 1924, the Mid-Suffolk Light Railway was absorbed and, although not identical, its engines were put into a single class, J64. This had not been allocated (although possibly intended for a small G.C.R. tank type as already mentioned) and it came conveniently next to the other 0-6-0T's under Stratford maintenance, where these Mid-Suffolk engines already went for overhaul.

Over twelve years were to pass before any more locomotives were absorbed. Although official control passed on 1st October 1936, the locomotives of the Midland & Great Northern Joint Railway were not added to L.N.E.R. stock until 1937.

On the M. & G.N. a letter classification had been used and this was continued until 28th July 1942 when the survivors were reclassified into the L.N.E.R. method, adding C17, D52, D53, D54, J40, J41 and J93 to the list. Any vacancies already existing in the corresponding wheel types were ignored and they were simply added to the end of the respective series. The G.N.-type 0-6-0's had already been absorbed into classes J3 and J4, of course.

On 1st November 1937 the L.N.E.R. took over from London Transport the working of the steam services between Rickmansworth and Verney Junction and bought the engines which had worked them hitherto. These had been Metropolitan classes G, H and K and in the alterations to diagram books at 31st December 1937 they became L.N.E.R. classes M2, H2 and L2 respectively. H2 could have become H1 if desired, that class having become vacant some fourteen months previously, but in Gresley's era, classifications were rarely used again, the exceptions being J84, J85 and Y10.

Additions from New Building and Rebuilding

By the time Gresley died in office in April 1941 sixteen classifications had been added by new building, the first examples appearing in the years indicated :—

A4	1935	P1	1925	V3	1939
B17	1928	P2	1934	V4	1941
D49	1927	U1	1925	W1	1930
J38	1926	V1	1930	Y1	1925
J39	1926	V2	1936	Y3	1927
K4	1937				

U (2-8-0 + 0-8-2), V (2-6-2) and W (4-6-4) were new wheel arrangements.

By substantial rebuilding three other new classifications came into being whilst Gresley was Chief Mechanical Engineer :—

A3 in 1927 (from A1, by fitting new boilers of 220lb. in place of 180lb. pressure) ;

A8 in 1931 (from H1, by rebuilding to 4-6-2T from 4-4-4T) ;

C9 in 1931 (from C7, by articulating the tender and fitting a booster engine).

Certain other rebuildings were of an equally substantial nature but did not involve new class designations. They were accommodated by creating a new " class part " and are dealt with in the section devoted to Locomotive Diagrams.

When Edward Thompson took over from Gresley, he did so without much warning and at almost the direst point in this country's struggle for survival in total world war. Thompson held ideas which differed substantially from those of his predecessor and the wind of change was not long in becoming apparent. He worked steadily towards a greatly simplified standardisation scheme for locomotives based about equally on new building of general utility types and substantial rebuilding of selected existing classes. To the classification list he added these five new class designations :—

K5 (which was a rebuild from K3 and of which only one was completed) ;

Y11 (for the petrol shunters which had hitherto been unclassified) ;

J45 (for diesel-electric shunters in May 1945 ; this was altered to DES1 in September 1945) ;

O6 (to cover L.M.S.-type 8F engines doing wartime duties on the L.N.E.R. and which were, in fact, L.N.E.R. stock) ;

J94 (to seventy-five 0-6-0ST's purchased from the Ministry of Supply).

Thompson also re-used three classes (A2, K1 and Q1) which had become vacant by scrapping and re-building, but he also created a number of others which are dealt with below under Changes in Classification. In any event, Thompson could only look forward to being in charge for a little over five years before reaching retiring age on 30th

June 1946. For more than four of these five years the country was still at war and in his last year vital political events took place which inevitably meant the end of the L.N.E.R. as an independent company.

On 1st July 1946 Arthur H. Peppercorn became C.M.E. for the last eighteen months of the L.N.E.R.'s existence. He added only one class, O7 in December 1946, to describe 200 standard War Department Austerity 2-8-0's which the L.N.E.R. purchased. He was, however, responsible for two new designs, both 4-6-2 passenger engines, but in neither case were new class symbols used and they are dealt with under the next heading.

Changes in Classification

Some hundreds of engines changed their original classifications as the result of rebuilding with larger, or different, types of boilers and this was a continuing process throughout the L.N.E.R.'s twenty-five years. This will be dealt with under the individual class headings ; here we are concerned only with classes which were redesignated.

During Gresley's era, there were only two moves of this kind. Class Y10 had become vacant in December 1925 by scrapping of its only engine. In June 1930 it was re-used for two new special purpose Sentinel shunting engines. The original classification scheme had allocated Z4 (probably because they were Service Stock) to the three G.E.R. crane tanks although they were of the 0-6-0 wheel type, but in April 1927 they became J92 at the end of the 0-6-0T series. This enabled the Z5 class to be split and the two smaller 0-4-2T's of G.N.S.R. class X became Z4 later in 1927, leaving the two larger ones of class Y as Z5.

In December 1942, and the following month, there was every indication that Thompson might deviate from the classification which had served for nearly twenty years. His experimental rebuild of a D49/2 Hunt 4-4-0 was reclassified D only, without any suffix number. That same month the first of his new engines, a general utility 4-6-0, went into traffic as class B. The following month an experimental rebuild to 4-6-2 from a P2 2-8-2 emerged as class A. These engines were prototypes for single standard designs for the wheel types concerned at that time planned by Thompson. In the last week of April 1943, however, the A became A2 and the B became B1 ; class A2 was vacant, but it was necessary to reclassify the two G.C.R. engines from B1 and in April 1943 they became known as B18. The solitary class D engine, however, remained as such until it was scrapped in November 1952. Official records are quite clear that it was class D only, despite the fact that Darlington painted D49 on the front buffer beam when the

engine was shopped in June 1944, and also that drawings in Doncaster Drawing Office refer to it as D49 Part 4.

Turning to mineral engines, in February 1944 Thompson rebuilt one of the numerous O4 class with the boiler and cylinders he had used on his B1 4-6-0's. This rebuild became O1 and the twenty G.N.R. engines hitherto in that class took the vacant O3 classification in March 1944, this never having been used previously. His next new design was a mixed traffic 2-6-4T, and on the appearance of the prototype in May 1945 (which took class L1)ʳ the twenty G.C.R. engines of that class were moved to L3, another class which had not been used before. In that same month, the eighteen Gresley A1 Pacifics which were still fitted with 180lb. boilers became class A10, also used for the first time, this move being to clear the way for another experimental rebuild, and A10 4470 reverted to class A1 on completion of this rebuilding in September 1945. Except for some later juggling with class parts in the A1, A2 and K1 classes, one more Thompson experimental rebuild remains to be mentioned. In August 1945 a Gresley B17 4-6-0 came out using the same boiler and cylinder arrangement as the Thompson B1 and O1 engines, and this rebuild took class B2. The six G.C.R. engines already in that class were transferred during the same month to class B19. Since that date there has been no alteration to the steam locomotive classification, although a few movements in class parts have occurred. These are set out in the section on Locomotive Diagrams.

Classification of Steam Railcars

These had class designations quite separate from the locomotives. The Clayton types were classed A, B and C, whilst the various types of Sentinel cars used D to H, Ha, and J.

Display of Classification on Engines

At Grouping, only the N.E.R., including the absorbed H. & B.R., and the N.B.R. engines carried any indication of their class. On the N.E.R. and H. & B.R. this was painted in letters and figures about 1½ inches high on the front buffer beam, the word "Class" being on one side of the drawhook and the class symbol itself on the other. N.B.R. engines had, from 1919, carried a small cast metal plate showing their class letter on their cab or bunker side sheets but, as mentioned earlier, this was entirely a power classification and such diverse wheel arrangements as 4-4-0 tender, 4-4-2 tank and 0-4-4 tank carried the same letter. These plates were retained until the 1939-45 war period, when many were removed, but quite a number survived the end of the L.N.E.R. (fig. 171).

After Grouping, engines repaired at Darlington and Gateshead continued to have their N.E.R. class painted on the buffer beam until as late as 1932. (The Darlington and Gateshead engine registers used N.E.R. classes until the end of 1929 and then changed to the L.N.E.R. symbols). In the early years of Grouping the two N.E.R. works repaired a number of engines for other sections, and certain J16 and J17 0-6-0's not only had their classes painted on, but these were the G.E.R. designation of F48 and G58 respectively. Some G.N.R. and N.B.R. engines were repaired in N.E.R. shops in 1924-25 but no photographic evidence has been located that any of the N.B. engines had buffer beam classifications, although G.N. 0-8-0 No. 3427 was noted with "Class K1" on the front buffer beam late in 1925. Conversely, N.E.R. J27's repaired at Stratford lost their buffer beam classes. Even the new K3's, which Darlington built in 1924-25 were sent out with "Class 2.6.0" on their front buffer beams, whilst Gresley Pacifics stationed in the N.E. Area had "Class 4.6.2" on them. However, Darlington soon commenced to paint the L.N.E.R. classes on the buffer beams of the standard L.N.E.R. designs and from 1932 changed to the L.N.E.R. system for N.E.R. types. In March 1938 instructions were given to all the other L.N.E.R. works to start painting L.N.E.R. classes on the engines they built or repaired (fig. 19) From April 1943 shed allocations were painted on the buffer beam and to make room for these the word "Class" was discontinued, the classification only being used thereafter (fig. 18).

From 21st March 1925 it became standard practice for all the works to indicate the class, along with the name of the works and the latest shopping date, inside the cab on or near to the roof, a practice inherited from the N.E.R. at Grouping.

Conclusion

The L.N.E.R. classification may not have been ideal, but it was reasonably informative and, of great importance, easy to remember. It has stood the test of time, not only of twenty-five years on the line which devised it, but of another fifteen years under the vicissitudes of a nationalised organisation. At the beginning of 1963 there were more than 1,250 engines still using it, and its advantages are well illustrated in Scottish Region notices where a typical entry of J83 compares with such clumsy references as 3FT C.R. 0-6-0T!

LOCOMOTIVE NUMBERING SYSTEM

Running numbers allocated to new engines could fall broadly into one of three categories— (1) the next available number at the end of the current list, (2) a gap in the existing list, or the number of a much older engine then transferred to a duplicate list, (3) a block allocation devoted to a particular class or wheel type. This third category was, of course, widely used on the Great Western Railway and in a simpler form on the Midland Railway, but only the G.N.R. of the constituent companies of the L.N.E.R. had shown any interest in it. In the years immediately preceding Grouping, the G.N., G.C. and G.E. Railways used the first two methods without any predisposition in favour of either, but in the case of the G.E.R., where gaps were filled, some order was maintained by having a series in sequence, usually for the new engines. The N.E.R. also followed the first two methods, except that transfer to a duplicate list had been discarded many years previously. From 1912 the N.B.R. had made no additions to capital stock (for which new numbers at the end of the main list would have been used) because new engines were charged to revenue and took blank numbers cleared by the transfer of older engines to the duplicate list.

Regular transfers were made to this duplicate list every six months. On the G.N.S.R. gaps were filled and occasional transfers made to the duplicate list.

The year 1921 can be cited as typical to show examples of the policy of each constituent company (except the H. & B.R. which built no new engines after 1915). Wartime effects had largely worn off and the shadow of Grouping had not begun to exert any influence. New engines that year on the G.N.R. (using their subsequent L.N.E.R. classifications to avoid confusion) were N2 1607-15 and 1729-70, K3 1005-9, O2 477-86, K2 1680-1704, and J6 631/2/3. These were nicely spread between extensions and gap-filling, and involved the transfer of two older engines, Nos. 633 and 1009, to the duplicate list. To G.C. stock that year were added B6 52/3, B7 36/7/8, 72/3/8, 458-66 and O5 19 and 22, every one of which involved the addition of the duplicate list suffix B to an older engine. It was a lean year for the G.E.R., the only new engines being N7 1002-11, which filled a gap, and J70 125/6/9 which sent the older tram engines to the duplicate list as 0125/6/9. The N.E.R. additions were B16 926-37/42/3, H1 1327/9/30, 1499, 1501/2/3/24-7, J72 2313-37 and J27

2338-43, a judicious blend between filling gaps and extending the list. Additions to stock on the N.B.R. provided a complete contrast to the method used by the N.E.R.; they first transferred the seven D51's and nineteen J34's built in 1879-81 to their duplicate list by renumbering them 1407-32, and then used the vacancies thus obtained in the capital list for new engines, C11 509/10, C16 511-6 and J37 33, 98, 101/3/4/5, 128/43/71/5, 272/3/99, 506/7/8/17/8. The G.N.S.R. only built two new engines in 1921, D40 45/6, the second one filling a gap and the former causing an 1866 built engine to be transferred to the duplicate list as 45A.

Such then were the established practices of the L.N.E.R. constituent companies in numbering their engines. The N.B.R. was clearly the odd man out and the general principle for the numbering of L.N.E.R. engines seemed unlikely to involve the wholesale renumbering of existing stock, whilst new engines might be expected to fill gaps and/or extend the list, and so it proved to be.

Stock Position at Grouping

G.N.R.—1359 engines numbered between 1 and 1770 of which twenty-six were carrying duplicate list numbers with the suffix letter A to identify them. In addition there was a Departmental service locomotive which appears to have been known as No. 3 Loco. Crane.

G.C.R.—1358 engines, 1252 Capital stock numbered 1-1252 and 106 Duplicate stock numbered 3B and 1156B.

G.E.R.—1336 engines plus seven which were regarded as service stock. The capital list numbers ran from 1 to 1900, but used none between 1312 and 1499, or between 1571 and 1789. On the duplicate list were four engines which carried a cypher in front of their running number, and there were three works engines in service stock which had lost their numbers in 1894 and had since been known as B, C and D. Although not at that time included in the stock total, there was also an unnumbered petrol shunting locomotive.

N.E.R.—2143 engines plus another eight allocated to service stock. All these had numbers in the capital list between 14 and 2365, also between 3013 and 3161. Those with numbers exceeding three thousand were the survivors of the H. & B. stock taken over nine months earlier. In addition there were thirteen electric locomotives numbered 1 to 13 in the capital list.

N.B.R.—1074 engines, those in the capital list numbered between 1 and 926 and those in the duplicate list (200 engines) carrying numbers between 1011 and 1471. This company had, in addition, a shunter known as Petrol No. 1.

G.N.S.R.—122 engines, numbered 1 to 115 plus seven with duplicate numbers carrying a suffix letter A.

The complete list of engines on the various duplicate lists at the time of Grouping was as follows :—

G.N.R.—C12 1009A ; E1 1000A ; J4 135/47/50/70/5A, 640A ; J7 156A ; J53 155A ; J54 139/53A, 633/4/5/7A ; J55 473A, 610/36/8A ; J56 608A ; J57 134/40/4/9A ; 0-6-0T 470A (Service Stock). Total 26.

G.C.R.—D8 508/10/1B ; D12 128B, 423/5/8/30/4/9/40-3/6B ; D50 506/7/9B ; G.C. " 12A " 169B ; E8 449/50B ; G3 1148-52/69B ; G.C. " 18 " 309B ; J12 31/2/4-8B, 458-74B, 501-5B ; G.C. " 7 " 10B, 11B ; J58 5B, 8B, 22B, 41B, 52B, 53B, 66B, 72/3/8B ; J59 272-7/9/80B, 336/8/9/40/2/67/8/70/1/2/4B, 413/4/5/7/8/20/1B ; J60 1153-6B ; J61 407B ; N6 1145/6/7B ; W.M.C.Q. 400B ; Y2 62/3B. Total 106.

G.E.R.—Y5 0228 ; Y6 0125/6/9. Total 4.

N.E.R.—Nil.

N.B.R.—D27 1321/3/4 ; D28 1322/61/87/8 ; D35 1434/9/42/8/9/52/3 ; D50 1390/1/2 ; D51 1401/2/4/5/6/11/24-9/54-71 ; E7 1239/45/6/7/9/56 ; G8 1320/5/6/7/34/8 ; J31 1070/82, 1114/22/32/3/4/7/8/40-4/6-9/62/4/6/78/80/3/8/9/90/5, 1200/6/8/14/21/3/4/7/96 ; J32 1297/8, 1300/4/5/10/1/2/4/5/9/29/37/9/41/3-6 ; J34 1364-70/7/80/1/3/6/93-7, 1400/7/9/10/2-23/30/1/2 ; J81 1216 ; J82 1289/91/4/9, 1306/28/30-3/5/6/48-59 ; J84 1257/9/70 ; J85 1168 ; J86 1173 ; Y9 1083/4/7-98, 1100-3 ; Y10 1011. Total 200.

G.N.S.R.—G.N.S. " K " 44A, 45A, 48A ; D47 49A, 50A, 52A, 54A. Total 7.

Alterations to Numbers, Grouping to February 1924

Whilst various forms and styles of livery were being applied throughout 1923, it was more than twelve months before any significant changes were made to any of the engine numbers. Between numbers 1 and 115, there were sixteen cases where seven different engines were running with the same number and even ignoring the duplicate numbering, there were forty-six cases of six engines with identical numbers. Clearly something effective had to be done, but it took more than a year to decide on a satisfactory scheme, coupled with more than six months experience of a tentative scheme, which in some cases only confounded the position still more.

NEW CONSTRUCTION.—In 1923, 126 new engines were added to stock and all these were given numbers in the series hitherto used by the constituent company which built or ordered them. Using their L.N.E.R. classes, the engines concerned were :—A1 G.N. 1472-81 ; A5 G.C. 3, 6, 7, 30, 45/6, 88, 154/6/8 ; B7 G.C. 475-82 ; B16 N.E. 1371-83, 2366-82 ; D16 G.E. 1780-

29

9 ; J27 N.E. 2383-92 ; J68 G.E. 31-40 ; N7 G.E. 990/1/2 ; N15 N.B. 19, 23, 31, 52/5, 60/7, 71/4-7, 519-28 ; O2 G.N. 487-94 ; Y7 N.E. 982-6. From September, new engines appearing with these numbers also carried the sectional suffix letter e.g. 1377D, 492N, 33E and 67B (see below).

The eighteen engines which took G.C. numbers caused four J58's and thirteen J12's with corresponding numbers to be transferred to the G.C. section duplicate list, B suffixes being applied to their numbers. The remaining engine whose number was required, J12 No. 479, was renumbered 971 in December 1923, the X4 class engine of this number having been withdrawn the previous April. It was anathema to the locomotive people at Gorton to have any blanks in their capital list.

On the G.E. Section there already existed J15's with the numbers 37/8/9, but No. 37 had been withdrawn about two months prior to the J68 appearing. Nos. 38 and 39, however, had the cypher added and became 038 and 039 in the duplicate list.

The numbers were clear for the N15's, due to the N.B.R.'s practice of transferring time-served engines to the duplicate list. Cowlairs had recently allocated Nos. 1472-81 to J34 class engines 519-28. No. 527 was withdrawn in February 1923 as such, but 528 lasted until July and is shown as 1481 in the Cowlairs withdrawal list.

The construction of the O2's caused J55 No. 494 to become 494A on 29th December 1923.

Completion of these orders for new engines in the early weeks of 1924 resulted in the final transfers to the duplicate lists : G.N. J55 No. 496 became 496A, G.C. J12 Nos. 483/4 became 483/4B and G.E. J14 No. 998 had the cypher painted above its brass number plate (which it retained with 998 on it), thus becoming 0998.

THE 1923 SUFFIX NUMBERING SCHEME.—The first steps at differentiating between engines carrying the same number were taken at the beginning of September 1923 when, during the first week of that month, engines emerging from Doncaster Works had a small letter N added to the end of their number. About a week later the other works followed suit, Gorton adding C, Stratford E, Darlington D (fig. 27), Cowlairs B and Inverurie S. This did not solve the problem entirely, because engines in the Great Central duplicate list, and those which had belonged to the North British Railway were now carrying the same suffix B. In simultaneous existence were G.C. J58 0-6-0T's and N.B. N15 0-6-2T's carrying the running numbers 7B, 52B and 78B, whilst 413B applied to a G.C. J59 0-6-0T and to a N.B. D30 4-4-0. This was clearly not the answer, although this attempted method of identification persisted for just on six months.

One at least of the G.N. duplicates (494) ran in L.N.E.R. livery with both the letters A and N after its number.

The 1924 Renumbering

On 6th February 1924 the Chief Assistant Mechanical Engineer at Darlington instructed his Chief Draughtsman and his Works Managers at Darlington and Gateshead as follows :—

" It has been arranged that the numbering of Locomotives should be :—

Existing Stock :— N.E. Section to retain present numbers
(H. & B. engines to be renumbered)
Other sections to add thousands to existing numbers as follows :—
G.N. 3 thousand
G.C. 5 thousand
G.N.S. Vacant numbers at end of G.C. section—this question to be settled between Mr. Thom and Mr. Heywood
G.E. 7 thousand
N.B. 9 thousand

Example : G.N. engine 300 would become 3300 and 1300 would become 4300.

This will mean that there will be no necessity to retain the suffixes lettered on any locomotives in the future. It will also mean that the H. & B. engines will have to be renumbered entirely and I enclose a statement showing the present and future numbering to be adopted.

The engines will be renumbered as they pass through the works for repairs and an advice of all alterations to this section's engines will be sent to you."

About the same date similar instructions were received at the other works and the outcome of the discussion between Messrs. Thom and Heywood was that G.N.S. engines had 6800 added to their existing numbers. The H. & B. engines had already had their original numbers increased by 3000 by the N.E.R. and they were now given the block of numbers 2405 to 2542 inclusive, following immediately upon the highest North Eastern number. Details and dates of the renumbering are given in the table opposite. It began on 27th February 1924 and by 27th October that year all except five of the 138 engines had been renumbered. Two more were done in November, one in December and another at the beginning of February 1925. The final one, however, did not receive its L.N.E.R. number (2477) until 24th November 1925, but it had run as " L & N E R 3096 " from July 1923, and there was no conflicting number on the G.N. Section.

30

RENUMBERING OF H. & B.R. LOCOMOTIVES

N.E.R. No.	1924 No.	Class	Date Reno.	N.E.R. No.	1924 No.	Class	Date Reno.	N.E.R. No.	1924 No.	Class	Date Reno.
3013	2405	N13	5/24	3070	2451	J23	5/24	3116	2497	J75	9/24
3014	2406	J28	7/24	3071	2452	J23	7/24	3117	2498	Q10	5/25
3015	2407	N13	7/24	3072	2453	J23	5/24	3118*	2499	Q10	4/24
3016*	2408	J28	5/24	3073	2454	J23	5/24	3119	2500	Q10	7/24
3017	2409	J28	5/24	3074	2455	J23	2/24	3120	2501	Q10	6/24
3018	2410	N13	4/24	3075	2456	J23	2/24	3121	2502	Q10	6/24
3019	2411	J28	5/24	3076*	2457	J23	6/24	3122	2503	Q10	5/24
3020	2412	J28	6/24	3077*	2458	J23	7/24	3123	2504	Q10	3/24
3021	2413	J28	7/24	3078	2459	J23	6/24	3124	2505	Q10	10/24
3022	2414	J28	9/24	3079	2460	J23	7/24	3125	2506	Q10	6/24
3023*	2415	N13	10/24	3080	2461	J23	8/24	3126	2507	Q10	10/24
3024*	2416	J28	6/24	3081	2462	J23	9/24	3127*	2508	Q10	3/24
3025	2417	J28	6/24	3082	2463	J23	9/24	3128	2509	Q10	5/24
3026	2418	J28	7/24	3083	2464	J23	2/24	3129	2510	Q10	6/24
3027*	2419	N13	8/24	3084	2465	J23	7/24	3130	2511	Q10	7/24
3028	2420	J28	5/24	3085	2466	J23	9/24	3131	2512	Q10	2/24
3029	2421	J28	7/24	3086	2467	J23	4/24	3132	2513	J23	2/24
3030	2422	J28	7/24	3087	2468	J23	9/24	3133*	2514	J23	7/24
3031	2423	J28	5/24	3088*	2469	J23	5/24	3134	2515	J23	4/24
3032	2424	J28	7/24	3089	2470	J23	8/24	3135	2516	J23	5/24
3033	2425	D24	5/24	3090	2471	J23	5/24	3136	2517	J23	6/24
3035	2426	D24	5/24	3091	2472	J23	2/24	3137	2518	J23	6/24
3038	2427	D24	4/24	3092	2473	J23	2/25	3138	2519	J23	7/24
3041	2428	D24	6/24	3093	2474	J23	7/24	3139	2520	J23	6/24
3042	2429	D24	7/24	3094	2475	J23	4/24	3140	2521	J23	5/24
3049	2430	J23	9/24	3095*	2476	J23	6/24	3141	2522	J23	8/24
3050	2431	J23	9/24	3096	2477	J23	11/25	3142	2523	J75	9/24
3051*	2432	J23	10/24	3097	2478	N11	5/24	3143	2524	J75	8/24
3052	2433	J23	6/24	3098	2479	N11	9/24	3144	2525	J75	3/24
3053*	2434	J23	9/24	3099	2480	N11	7/24	3145	2526	J75	10/24
3054*	2435	J23	6/24	3100	2481	N11	11/24	3146	2527	J75	12/24
3055	2436	J23	9/24	3101	2482	N11	2/24	3147*	2528	J75	9/24
3056	2437	J23	9/24	3102	2483	N12	9/24	3148	2529	J75	5/24
3057	2438	J23	8/24	3103	2484	N12	10/24	3149*	2530	J75	9/24
3058	2439	J23	5/24	3104	2485	N12	6/24	3150	2531	J75	7/24
3059	2440	J23	2/24	3105	2486	N12	4/24	3151	2532	J75	5/24
3060	2441	J23	6/24	3106	2487	N12	9/24	3152	2533	N13	7/24
3061	2442	J23	5/24	3107	2488	N12	10/24	3153	2534	N13	6/24
3062	2443	J23	10/24	3108	2489	N12	2/24	3154	2535	N13	8/24
3063	2444	J23	6/24	3109*	2490	N12	10/24	3155	2536	N13	7/24
3064*	2445	J23	6/24	3110*	2491	N12	11/24	3156	2537	N13	7/24
3065	2446	J23	5/24	3111*	2492	J75	9/24	3157*	2538	J28	5/24
3066	2447	J23	7/24	3112	2493	J75	9/24	3158	2539	J28	5/24
3067	2448	J80	5/24	3113	2494	J75	8/24	3159	2540	J28	9/24
3068	2449	J80	9/24	3114*	2495	J75	6/24	3160	2541	J28	2/24
3069	2450	J80	5/24	3115	2496	J75	9/24	3161	2542	J28	6/24

*These engines are known to have carried the D suffix.

RENUMBERING OF G.C.R. DUPLICATE LIST LOCOMOTIVES

G.C. No.	L.N.E. No.	Class	Date Reno.	G.C. No.	L.N.E. No.	Class	Date Reno.
1152B	6402	G3	10/25	460B	6449	J12	*
1151B	6403	G3	10/24	459B	6450	J12	10/24
1150B	6404	G3	5/25	421B	6451	J59	6/25
1149B	6405	G3	2/25	420B	6452	J59	Scr. as 420B
1148B	6406	G3	1/26	418B	6453	J59	§
1169B	6407	G3	11/25	417B	6454	J59	Scr. as 417B
1156B	6408	J60	2/26	450B	6455	E8	Scr. as 450B
1155B	6409	J60	12/24	449B	6456	E8	Scr. as 449B
1154B	6410	J60	9/24	3B	6457	J12	4/25
1153B	6411	J60	5/24	34B	6458	J12	11/24
1147B	6412	N6	10/24	30B	6459	J12	Scr. as 30B
1146B	6413	N6	8/25	483B	6459	J12	12/25
1145B	6414	N6	5/25	128B	6460	D12	Scr. as 128B
510B	6415	D8	12/24	415B	6461	J59	Scr. as 415B
506B	6416	E2	Scr. as 506B	413B	6462	J59	Scr. as 413B
505B	6417	J12	8/24	443B	6463	D12	§
504B	6418	J12	11/25	442B	6464	D12	*
503B	6419	J12	Scr. as 503B	439B	6465	D12	Scr. as 439B
484B	6419	J12	Scr. as 484	430B	6466	D12	5/25
502B	6420	J12	7/25	428B	6467	D12	§
501B	6421	J12	8/24	425B	6468	D12	Scr. as 425B
471B	6422	J12	11/24	407B	6469	J61	6/25
470B	6423	J12	4/25	374B	6470	J59	*
37B	6424	J12	§	371B	6471	J59	Scr. as 371B
35B	6425	J12	5/24	367B	6472	J59	Scr. as 367B
7B	6426	J12	§	342B	6473	J59	§
6B	6427	J12	1/25	340B	6474	J59	Scr. as 340B
46B	6428	J12	7/24	339B	6475	J59	2/26
45B	6429	J12	12/24	336B	6476	J59	10/24
63B	6430	Y2	6/26	309B	6477	—	Scr. as 309B
62B	6431	Y2	7/28	280B	6478	J59	9/24
482B	6432	J12	3/24	279B	6479	J59	Scr. as 279B
481B	6433	J12	§	276B	6480	J59	Scr. as 276B
480B	6434	J12	1/25	275B	6481	J59	4/25
478B	6435	J12	Scr. as 478B	272B	6482	J59	3/26
477B	6436	J12	6/24	8B	6483	J58	11/24
476B	6437	J12	6/24	53B	6484	J58	10/25
475B	6438	J12	Scr. as 475B	52B	6485	J58	9/24
474B	6439	J12	§	88B	6486	J58	§
473B	6440	J12	2/25	5B	6487	J58	*
472B	6441	J12	5/24	158B	6488	J58	3/25
469B	6442	J12	8/24	41B	6489	J58	11/25
466B	6443	J12	*	156B	6490	J58	*
465B	6444	J12	Scr. as 465B	73B	6491	J58	§
464B	6445	J12	9/24	78B	6492	J58	Scr. as 78B
463B	6446	J12	Scr. as 463B	72B	6493	J58	§
462B	6447	J12	Scr. as 462B	22B	6494	J58	*
461B	6448	J12	§				

* Renumbered, date unknown.

§ Not known whether renumbered, though Nos. 443B, 6439/48/53/67/73/86/91/3 did appear as such in the Gorton scrap list.

RENUMBERING OF N.B.R. DUPLICATE LIST LOCOMOTIVES

N.B.No.	L.N.E.No.	Class	N.B.No.	L.N.E.No.	Class	N.B.No.	L.N.E.No.	Class
1355	9018	J82	1097	9938	Y9	1387	9995	D28
1390	9231	D50	1098	9939	Y9	1388	9996	D28
1391	9232	D50	1100	9940	Y9	1439	9997	D35
1392	9268	D50	1101	9941	Y9	1448	9998	D35
1343	9275	J32	1102	9942	Y9	1168	9999	J85
1320	9283	G8	1082	9943	J31	1173	10000	J86
1325	9284	G8	1114	9944	J31	1259	10001	J84
1326	9285	G8	1122	9945	J31	1291	10002	J82
1479	9294	J34	1132	9946	J31	1294	10003	J82
1477	9316	J34	1133	9947	J31	1299	10004	J82
1323	9319	D27	1137	9948	J31	1306	10005	J82
1327	9321	G8	1138	9949	J31	1328	10006	J82
1334	9323	G8	1140	9950	J31	1330	10007	J82
1338	9328	G8	1141	9951	J31	1331	10008	J82
1364	9341	J34	1142	9952	J31	1332	10009	J82
1365	9342	J34	1143	9953	J31	1333	10010	J82
1366	9343	J34	1144	9954	J31	1011	10011	Y10
1369	9344	J34	1146	9955	J31	1335	10012	J82
1370	9345	J34	1147	9956	J31	1336	10013	J82
1377	9346	J34	1148	9957	J31	1348	10014	J82
1470	9394	D51	1149	9958	J31	1349	10015	J82
1471	9395	D51	1162	9959	J31	1350	10016	J82
1393	9481	J34	1164	9960	J31	1351	10017	J82
1394	9482	J34	1166	9961	J31	1352	10018	J82
1395	9483	J34	1178	9962	J31	1353	10019	J82
1397	9529	J34	1180	9963	J31	1354	10020	J82
1400	9530	J34	1183	9964	J31	1356	10021	J82
1409	9538	J34	1188	9965	J31	1357	10022	J82
1410	9544	J34	1189	9966	J31	1358	10023	J82
1413	9545	J34	1190	9967	J31	1359	10024	J82
1415	9549	J34	1195	9968	J31	1401	10025	D51
1417	9559	J34	1200	9969	J31	1402	10026	D51
1418	9560	J34	1206	9970	J31	1404	10027	D51
1419	9565	J34	1208	9971	J31	1406	10028	D51
1420	9693	J34	1223	9972	J31	1411	10029	D51
1421	9694	J34	1224	9973	J31	1425	10030	D51
1422	9696	J34	1227	9974	J31	1426	10031	D51
1430	9697	J34	1297	9975	J32	1427	10032	D51
1432	9698	J34	1304	9976	J32	1428	10033	D51
1472	9699	J34	1311	9977	J32	1429	10034	D51
1474	9700	J34	1312	9978	J32	1455	10035	D51
1475	9701	J34	1314	9979	J32	1456	10036	D51
1476	9702	J34	1315	9980	J32	1457	10037	D51
1380*	9703	J34	1337	9981	J32	1458	10038	D51
1386*	9704	J34	1339	9982	J32	1459	10039	D51
1083	9835	Y9	1345	9983	J32	1460	10040	D51
1084	9927	Y9	1346	9984	J32	1461	10041	D51
1087	9928	Y9	1070	9985	J31	1462	10042	D51
1088	9929	Y9	1239	9986	E7	1464	10043	D51
1089	9930	Y9	1245	9987	E7	1465	10044	D51
1090	9931	Y9	1246	9988	E7	1466	10045	D51
1091	9932	Y9	1247	9989	E7	1467	10046	D51
1092	9933	Y9	1249	9990	E7	1468	10047	D51
1093	9934	Y9	1256	9991	E7	1469	10048	D51
1094	9935	Y9	1321	9992	D27	1470	10049*	D51
1095	9936	Y9	1322	9993	D28	1471	10050*	D51
1096	9937	Y9	1361	9994	D28			

*J34 Nos. 1380/6 were originally intended to become Nos. 9394/5 but instead were reallocated 9703/4. In consequence D51 Nos. 1470/1 were transferred to Nos. 9394/5 from their original position at 10049/50.

The engines on the duplicate lists of the G.N. and G.E. followed the above pattern, with 3000 and 7000 respectively added to their numbers. Thus 1009A became 4009A and 038 became 07038 (fig. 25), for example ; two of the G.N. engines, Nos. 3155A (fig. 26) and 4009A actually survived as such until the 1946 renumbering took place, although 3155A could have become 3155 on the withdrawal of the R1 of that number in December 1927. None of the G.N.S. duplicates received their 1924 numbers, the last being withdrawn in January 1926 still as 52A.

Why the G.C. Section could not have also followed this system by adding 5000 to its duplicate numbers has never been apparent. Apart from the handful of engines from the L.D. & E.C. using duplicate numbers, all the G.C. duplicates were at least thirty-five, and the majority of them well over forty, years old. Steady inroads were being made into them each year and their elimination was within sight. Gorton, however, chose to deal with them quite differently and, to those still in stock on 15th January 1924, the numbers 6402 to 6494 inclusive were allotted, on the basis of the older the engine, the higher the number. This had the effect of reversing the sequence in which most of the engines had been numbered originally. Before this renumbering was actually started, J12's Nos. 30B and 503B (which were to become 6459 and 6419 respectively) were withdrawn on 25th January 1924, and so Nos. 6459 and 6419 were allotted again to J12's Nos. 483 and 484 whose numbers in the capital list were needed for the last two engines of the B7 class then approaching completion. The former numbers of the engines allotted Nos. 6402 to 6494 are detailed in the table on page 32 ; this also gives the available information on which numbers were actually changed and when. The choice of the number 6402 for the start of this scheme was determined by four factors (i) the highest G.C. capital list number of 1252, (ii) which had been extended to 1377 by the numbers allocated to 125 R.O.D. 2-8-0's bought from the Ministry of Munitions, officially added to stock in January 1924, (iii) the addition of 5000 to all G.C. numbers and (iv) the ordering of twenty-four D11 4-4-0's for Scotland to which numbers 6378 to 6401 had been given.

The N.B. Section too had had their own ideas about dealing with duplicate list numbers other than by simply adding 9000 to them. Early in 1924 they decided to compress their duplicate numberings into the smallest compass by filling up all the blanks existing in their capital list at that time and then adding the remainder to the end of the list by using numbers 9927 to 10050 inclusive, the object being apparently to reduce five-figure numbers to a minimum. The table on page 33 sets out the numbers allotted in this scheme. Y9

class 9929 (on 10th April) and D50 class 9231 (on 30th April) were the first to be done, Nos. 9232, 9345, 9538, 9835, 9989 (fig. 23), 9990 and 10023 appeared in May, 9932 and 10007 came out in June and 9942 in July, after which the scheme was dropped in favour of the straightforward addition of 9000 to the N.B. duplicate numbers. Of the twelve engines which received numbers under this short-lived scheme, No. 9232 became 10391 (i.e. old number plus 9000) in August 1924, whilst Nos. 9231, 9345, 9538, 9835, 9932/90 were similarly altered in September, Nos. 9929/42/89 in October, and Nos. 10007/23 in November. One other engine took the number 9995 whilst in the works, but before it went into traffic on 8th October this was changed to 10387.

By the time the general renumbering had got under way, three small companies had been absorbed. The Colne Valley & Halstead and the Mid-Suffolk Light Railways, whose engines were normally serviced by Stratford, naturally took numbers at a convenient place in the G.E. Section and they used the series 8312-7, but the other company, the East & West Yorkshire Union, came within Doncaster's orbit and their engines filled a gap by taking Nos. 3112-5. This was by no means the first gap—they could equally well have become Nos. 3016-9.

Numbering of New Engines, 1924 to 1941

Following well established principles within the Group, filling of gaps proceeded simultaneously with extensions to the list, and continued thus until the end of the Gresley regime. The results were untidy, but interesting.

By choosing a round number (2400) for their first Pacific, the N.E.R. had skipped Nos. 2393-9 and three of these, 2393/4/5, were put on the two Mikados and the Garratt which were built in 1925, but the other four were left vacant. Apart from this the next available number was 2543 and in 1924-25 Gresley Pacifics took Nos. 2543-82 and a batch of J20's 2583-94. Again a small gap was left because the N7's and N2's built in 1927-29 were allocated Nos. 2600-90 followed by the J39's built in 1928-29 which took Nos. 2691-2742. In the same years A3 Pacifics were given Nos. 2743-52 and by 1930 number 2797 had been reached with D49's 2753-60, K3's 2761-9, J39's 2770-88, J50's 2789-94 and A3's 2795/6/7. But there had been some anticipation in December 1928 ten B17's used Nos. 2800-9 whilst in September 1930 the V1 class came out beginning at No. 2900. To redress the balance, the gap left in 1925 at 2595-9 was used for five A3's built in 1930, but in the same year the

34

number 10000 appeared on the Gresley-Yarrow water-tube boiler 4-6-4. By the end of 1931 the B17's had reached No. 2836 and V1's were up to 2927 ; but in that and the following year Nos. 2954-61 were taken by O2's and 2962-80 by J39's, whilst the small gap at 2798/9 was filled by two S1 hump-shunting engines. The B17's were extended to No. 2842 in 1933 and that year saw the commencement of filling the gaps between Nos. 2430 and 2512 caused by withdrawal of the older H. & B. engines. By 1936 B17's were up to No. 2861 with others on order up to 2872, and all other numbers between 2897 and 3000 had been used. Attention then turned to extensions and filling of gaps in what had been the Great Northern Section list. In consequence the first five Green Arrows came out as Nos. 4771-5 and gaps at 4482-98 and 3813-32 were filled by A4's and K3's respectively. In Gresley's last years, construction and orders placed extended the list from 4776 to 4899 with V2's and 4900-3 with A4's, whilst gaps were filled at 3401/2 with class V4, 3441-6 with class K4, 3833-57 with class O2, 4462-9, 4499 and 4500 with class A4. In addition, V2's beginning at 3641 were destined to reach 3695, and a batch of J39's took Nos. 3081-98.

In the Great Central range, a further purchase of Government 2-8-0's had taken Nos. 6495-6642, whilst in the Great Eastern series Nos. 8571-80 were used for ten new B12's and Nos. 8400-4 for some Sentinel shunting engines. There was also a solitary example of a Y1 Sentinel filling a gap (9529) in the N.B. series.

Meanwhile in every year from 1924 to 1940 inclusive new engines were utilising gaps in the N.E. Section lists caused by withdrawals, ranging from 17 to 2006 with engines in classes as diverse as A5, D49, J38, J39, J50, J72, K3, N2, N7, P2, Q7, T1, V1, V3, Y1 and Y3. New engines destined for the North Eastern Area generally filled breaks in that section's list whereas those for the rest of the L.N.E.R, were numbered in the gaps below No. 3000, as recorded above.

" What might have been " began in 1931 when a series of twenty-three J39's was ordered and allotted Nos. 2962-84. The first fifteen, for the Southern Area, came out as Nos. 2962-76, but instead of the remainder going to the Scottish Area as originally intended, only the first four, Nos. 2977-80, did so. The last four, which were to have been Nos. 2981-4, were diverted to the North Eastern Area, who wished to have numbers in line with their other engines of this class, so these four appeared as Nos. 1453/69/71/80, although their original motion parts were stamped 2981-4.

Another attempt to use 2981 was made in 1934, for this was the number originally allotted to the first P2, *Cock o' the North*.

For publicity purposes it was, however, changed to No. 2001 which had been borne by the first 4-6-0 passenger engine in this country, built by the N.E.R. in 1899. The original motion of the P2 was noted with 2981 stamped on it.

On 16th March 1936 a batch of seventeen streamlined Pacifics of class A4 was ordered ; six for the Southern Area were to be Nos. 2063/77, 2515/6/9/20, six for the North Eastern Area Nos. 2031/6/9/49/52/64 and five for the Scottish Area Nos. 2111-5. But on 13th October instructions were issued to change these numbers to 4482-98 and that is how they appeared. Motion parts of Nos. 4482-7 were, however, noted as being stamped 2063/77, 2515/6/9/20, but Nos. 4488 onwards were stamped as such.

The first five V2's were to have been numbered 637/9/40/64/70. No. 637 was actually so painted but was altered to 4771 before entering traffic and the others became 4772-5.

Sundry Changes

The former G.E. petrol shunter was given the number 8430 by March 1927, although it is believed this actually took place in 1925. Hitherto it had not borne a number, simply being known as *Peggy*, after the shunt horse it displaced. The similar machine on the N.B. Section, officially known as Petrol No. 1, was displaced by a Sentinel steam shunter in 1928 and, after finding temporary employment at Connah's Quay, was then transferred to work at Ware on the G.E. Section, where it became No. 8431 in July 1930.

In November 1926, three standard Sentinel shunters were purchased for departmental use on the G.N. Section, but unlike the corresponding engines on the G.E. Section, they ran without numbers (fig. 31). At first they were simply identified by the places at which they worked viz. Boston, Peterborough and Doncaster and these names were painted on their underframes in their early days but seem soon to have worn off. In April 1930 they were given numbers 4801/2/3 respectively.

Class J54 No. 3920 was transferred to departmental stock in December 1928 for use in the yard at Doncaster Works and was renumbered Service Stock No. 3 (fig. 29). In April 1930 it was again renumbered, 4800, but by 1937 this number was required to enable an order for twenty-eight V2's to be numbered consecutively from 4776 upwards. So, on 28th August 1937, the saddletank was renumbered 4990. The three Sentinels, Nos. 4801/2/3, mentioned above were also affected by the V2 numbering and were altered to Nos. 4991/2/3 in September, March and April 1937 respectively.

Engines Absorbed, 1937

Although operation of the Midland & Great Northern Joint Railway was taken over by the L.N.E.R. on 1st October 1936, the 86 M. & G.N. locomotives were not at first added to stock. However for all purposes other than financial they were regarded as L.N.E.R. stock from October 1936 and their position in the L.N.E.R. numbering system was soon made clear. Most of these engines were scheduled to be maintained at Stratford, and the authorities there simply looked on the whole of them as duplicate list engines, consequently their M. & G.N. numbers were prefixed by a cypher (fig. 34). Much the same effect could have been achieved in a more kindly way had Stratford only thought fit to increase their numbers by 8600. The first to be renumbered were 01 on 20th October and 052 and 058 on 22nd October 1936, all still with M. & G.N. on the tender, but No. 07 also out of Melton Constable shops on 22nd October, was repainted in L.N.E.R. lined black livery. Twenty-two were withdrawn still bearing their M. & G.N. number unaltered—these were Nos. 3, 4, 14/7/8, 23/6/8, 36/7/9, 45/8, 57, 66/7/8, 72/4/5, 80 and the works engine 16A. By early 1938 all the others had received the cypher prefix except No. 61, and this one completed the renumbering in January 1939.

On 1st November 1937 three classes totalling eighteen engines were taken over from the London Passenger Transport Board. The numbers they took were blanks in the Great Central series, the four 0-6-4T's becoming Nos. 6154-7 and the six 2-6-4T's following with Nos. 6158-63, but the eight 4-4-4T's were given Nos. 6415-22. They were sent to Stratford for repair and beginning with No. 6417 on 3rd March 1938, their renumbering was completed when 6155 received its new number on 21st October 1939.

The 1942 Partial Renumbering

A partial renumbering to clear the numbers 8301-8900 inclusive was begun at Stratford on 14th October 1942 to make way for Thompson's first new design, the standard B1 4-6-0 then building at Darlington and to avoid confusion with L.M.S.-type 8F 2-8-0's being built

at Doncaster as a war emergency measure. The engines affected—and their new numbers—were :—

F7 class 8301/4/5/7/8/10 to become 7593-8
Y1 class 8400/1/2 to become 7772/3/4
Y10 class 8403/4 to become 7775/6
Petrol Shunters 8430/1 to become 7591/2
B12 class 8500-5/7-80 to become 7415-94
D15/D16 class 8780-8900 to become 7650-7770.

The new numbers were already vacant except those required for the B12's : thirteen of these, 7416/27/63/6/77/8/90/2/4/6/7, 7503/6, were still occupied by surviving E4's, and, together with the other five of this class, 7407/8/9/11/4, they were duly allotted numbers 7791-7808. By the third week of January 1943, thirty-five of the numbers had been altered (fig. 53), including three F7's done at St. Margaret's shed, Edinburgh and the way was more than clear for the first batch of B1's to carry the numbers 8301-10.

After No. 8574 had become 7488 on 23rd January 1943, Stratford Works discontinued this scheme, but news of this change of policy must have been slow in reaching out-stations, for the District Loco. Running Superintendent at Norwich renumbered 8403/4 to 7775/6 during February and on 1st April 8400 became 7772. Of the five Sentinels concerned, this only left 8401 at Lowestoft Sleeper Depot with its original number, and this it continued to retain. Whilst the scheme was in operation, No. 8786 was wrongly renumbered 7756 instead of 7656 and it ran thus for a few days in November 1942 before being corrected. Listed below are the engines which were actually renumbered. They retained their new numbers until 1946, when the complete renumbering of L.N.E.R. stock was undertaken, except that 7656 reverted to 8786 and 7665 to 8795 in August and July 1944 respectively. This was necessary because in that year the L.N.E.R. took into stock (using its own livery and numbering) twenty-five L.M.S.-type 8F 2-8-0's built at the Brighton Works of the Southern Railway, which were numbered 7651-75.

As it transpired, none of the E4 class need have been renumbered, all the B12's which were altered taking up numbers already

1924 No.	1942 No.	Date Reno.	1924 No.	1942 No.	Date Reno.	1924 No.	1942 No.	Date Reno.	1924 No.	1942 No.	Date Reno.	1924 No.	1942 No.	Date Reno.
7407	7791	11/42	8307	7596	10/42	8523	7437	11/42	8574	7488	1/43	8842	7712	12/42
7411	7794	10/42	8308	7597	10/42	8535	7449	12/42	8577	7491	10/42	8857	7727	12/42
7427	7797	1/43	8310	7598	10/42	8553	7467	11/42	8786	7656	11/42	8858	7728	1/43
7490	7802	11/42	8400	7772	4/43	8556	7470	11/42	8795	7665	12/42	8870	7740	12/42
7496	7805	10/42	8402	7774	1/43	8558	7472	1/43	8822	7692	12/42	8894	7764	1/43
8301	7593	10/42	8403	7775	2/43	8562	7476	12/42	8825	7695	12/42	8900	7770	12/42
8304	7594	12/42	8404	7776	2/43	8565	7479	12/42	8837	7707	11/42	—	—	—
8305	7595	10/42	8512	7426	1/43	8568	7482	10/42	8838	7708	11/42	—	—	—

vacant, but this of course is only hindsight. No B12's at Scottish sheds were altered, and all those done in England were B12/3. Only a single D15 (8894) was changed, but No. 8900 *Claud Hamilton* was one G.E. engine to lose its link with its original number.

The 1943 Thompson Complete Renumbering Scheme

This was the first attempt by the L.N.E.R. at systematic numbering and at allocating blocks of numbers to individual locomotive classes. Since 1853 at Doncaster and 1864 at Darlington, numbering of engines had followed a policy of expediency and seldom had the original number bestowed on an engine been altered. Even if thought was given to it, the opportunity for general renumbering presented at the time of the Grouping was not taken as, for example, it was on the L.M.S., but there, of course, the Midland Railway, which had carried through a successful block renumbering some sixteen years earlier, established itself in the lead. The L.N.E.R. method, haphazard though it might be, did at least enable the original identity of an engine to be recognised readily in the majority of cases, thus some sort of individuality was retained. However, the days of common user and of mass-production were at hand, so it was definitely a case of "other times, other manners." The new scheme was prepared in the C.M.E.'s Office at Doncaster and provision was made for all locomotives (steam, electric, and internal combustion) which were in stock on 4th July 1943. In its printed form (which extended to 106 pages) it was dated December 1943 and engines withdrawn between July and the end of November did not appear, although there were the corresponding blank spaces.

Under the scheme the broad division of locomotives for renumbering was as follows :—

New Numbers	Engines Covered
1- 999	Largest express passenger tender
1000-1999	Six-coupled passenger and mixed traffic tender
2000-2999	Four-coupled passenger tender
3000-3999	Eight-coupled freight tender
4000-5999	Six-coupled freight tender
6000-6999	Electric
7000-7999	Passenger tank
8000-8999	Shunting tank
9000-9999	Mixed traffic and freight tank
10000	Class W1

The blocks of numbers allocated to the individual classes are set out in the table on page 39. In each class individual engines were dealt with in order of building, the oldest coming first. This, at least, was the intention, but there were a few departures from it, one very deliberate, and the others straightforward errors. When it is realised that the scheme was drawn up in the middle of the war, with man-power shortage, bombing and blackout as daily hazards, every credit is due to those who drafted it for the very few slips indeed which they made. Having decided to rationalise the numbering completely, it must have been disappointing when, entirely for prestige reasons connected with their names, four of the A4 Pacifics were taken entirely out of context and given numbers 1 to 4, instead of 609, 608, 596 and 611 respectively which were their proper places. But one can perhaps understand the Chairman of Directors looking with more favour on number 1 than 609 for the engine which carried his name.

Odd features of this great renumbering were that only three engines kept their former numbers, J3 class Nos. 4125/6 by sheer coincidence, and W1 No. 10000. In addition three Stratford Works crane engines which had lost their G.E.R. numbers in 1894 for the letters B, C and D regained numbers, becoming 8667/8/9. A further remarkable coincidence was the direct exchange of numbers 4574-89 and 9454-69 between classes N1 and J37.

In the block of numbers from 8490 to 8636, allocated to the J67 and J69 classes, blanks were left for the engines sold to the War Department in 1940. Presumably at the time the scheme was prepared a possibility existed of their eventual return to L.N.E.R. stock. Similarly, with the O4 class new numbers were allotted to the engines sent overseas in 1941 but not officially written off until the end of 1943. In passing it may be mentioned that a masterly effort was made to sort out the R.O.D.'s in the renumbering scheme, on the following basis :—

3500	Old No. 5966.
3501-3625	Original G.C.R. engines.
3626-8	G.C.R. R.O.D. engines 5001/5/8.
3629-42	Nasmyth Wilson-built R.O.D. engines.
3643-69	Kitson-built R.O.D. engines.
3670-3734	R. Stephenson-built R.O.D. engines.
3735-3901	N.B. Loco.-built R.O.D. engines.
3902-20	G.C.R. engines, rebuilds from class O5.

Later, this carefully arranged order of the O4 class was to be completely upset (see page 40).

One other oddity concerned the B12 class where a gap was left for No. 1506, the 4-6-0 which the G.E.R. withdrew following the accident at Colchester in July 1913. Incidentally this class received back their original pre-Grouping numbers.

During January to April 1944, several engines both at Doncaster and Darlington Works had numbers in the new series applied temporarily, usually on one side only, and mainly for photography. On 27th January 1944 a Q1 0-8-0T, newly rebuilt, was painted shop grey on one side with NE 9925 applied by transfers on the tank. This was the starting number of the block for the Q1 class, but after being photographed, the engine was painted black and its proper number, 5044, restored. A month later V2 No. 4797 was renumbered 2570, with which it had no connection, and this seems to have been done simply to determine how long it took. On 4th April J50 No. 2789 was painted grey and renumbered 8900 (a J50 number but not its own) and the newly-rebuilt A2 No. 2006 was similarly painted but given its own number 995. Both were done on one side only for official photography. Three weeks later A3 No. 2747 was similarly treated but given the number 500, not its own but at least the starting number for its class. Then on 5th May when A3 No. 2749 arrived for repair, its number was obliterated on *both* sides of the cab and white stencilled numbers, smaller than standard, were applied, but these showed 554 instead of its intended number of 558. At Darlington the first A2/1 Pacific was photographed as No. 884 before being put into traffic on 13th May as No. 3696. If this engine had been built as a V2 2-6-2, as originally ordered, 884 would have been its intended number, but the printed scheme of December 1943 did not include these A2/1 class engines either as 4-6-2 or 2-6-2 types. These were all temporary changes, but from them the authorities had concluded that the complete renumbering of more than six thousand engines was not a feasible proposition until the war ended, and so the general renumbering was put into abeyance.

Temporary Alterations in 1944-45

From Doncaster Works in July 1944 appeared two new 350 h.p. diesel-electric shunting engines numbered 8000/1—their correct numbers in the complete renumbering scheme. To avoid duplication with engines already bearing these numbers, N7's 8000-11 were altered to 7978-89 between the end of July and the first few days of September. This was simply a temporary expedient.

For hauling officers' saloons, D3 4-4-0 No. 4075 was fitted at Doncaster in September 1944 with a new double-window cab and a plethora of polished brass and copper fittings. It first came from Plant towards the end of that month painted shop grey and renumbered 1, but a few days later was repainted green and the number altered to 2000, this being the starting number for 4-4-0 types in the general scheme. In consequence, two North Eastern Area engines had their numbers changed, one of them twice. During the week ending 30th September electric locomotive No. 1 was altered to 4075, but during the week ending 21st

October it reverted to number 1. In that same week J25 0-6-0 No. 2000 was altered to 2050, a number which was already vacant.

Finally, between mid-May and mid-June 1945, ten J50's Nos. 3157-64/6/7 were renumbered 3180-9 to clear the way for a further series of L.M.S.-type 8F 2-8-0's which were to carry L.N.E.R. numbers 3148-67. Although J50 No. 3189 was noted ex-works after repair on 15th September 1945, it was still carrying 3167 on its number plates ; on the same day, in Doncaster Erecting Shop, the first of these twenty 2-8-0's was noted with both its L.N.E.R. number 3148 *and* its L.M.S. number 8540 stamped into the motion parts! However, the next 2-8-0, No. 3149, bore that number only.

The Complete Renumbering of 1946

On Sunday 13th January 1946 the first moves were made to renumber all L.N.E.R. locomotives in accordance with the scheme prepared in 1943. The majority of the changes were made at the running sheds, mainly at week ends, and usually on the Sunday. In addition, engines entering works for overhaul during 1946 were given their new numbers where these were vacant. The first engine to be renumbered cannot be established as seventeen were changed on that first Sunday, all of them in Scotland. The job was ostensibly completed just over twelve months later by the renumbering of O4 No. 6559 to 3639 on 18th January 1947. During that time, 6263 engines were renumbered, 47 of them twice, whilst 219 engines in the original list prepared in July 1943 were scrapped without being renumbered since the list was compiled. However, at the close of this huge undertaking, one curious exception to the scheme remained. In June 1946 a Sentinel 0-4-0T, Y1 No. 8401, in Service Stock had been renumbered 7773 (fig. 36), the number it should have received under the 1942 scheme It was not until August 1951 that it became correctly, 8131.

Selection of the engines to be renumbered was not, indeed could not be, done other than in a carefully planned programme if duplication and confusion were to be avoided. Al the early renumberings were designed to clear the numbers 1000 to 1189 inclusive so that these could be utilised by the ten existing B1' and the further 180 of this class then on order Some of the numbers required, such as 1019 20/1, were already vacant, but to clear 108 involved a chain of ten engines, 3365◄—Q1 1311◄—B5 5186◄—J10 5099◄—J21 1576◄—B1. 8576◄—J69 7268◄—G5 1762◄—K2 4672◄—J1 8252◄—J71 1083. The clearance of the require 190 numbers had been achieved by 14th Apri and 439 engines had been affected by this stag alone. On 10th March a similar plan was begu

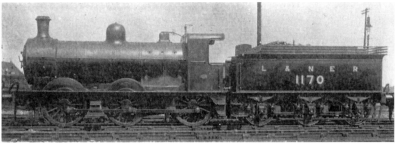

Fig. 20   Class J3 No. 1170. As lettered " L & N E R ". Later
pattern of G.N.R. Stirling tender

Fig. 21   Class D13 No. 8026. G.E.R. 2790-gallon tender
originally built to carry oil fuel

Fig. 22   Class X4 No. 5969 at Trafford Park shed, June 1926

Fig. 23 Class E7 No. 9989 at Dunfermline shed, July 1924.
As renumbered under N.B. Section 1924 duplicate
scheme. N.B.R. 1652-gallon tender

Fig. 24 Class D24 No. 2426 at Cudworth shed, lettered "L.N.E.R."
H. & B.R. 3500-gallon tender

Fig. 25 Class J15 No. 07038 at Stratford shed, June 1930.
With G.E. Section duplicate list number

Fig. 26   Class J52 No. 3155A at Doncaster shed,
September 1934.
With G.N. Section duplicate list number

Fig. 27   Class J22 No. 606D at Darlington Bank Top shed, 1924.
With 1923 sectional suffix

Fig. 28   Class Q5 No. 657 at Shildon shed, June 1926. Grenade and
chevrons on cabside to commemorate service overseas
during First World War

Fig. 29   Class J54 Service Stock No. 3 at
Doncaster Works. With Southern
Area load class tablet on vacuum
standpipe

Fig. 30   Class J92 D Works and another at
Stratford Works, October 1945.
Wartime lettering " N E "

Fig. 31   Class Y1 Sentinel locomotives for departmental service
at Boston, Peterborough and Doncaster. Later numbered
4801/2/3 respectively

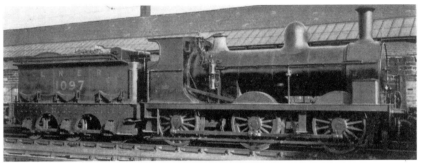

Fig. 32   Class " 398 " No. 1097 at Shildon shed, July 1926.
N.E.R. 2200-gallon tender

Fig. 33   Class D19 No. 1619 at Selby shed, June 1929.
Three-cylinder compound.   N.E.R. 3940-gallon tender

Fig. 34   Class D52 No. 013 at Peterborough, May 1937.
M.R.-type panelled tender

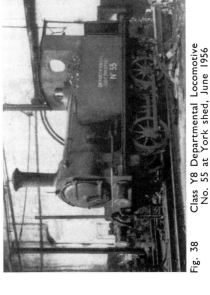

Fig. 36   Class Y1 Sentinel No. 7773 at Lowestoft Harbour, June 1948. As incorrectly renumbered under the 1946 scheme

Fig. 38   Class Y8 Departmental Locomotive No. 55 at York shed, June 1956

Fig. 35   Class J79 No. 1662D. With 1923 sectional suffix to number

Fig. 37   Class Y11 petrol locomotive No. 68189 at Ware, April 1949. Temporarily renumbered in the B.R. 60,000 series

Fig. 39   Class J6 No. E4216 at Spalding shed, May 1948. In British
               Railways livery with E prefix above number.

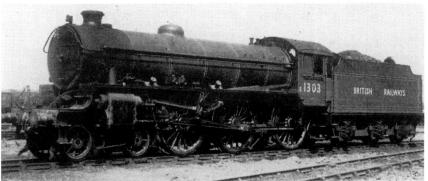

Fig. 40   Class B1 No. E1303 at York shed, June 1948. In L.N.E.R.
         green, with British Railways E prefix in front of number.
         L.N.E.R. Group Standard 4200-gallon tender with high
                              front shield

Fig. 41   Class A3 No. 531 *Isinglass* at Doncaster Shed, 1946. With
                          1946 interim number

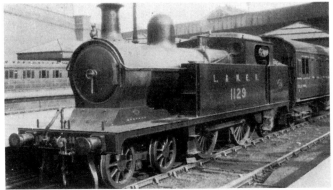

Fig. 42   Class C14 No. 1129 at Nottingham Victoria
As lettered "L. & N.E.R." and retaining
G.C.R. number plate

Fig. 43   Class D20 No. 1051 at King's Cross shed in 1924.
As lettered "L & N E R"

Fig. 44   Class D30 No. 427B *Lord Glenvarloch* at Eastfield shed,
October 1923. With 1923 sectional suffix to
number and Cowlairs paint date on leading edge of
footplate angle iron. N.B.R. 4235-gallon tender.

Fig. 45   Class N7 No. 916 at King's Cross Shed.   In lined black livery

Fig. 46   Class J15 No. 7942. Retaining G.E.R. grey livery but with
L.N.E.R. number. G.E.R. 2640-gallon tender

Fig. 47   Class A4 No. 2512 *Silver Fox* at King's Cross shed, 1938.   In
silver-grey livery with name painted on side of boiler casing.
Corridor tender

Fig. 48   Class D16/2 No. 8787 at King's Cross, circa 1934. In special
green livery for working Royal trains

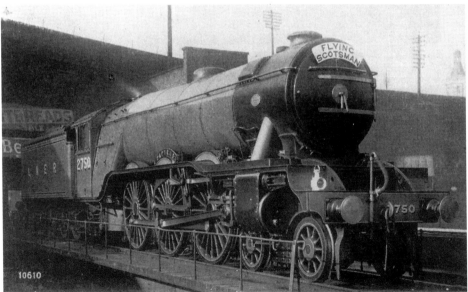

Fig. 49   Class A3 No. 2750 *Papyrus* at King's Cross. With corridor tender

Fig. 50   Class B12 No. 8517 at Stratford shed, 1928.   With number positioned
above beading on cab side.   G.E.R.   3700-gallon tender and A.C.F.I.
feed water heater

Fig. 51   Class D21 No. 1237 at Selby in October 1935.   With number within
beading of rear splasher.   N.E.R. 4125-gallon tender

Fig. 52   Class D17/2 No. 1921 at London Road shed, Carlisle,
April 1930.   With number centrally placed on splasher.
N.E.R. 3940-gallon tender

Fig. 53   Class E4 No. 7794 at Cambridge shed, April 1946.
1942 number and wartime livery. With side window
cab fitted when in N.E. Area. G.E.R. 2640-gallon tender

Fig. 54   Class J36 No. 5211 at Bathgate shed, 1947.
Post-war green livery with Gill Sans lettering.
N.B.R. 2500-gallon tender

Fig. 55   Class J11 No. 4400 at Mexborough shed, September 1948.
Number hand painted under 1946 renumbering scheme.
G.C.R. 3250-gallon tender

BLOCK RENUMBERING SCHEME—1943

Numbers Allocated	Class	Numbers Allocated	Class	Numbers Allocated	Class
1-4	A4	3460-3474	Q7	8090/1	Y8
500-578	A1 & A3	3475-3494	O1	8092-8124	Y9
580-613	A4	3500-3920	O4	8125-8129	Y4
700-883	V2	3921-3987	O2	8130-8153	Y1
990-995	P2 & A2	3990/1	P1	8154-8185	Y3
1000-	B1	4100-4103	J40	8186/7	Y10
1300-1312	B5	4105-4167	J3 & J4	8188/9	Y11
1313-1327	B15	4170-4279	J6	8190/1	Z4
1328-1330	B6	4280-4453	J11	8192/3	Z5
1331-1341	B8	4460-4535	J35	8200-8203	J62
1342-1351	B9	4536-4639	J37	8204-8210	J63
1360-1397	B7	4640-4674	J19	8211-8215	J65
1400-1468	B16	4675-4699	J20	8216-8226	J70
1470/1	B18	4700-4988	J39	8230-8316	J71
1472-1477	B2	5000-5014	J1	8317-8319	J55
1480-1485	B3	5015-5024	J2	8320-8354	J88
1490-1499	B4	5025-5123	J21	8355-8364	J73
1500-1580	B12	5126-5209	J10	8365	J75
1600-1672	B17	5210-5346	J36	8366-8369	J60
1699	B13	5350-5479	J15	8370-8388	J66
1700/1	V4	5480-5499	J5	8390-8441	J77
1720-1794	K2	5500-5589	J17	8442-8481	J83
1800-1992	K3	5600-5644	J24	8482-8489	J93
1993-1998	K4	5645-5729	J25	8490-8636	J67 & J69
2052-2054	D53	5730-5779	J26	8638-8666	J68 & J67
2057/8	D13	5780-5894	J27	8667-8669	J92
2059-2074	D31	5900-5934	J38	8670-8754	J72
2075/6	D42			8757-8889	J52
2100-2106	D6	6000	{ Electric Mixed Traffic	8890-8991	J50
2108-2114	D17			9050-9069	L1
2115-2148	D3	6480/1	{ Electric Shunting	9070-9073	L2
2150-2201	D2			9075-9077	M2
2202-2216	D1	6490-6499	{ Electric Freight	9080-9084	M1
2217-2223	D21			9085-9088	N11
2225-2256	D41	6999	{ Electric Express	9089	N12
2260-2280	D40			9090-9109	N10
2300-2333	D9	7092-7094	F7	9110-9119	N13
2340-2397	D20	7095-7103	F1	9120-9125	N14
2400-2415	D29	7104-7113	F2	9126-9224	N15
2416-2442	D30	7114-7150	F3	9225-9248	N4
2443-2454	D32	7151-7187	F4	9250-9370	N5
2455-2466	D33	7188-7217	F5	9371-9401	N8
2467-2498	D34	7218-7239	F6	9410-9429	N9
2500-2620	D15 & D16	7240-7349	G5	9430-9485	N1
2650-2659	D10	7350-7399	C12	9490-9596	N2
2660-2694	D11	7400-7439	C13	9600-9733	N7
2700-2775	D49 & D	7440-7451	C14	9770-9789	A7
2780-2797	E4	7452-7481	C15	9790-9799	A6
2800-2891	C1	7482-7502	C16	9800-9842	A5
2892/3	C2	7503/4	C17	9850-9894	A8
2895-2898	C5	7505	G10	9900-9905	S1
2900-2925	C4	7510-7516	H2	9910-9922	T1
2931-2948	C6	7600-7691	V1 & V3	9925-	Q1
2950-2997	C7	8000-	Diesel	9999	U1
3200-3243	Q4	8080	Y5	10000	W1
3250-3339	Q5	8081/2	Y6		
3340-3459	Q6	8083-8089	Y7		

to clear Nos. 1190-1339 for a further 150 B1's. It took until 1st September to deal with the 329 engines affected, but there was now a complication in that the scheme propounded in 1943 had allowed for a maximum of 300 B1's; the numbers from 1300 upwards were to be occupied mainly by G.C. 4-6-0's. As shown above, one of the early moves to clear No. 1083 had involved the renumbering of B5 No. 5186 to 1311, but on 24th March this engine's number was again changed and, along with No. 1312 (fortunately only two had then come into the affected area), they became Nos. 1689/90. The change of plan involved nine classes, as follows :—

B5 class from 1300-12 to 1678-90
B15 class from 1313-27 to 1691-8 (seven had already been withdrawn)
B6 class from 1328/9/30 to 1346/7/8
B8 class from 1331-41 to 1349-59
B9 class from 1342-51 to 1469-78
B18 class from 1470/1 to 1479/80
B19 class from 1472-7 to 1490-3 (two had been withdrawn in 1944-45)
B3 class from 1480-5 to 1494-9
B4 class from 1490-9 to 1481-9 (one had been withdrawn in 1944)

During April there were also second thoughts about the numbers allocated to the 4-6-2 and 2-6-2 tender engines, and these were changed as follows :—

A4 class from 580-95/7-607/10/2/3 to 5-34 (but not in same sequence)
A3 and A10 classes 501-78 to 35-112 (now in order of original number, *not* age)
A1 class from 500 to 113 (this was the rebuild of No. 4470)
A2/2 class from 990-5 to 501-6
A2/1 class from 3696-9 to 507-10 (these were not built at the time of the 1943 scheme)
V2 class from 700-883 to 800-983.

Justification for these alterations is indeed hard to find. The A4 changes certainly brought another four of the personal prestige named engines to the lower numbers and the rest were then dealt with in order of age. But on the A3 and A10 classes the number/age principle was completely abandoned. Nor has there ever been the faintest indication of a possible need to move up the V2 numbers by a hundred.

The last of the Gresley Pacifics to be renumbered into the 500-615 series was No. 4485 which became No. 587 on 19th April : by then there were three A10's (502/11/38), seventeen A3's (507/8/17/8/20/1/2/8/31/7/42/5/58/61/5/70/5) and five A4's (585-8, 605) already renumbered (fig. 41). The first to change to the new series were Nos. 4484 to 25 and 4480 to 111, both on 4th May, but it was not until No. 521 became 53 on 30th November that these alterations were completed. One of the A2/2 class ran as No. 994 from 25th April to

12th May when it was renumbered 505. In the V2 class nineteen had, by 18th April, become Nos. 701/10/1/4/8-22/9/33/50/62/71/95/9, 805/9/71 and it took from 5th May (722/822) to 18th October (771/871) to clear this change of mind. About this time there were second thoughts about the numbers allocated to Thompson's new Pacifics approaching completion at Doncaster. They were to have been Nos. 200-14, but on 22nd June the first one had 500 stamped over 200 on its motion, the second had 511 stamped over 501 but the third had 512 only, and when they did go into traffic, it was as Nos. 500/11-24.

A further small adjustment was made to the numbers originally given to classes Y5, Y6 and Y7 in the 1943 list. Y7 No. 1798, which was due to become 8083, was withdrawn on 12th January 1946, thus leaving its new number vacant. The Y5 and the two Y6's which were originally to become Nos. 8080/1/2 respectively, were moved up one place to 8081/2/3. The purpose behind this move was to allow numbers 8006-80 to be given to a batch of seventy-five 0-6-0ST's purchased from the War Department in June 1946 and classified J94 on the L.N.E.R. This alteration seems rather pointless when the J94's could equally well have become Nos. 8005-79 as 8005 was never required in the 1946 numbering.

Some three weeks before the complete renumbering was finished, the L.N.E.R. purchased 200 " Austerity " 2-8-0's taking them into stock as from 28th December 1946 and designating them class O7. Their W.D. numbers needed changing, of course, and L.N.E.R. numbers 3000-3199 were allotted to them. This involved renumbering the O6 class and from 3100-67 they went to 3500-67. But fifty-nine class O1 and O4 were then using most of these numbers, so they too were moved on : it was decided to take those occupying numbers between 3500 and 3569 inclusive and drop them into the blanks existing between 3572 and 3809. These blank numbers resulted from the fact that the O4's sent overseas in 1941 were still officially in stock in July 1943 when the renumbering scheme was prepared. Engines 3503 and 3537 were renumbered 3582 and 3693 on 1st February 1947 and the move was completed when 3548 became 3727 on 6th April 1947. Meanwhile the O6 move started with 3112/44/59 becoming 3512/44/59 on 2nd February and was completed when 3148 became 3548 on 20th April 1947. The renumbering of the O7 class proceeded simultaneously, starting on 1st February with 3007/9, and finishing on 26th April 1947 with 3010. So much for the nicely worked out scheme of block numbering with engines in order of age ; all the good work done in sorting out the O4 and O1 classes was lost completely.

When Thompson's prototype standard 2-6-4T had been built in May 1945, it carried the number 9000. The production batch ordered from Darlington by the L.N.E.R. in 1947 were allotted numbers 9001-29, the first three coming out as 9001/2/3 in L.N.E.R. livery. Even before these engines began to appear, it was realised that there were not enough spare consecutive numbers in the 9000 range to accommodate additional L1's authorised to be built by contractors. Pending a decision whether this class was to be regarded as mixed traffic or passenger tanks for numbering purposes, the first fifteen engines of the Darlington batch appeared with 9000-series numbers. Eventually Doncaster decided that the L1's should be numbered in the passenger tank range and, between the middle of April and the end of July, No. 9000 and the first fifteen engines of the production batch were renumbered 67701-16. Meanwhile the remaining Darlington-built engines came out as 67717-30.

Renumbering after Nationalisation

This was Grouping all over again but on an even bigger scale. During the month of January no changes were made, but from the beginning of February, L.N.E.R. engines came out of shops with an E prefix to their existing number (fig. 40), and this continued for about six weeks. In some instances the E was positioned above the engine number (fig. 39). As far as is known, Cowlairs Works never used the E prefix. Early in March, British Railways announced its renumbering arrangements whereby L.N.E.R. steam locomotives were to add 60,000 to their existing numbers, the only exception being that No. 10000 would become 60700. The diesel-electric shunters would take numbers beginning at 15000 and the electric locomotives would begin at 26000.

The first applications of this scheme appear to have been on 17th March 1948 when No. 60066 emerged from Doncaster and No. 62300 from Gorton and in that same week Nos. 62536, 67237 and 69659 were also done at Stratford. No. 61065 appeared from Darlington the following week and also by 20th March Nos. 62215, 62479, 65228 and 68111 were all ex-Cowlairs, whilst No. 64485 was Inverurie's first on 19th March.

Of new engines then building, A2 class E527 to E531 had the intermediate style and were followed by 60532, B1's E1288 to E1303 preceded 61304, whilst in L1 class there were E9004 to E9012, then 69013/4/5 followed by 67717 (see above).

The addition of 60,000 to the numbers proceeded steadily as the engines went to works for overhaul and by early 1952 only a handful remained with their L.N.E.R. numbers. These gradually diminished but even at the beginning of 1954 eleven had still not received their new numbers. Of these, three C15's (7461/5/70), three Y9's (8096, 8103/9), and Y1 E8143 were scrapped that year without being renumbered. In June 1954 No. 8091 became Departmental No. 55 and in September and October Nos. 8110 and 8183 became 68110 and 68183. This left one only, J67 No. 8568, which was still around Stratford as L.N.E.R. 8568 until early in 1956 when it went into works, not for scrapping as expected, but for a general repair. It returned to traffic on 7th April 1956 as 68568 and L.N.E.R. numbers finally ceased to exist.

Mention has been made that the L.N.E.R. diesel-electric shunter numbers were to begin at 15000 and the electrics at 26000, but the only early move in this direction affected the two small electric locomotives, Nos. 6480/1, which worked solely on the Quayside branch at Newcastle: they became Nos. 26500/1 in April 1948. In due course, numbers 26502-11 were applied to the former Newport-Shildon locomotives 6490-9, but except for 26510 which had been rebuilt at Doncaster in 1942, they remained in store until sold for scrapping on 21st August 1950 together with the Raven experimental 4-6-4 electric whose number 6999 was altered to 26600. The rebuilt engine, No. 26510, went to Ilford car sheds in August 1949 and its number was changed again in February 1959, this time to Departmental No. 100. There remained the 1941-built prototype for the Manchester-Sheffield electrification No. 6701, which had become No. 6000 under the 1946 renumbering: in March 1952 it became No. 26000.

The diesel-electric shunters Nos. 8000-3 were duly renumbered 15000-3 although it took from June 1950 to June 1952 to effect this change, but the petrol shunters Nos. 8188/9 were given much earlier attention. Originally it was intended that they should be renumbered 68188/9: No. 8189 received its 60000 series number in December 1948 (fig. 37), but in May 1949 they were altered to 15098/9 respectively and in the same month another engine of this type joined them as 15097. Although purchased by the L.N.E.R. in August 1925 for use at Greenland Creosote Works, West Hartlepool, this last-mentioned engine had never been shown in stock returns and had never had a running number. Known simply as L4 by the N.E. Area Engineer's Department (by whom it had been purchased as " departmental equipment "), it received no other recognition by the L.N.E.R. and even the complete 1946 renumbering passed it by. Its existence was unknown to the C.M.E.'s Department until 1949, when the Civil Engineer requested a replacement for it.

Orders were placed in 1949 for a further fifty B1's and also for seventy K1's. The numbers they were given caused further renumberings. Forty of the B1's from the North British

Locomotive Co. were allotted Nos. 61360-99, but eleven of these numbers were still occupied by the B7 class. Thus in the last week of April and the first two of May 1949, the B7's then numbered 1365/7/75/7/81/2/7/8, 61391, 1392 and 61396 moved to Nos. 61702-7/9-13, which had not previously been used. The other ten B1's, to be built at Darlington, were allotted Nos. 61400-9 all of which were then occupied by B16's. The latter, then numbered 61400/1/2, 1403, 61404-7, 1408/9 became 61469-78 during December 1949, the B9 class hitherto using these numbers all having been withdrawn. The seventy K1 class from the North British Locomotive Co. were given numbers 62001-70 of which all except 62059/60/5 were vacant at the beginning of 1949, these being occupied by D31's. No. 62065 was withdrawn in April, and the other two (along with the remaining D31, No. 62072) moved to 62281/2/3 in June/August 1949.

One more change remains to be recorded,

and concerns the 200 class O7 " Austerity " 2-8-0's Nos. 3000-3199 which were steadily becoming 63000-63199. Early in 1949, British Railways decided to renumber these, together with other engines of this type inherited from the other Regions, so Nos. 3000-3100 built by the N.B. Loco. Co. were allotted Nos. 90000-90100 and the Vulcan-built engines, Nos. 3101-99, went to 90422-520. No. 90432 was the first to be done in February 1949 and No. 90096 the last in December 1951.

The 1952 Departmental Stock List

In August 1952 it was decided to number separately the service locomotives belonging to the Eastern and North Eastern Regions. The basis was for the G.N. Section to begin at 1, G.E. Section at 31 and N.E. Section at 51 (fig. 38). Those concerned together with later additions, and with their normal locations, are appended.

Dept. No.	Class	Previous No.	Reno.	Normal Location	Withdrawn
1	J52	68845	11/52	Doncaster Loco. Works	2/58
2	J52	68816	11/52	,, ,, ,,	3/56
2	J52	68858	3/56	,, ,, ,,	2/61
3	Y3	68181	11/52	Ranskill Wagon Works	11/59
4	Y1	68132	12/52	,, ,, ,,	6/59
5	Y3	68165	3/53	Doncaster Carr Wagon Works	11/58
6	Y1	68133	3/53	Peterborough Engineers Dept.	11/55
7	Y3	68166	3/53	Boston Hall Hills Sleeper Depot	
8	Y3	68183	10/55	Peterborough Engineers Dept.	1/59
9	J52	68840	1/58	Doncaster Carriage Works	2/61
10	J50	68911	2/61	Doncaster Loco. Works	
11	J50	68914	2/61	,, ,, ,,	
12	J50	68917	3/63	,, ,, ,,	
21	Y3	68162	3/56	Cambridge Engineers Dept.	7/60
31	J66	68382	8/52	Stratford Loco. Works	11/59
32	J66	68370	9/52	,, ,, ,,	9/62
33	Y4	68129	9/52	,, ,, ,,	
34	Y7	68088	9/52	,, ,, ,,	10/52
35	J92	68668	9/52	,, ,, ,,	11/52
36	J66	68378	11/52	,, ,, ,,	1/59
37	Y1	8130	5/53	Lowestoft Engineers Dept.	3/56
38	Y3	8168	5/53	,, ,, ,,	2/59
39	Y1	8131	8/53	Norwich Engineers Dept.	4/63
40	Y3	8173	5/53	Lowestoft Sleeper Depot	
41	Y3	8177	5/53	,, ,, ,,	
42	Y3	8178	3/53	Cambridge Engineers Dept.	7/60
43	J69	68532	1/59	Stratford Loco. Works	8/59
44	J69	68498	8/59	,, ,, ,,	9/62
45	J69	68543	11/59	,, ,, ,,	9/62
51	Y1	68136	11/52	Faverdale Wagon Works	10/56
53	Y1	68152	4/54	York Engineers Yard	3/59
54	Y1	68153	10/54	Darlington Geneva P.W. Yard	6/61
55	Y8	8091	6/54	York Motive Power Depot	11/56
57	Y3	68160	10/56	Faverdale Wagon Works	2/61
100	EB1	26510	2/59	Ilford Car Sheds	

NOTE.—Departmental Locomotives Nos. 52/6, 81-8, 91/2 are diesel-mechanical locomotives added to stock by British Railways.

J50 class 0-6-0T's Nos. 68928/61/71/6 have been allocated Departmental Nos. 13-16.

LIVERIES

BEFORE GROUPING

Before dealing with L.N.E.R. liveries a brief résumé of the situation as at the end of 1922 is necessary because many engines ran for years after Grouping in their old colours whether or not renumbered and/or lettered.

On the G.N.R. all engines had been grass green, but this had given way to grey for goods engines (and certain passenger engines) as an economy measure during the 1914-18 War. The number was shown in small figures on the cab or bunker sides, and the letters " G N R " on the tender or tank. The G.C.R. employed two very fine liveries—Brunswick green with red, black and white lining for passenger engines and black with red and white lining for goods—and all engines had the full name " GREAT CENTRAL " on the tender or tank, the number being usually shown on a large cast plate on the cab or bunker, although many older engines still had the small transfer numerals previously used. Another First World War casualty was the striking royal blue of the G.E.R., and in the absence of supplies of the necessary paint, engines were finished in a very uninteresting grey with no lining. The number was shown on a large cast plate on the cab or bunker and also latterly by means of 19in. yellow numerals which replaced the letters "G E R " on the tender or tank. A few engines remained blue until after Grouping.

On the N.E.R. distinct passenger and goods liveries were applied being Saxony green of different shades with black and white lining, and black with red lining respectively. The passenger engines had large cast number plates on the cab or bunker and the full title " NORTH EASTERN " on the tender or tank (small tank engines had " N.E.R.") whilst goods engines had small number plates on the cab and large numerals flanked by the letters " N.E." on the tender. During 1922 a number of Hull & Barnsley engines were re-painted in the appropriate N.E.R. livery instead of the original owners' invisible green (i.e. black) with blue, vermilion and yellow lining.

The most complex livery situation was to be found on the N.B.R. where up to 1914 all engines had been bronze green (which varied considerably in shade) with red, yellow and black lining. In that year black with double yellow lining was introduced for goods engines, and about October 1921 two new styles were brought in—unlined green for duplicate list passenger engines and unlined black for goods engines. N.B. engines were so well painted that several examples of goods engines in lined bronze green livery came into the Grouping and two even got their 1924 numbers while still in this livery. Large engraved number plates were affixed to cab or bunker and large numerals between the letters " N.B." appeared on the tender or tank. The Great North of Scotland had also used Brunswick green, but as from 1914 when Heywood came from the Taff Vale, black with red and yellow lines was used instead, and this livery actually survived on the 0-4-2T's until after 1939. The Brunswick green lasted on one engine until after Grouping.

The liveries of the small companies absorbed in 1923-24 were as follows : Colne Valley & Halstead Railway—black with red lining ; Mid-Suffolk Light Railway—dark red with yellow and vermilion lining ; East & West Yorkshire Union Railways—unlined black.

Of the engines taken over in 1936-37, the M. & G.N. were red-brown lined black and yellow (previously their livery had been yellow) with raised brass numerals on the cab or bunker and letters "M & G N " on tender or tank, whilst the London Transport (ex-Metropolitan) were dark red with black and yellow lining, numbers on the bunker and full wording " LONDON TRANSPORT " on tank.

AFTER GROUPING

The L.N.E.R. directors were not long in giving consideration to the choice of locomotive and rolling stock liveries, and preliminary inspections of engines and carriages were reported to have taken place in December 1922. When the Board met at York on 31st January 1923, eight engines were on view as follows :—

C7	2169	in N.E.R. green
Q6	2237	in N.E.R. black with red lining
C1	1418	in G.N.R. green
O2	484	black with red lining (N.E.R. style but with G.N.R. number on cab instead of N.E.-type plate)
C11	874	in N.B.R. bronze green
D11	503	in G.C.R. green
B7	474	in G.C.R. black with red and white lining
A5	451	in G.C.R. green

These were all lettered " L. & N.E.R." with large numerals on tender or tank sides, except that the two engines painted at Doncaster (Nos. 484 and 1418) had no stops after the letters.

A further exhibition was held at Marylebone on 22nd February 1923 when the directors inspected twelve engines as under :—

D11 503, B7 474, C11 874 and C7 2169 as at York in the previous month and

B12	1534	in G.N.R. green
A5	449	in G.N.R. green
A5	3	in G.C.R. green
A1	1472	in G.N.R. green
B16	2368	in N.E.R. black with red lining
C11	876	in G.N.R. green
O4	1183	in N.E.R. black with red lining
C7	2207	in G.N.R. green

The G.N.R. green livery used had been slightly modified (e.g. it was without the olive green edging and only the B12 had the chocolate framing) and it would appear that this had already been tentatively chosen as the new passenger tender engine livery just as the N.E.R. black with red lining seems to have been selected for tank and goods engines. These were now confirmed. It will be noted that some of the constituent companies' current liveries were not considered—the greys of the G.N.R. and G.E.R., the black of the G.N.S.R., and the unlined green and black of the N.B.R. Nor were any former liveries shown and it was a disappointment to many that the old G.E. blue was not given a trial.

In the meantime engines had continued to appear from the various works in the appropriate pre-Group liveries, modified in some cases by omission of lettering or coats of arms, the style " L. & N.E.R." in 7½in. shaded letters with large numbers on tender or tank coming into all-line use in March 1923 (fig. 42). As from May 1923 the new standard liveries were generally adopted, with the stops (which had not been used by Doncaster, following normal G.N.R. practice) omitted from the lettering " L & N E R " (fig. 43). By this time 12in. numerals, like the G.N.R. style (which however were only up to 7½in. high), were being applied. There were two varieties of these letters and numbers, gold for passenger engines and yellow for goods, and they remained standard until nearly the end of the L.N.E.R.'s existence. They were beautifully shaded in red, pleasing in character and most important of all were clearly legible at a distance (fig. 17). The number was also shown in 4½in. figures on the front buffer beam of all engines (fig. 19) ; tank engines often displayed no number at the rear but some showed it on the rear buffer beam and others on the back of the bunker (figs. 153/71).

Further changes occurred between June and September 1923 with the dropping of the " & " and the introduction in the latter month of the 4½in. high sectional suffix to the number (Great Northern—N, Great Central—C, Great Eastern—E, North Eastern—D, North British —B and Great North of Scotland—S) (fig. 44). The various works did not keep strictly in step with the foregoing developments. These suffixes were discontinued after the introduction of the sectional renumbering in February 1924 (see chapter on numbering), and it should be mentioned that the small N.E.R. goods engine type of combined number and dateplate had been adopted as standard although Gorton continued to use the large G.C. pattern for some time, even to the extent of casting new plates with the 1924 numbers (fig. 125). In 1923-24 there were many freak liveries, principally due to changes being made to lettering and/or numbering while the engines remained in pre-Group livery, and the most notable of these will be dealt with in detail under the individual class headings. Apart from such oddities, it was regular practice at Stratford for several years to repaint engines in G.E.R. grey livery with L.N.E.R. 1924 numbers painted in G.E. style and without lettering (fig. 46). Class F4 No. 7099 was the last to run in this style, being withdrawn in May 1932.

The green livery was confined to passenger tender engines, which was usually interpreted as those having a driving wheel diameter greater than 6ft. 0in., but Cowlairs with sound commonsense included the Glens and later the Intermediates and even the superheated West Highland Bogie—the last-named having only 5ft. 7in. coupled wheels. The N.E. Area also made a special exception of the single-driver tank engines of classes X1, X2 and X3 as they were frequently used for official saloon haulage. The full list of classes was as follows :—

A1 (later A10), A2, A3, B1 (later B18), B2 (later B19), B3, B4, B12, B14, B17, C1, C2, C4, C5, C6, C7, C8, C10, C11, D1, D2, D3, D4, D5, D6, D7, D8, D9, D10, D11, D12, D13, D14, D15, D16, D17, D18, D19, D20, D21, D22, D23, D24, D25, D26, D28, D29, D30, D31, D32, D33, D34, D36, D38, D40, D41, D42, D43, D44, D49, E1, E5, " 901," X1, X2, X3, X4.

As from May 1928, when the London-Edinburgh non-stop running was inaugurated, the Gresley Pacifics had their numbers put on the cab instead of the tender in order to facilitate exchange of corridor tenders. These were still lettered " L N E R " but now in 12in. instead of 7½in. letters to conform with the size of the numbers, and the style was authorised for all classes in November 1928 although not actually applied until the early months of 1929 (fig. 49). In the meantime (from June 1928) the number of green classes had been reduced as an economy measure, and the goods engine livery was altered to unlined black ; secondary passenger engines, both tender and tank, continued to receive red lining (fig. 45).

The selection of classes for the green livery was arbitrary and those which qualified were :—
A1 (later A10), A2, A3, B1 (later B18), B2 (later B19), B3, B4, B12, B17, C1, C6, C7, C8, C11, D49, X1, X2 and X3. Later additions down to 1941 were A4, C9, K4, P2, V2 and V4. The anomaly of painting the G.C. Atlantics black will be observed, and another peculiarity arose from differing works practices in that B12's were turned out of Inverurie painted black. For Royal train working two Clauds, Nos. 8783/7, were kept green (fig. 48) and No. 8900 *Claud Hamilton* itself also received this favoured treatment after rebuilding in 1933. Inverurie was adept at making good paintwork last and thus it came about that many G.N.S. 4-4-0's and D31's ran in green with the numbers on the cab well into the 1930's.

Many engines (especially G.N. classes) had cabs which were too short to permit the use of standard size numerals, and smaller figures (7½ or 9in.) of the same style were employed on these (fig. 111). Even after 1929 7½in. " L N E R " lettering continued to be used on many small tenders, principally in Scotland. Slight modifications were necessary on certain G.C., G.E., N.E. and G.N.S. tender classes where beading interrupted the cab side ; after some experimenting with figures high up on the cab side (fig. 50) or within the beading (fig. 128), the beading was removed from many classes, but on N.E. engines the number was placed within the beading which was left in position (figs. 51 and 52), as it also was on the G.C. classes with the exception of some D9's which had it removed. A few G.E. 0-6-0's also carried their numbers high up on the cab side for a time due to the fact that Stratford had not troubled to move the L.N.E.R. cast number plates from the middle of the cab side.

Throughout the whole L.N.E.R. period there were detail differences in finish as between the various shops (and even an individual Works' practice could vary slightly), a typical instance being the painting of outside cylinders of engines in green livery—Doncaster used black, whilst Darlington used green. The shades of green also varied, that applied at Darlington being more yellow, with the Stratford green not so light but lighter than that of Doncaster and the remaining works. Another variant was alignment of lettering on tenders. In some cases it was coincident with the cab-side numbers on the engine and in other cases centrally on the tender irrespective of the height from ground of the cabside numbers. An example of the former was seen in B17's painted at Darlington and the latter as painted at Stratford or Gorton.

A new livery was introduced in 1935 for the A4 class which was painted silver-grey (fig.

47) to match the " Silver Jubilee " train, the colour having been tried out on No. 4800, one of the Doncaster Works shunters. Later examples of streamlined Pacifics were turned out in the standard green livery, but Nos. 4488-92/5/6 were specially painted Garter blue with red wheels for working the " Coronation " and " West Riding Limited " expresses. In 1938 this blue livery was adopted for the whole class, also the solitary W1 No. 10000 upon its rebuilding, this engine having previously always been dark grey. The original blue engines had stainless steel numbers and letters (fig. 3), and for the first time Gill Sans type was used for these although this had been employed for all printing and many painted notices by the L.N.E.R. since November 1932.

For economy reasons unlined black was adopted for all engines as from November 1941, and from July 1942 the lettering was changed from " L N E R " to " N E " (fig. 53). One other variation came into use during the 1939-45 War, namely the " totem " on a metal plate on the bunkers of the Q1 0-8-0T rebuilds (fig. 84). These " totems " had white letters on a blue ground. The pioneer electric locomotive for the Manchester-Sheffield line, No. 6701, also had the " totem," painted in gilt, on its cab doors when it was built in 1941 ; it was however also lettered " L N E R" in the centre of the body side.

One of the most welcome post-war announcements was that the L.N.E.R. intended to paint *all* engines green (except the A4's and W1 which were again to be blue). Unfortunately the works were too busy in the immediate post-war period to put this fully into effect, but the A4's were repainted blue and all fitted with stainless steel numerals and letters, and the other Pacifics green. Cowlairs Works in particular made a commendable effort painting secondary passenger and selected shunting engines green. Details of the actual engines painted green down to the end of the L.N.E.R. era will be given in the class articles, but here it may be recorded that representatives of the following classes were dealt with : A1, A2, A3, A10, B1, B2, B3, B4, B12, B17, D3, D11, D16, D29, J36 (fig. 54), J50, J69, J71, J72, J83, K2, K3, K4, L1, N2, V2, V4. One notable example was the D3 2000 which had the L.N.E.R. coat of arms on the tender between the letters N and E, being intended for special saloon haulage (fig. 8). The only other L.N.E.R. engine ever to be so adorned was the Wembley Exhibition engine No. 4472 *Flying Scotsman*, which had the company's coat of arms on the cab sides from 1924 until 1928 (fig. 9). An experimental royal blue livery was tried on the rebuilt A1 4470 in 1945.

In 1946 the complete renumbering of the L.N.E.R. locomotive stock was undertaken (see chapter on numbering) and this involved the use of a considerable number of the characteristic transfers. To conserve supplies of these, recourse was often had to hand painting, usually in small figures utterly at variance with traditionally high L.N.E.R. standards (fig. 55). At length 12in. unshaded Gill Sans numbers and letters were officially adopted as from December 1946 (fig. 132).

For the historian, the L.N.E.R. was a most helpful railway by reason of its policy of inscribing a paint-date on all engines on emergence to traffic after general (and also certain intermediate) repairs. The usual format, which had been previously in use on the N.E.R., was generally introduced in March 1925 and indicated the month and year, followed by an abbreviation for the name of the works, and the word "Type" or "Class" followed by the Diagram Book Classification. All this was painted in white high up on the inside of the right-hand cab side-sheet either in italicised script or Gill Sans. Again however there were variations; prior to April 1925 the N.B. works had painted the day/month/year date of release to traffic on the leading end of the right-hand footplate valance preceded by a letter denoting the particular works (A—Cowlairs, K—Kipps, M—St. Margaret's), and some years after Grouping Inverurie adopted this style (still in use there, incidentally) but showing in figures only the month and year preceded by the letter "I." During 1944-46 Darlington showed the paint date (month and year) in small figures above the engine number on the cab or tank side. Doncaster was very thorough and, even after the introduction of the standard method, showed both inside the cab side sheet and tender side sheet the actual date ex-Works.

Steam railcars when first introduced were painted teak but soon red and cream livery was adopted, followed by green and cream, paint-dates being shown (as on carriages) on the solebars. Some railcars were painted brown all over during the 1939-45 War. Diesel railcars were painted blue and primrose (later green and cream), whilst Tyneside multiple-unit electric stock was successively teak, red and cream and blue and cream.

Generally speaking pre-Grouping liveries disappeared within the first few years of Grouping but exceptions lingered on, the most notable being the N.E.R. electric No. 5 which was never repainted in L.N.E.R. livery although still in stock at the end of 1947.

TYPICAL PAINTING SPECIFICATIONS

GREEN LIVERY—GRESLEY CLASS A1—1924 AND *1928

* From 1928 the engine number was put on the cab side instead of on the tender and the lining on the front buffer-beam was modified.

Boiler	Green§.
Clothing bands & angle-iron to cab	Black, edged with 3/16″ white line.
Mud plugs	Black, with 1/4″ black surround and 3/16″ white line outside.
Handrails	To be left bright.
Smokebox	Black.
Handrails, handles and hinges	To be left bright.
Cab	Green, edged with black (2″ at bottom, 1/2″ at front and rear) and 3/16″ white line inside.
Roof	Black.
Windows	Beading black all round edged with 1/4″ black border and 3/16″ white line outside.
Handrails	Green.
Doors	Green, unlined.
Numerals	*12″ Gold, with red shading, base of numbers 2′ 8″ from footplate.
Front spectacle plate	Green, with 1/4″ black edge and 3/16″ white line inside.
Spectacles	Edged with 1/4″ black and 3/16″ white lines.
Splashers	Green, with black beading round top and 2″ black edge at base, all with 3/16″ white line inside.
Footplate angle-iron and footsteps	Black, with 3/16″ red line 1/2″ from bottom edge and from front buffer-beam.
Frames	
Portion above footplate	Black, with 3/16″ red line 1/2″ from top edge.
Fall plate	Black, with 3/16″ red line 1/2″ from edges.
Main portion of frames below footplate	Black, with 3/16″ red line 1/2″ from bottom edge and from cut-outs.
Horn blocks, spring gear, brake gear	Black.
Inside of frames, cross-stays, axles	Red.
Trailing axleboxes	Black, with 3/16″ red line 1/2″ from edges.
Outside cylinders and clothing	Black.
Wheels	Green, with 1 3/4″ black rim edged inside with 3/16″ white line and black centres with 3/16″ white line outside.
Front buffer-beam	Red, with 3/4″ (1/2″*) black edge and 1/4″ (3/16″*) white line inside.
"No." and figures (on either side of drawhook)	4 1/2″ gold, with brown and black shading.
Tender	Green, with 2″ black border top and bottom edged inside with 3/16″ white line, lined (sides and back) with 2″ black edged on both sides with 3/16″ white line (lining 7″ from front, 4″ from bottom and 9″ from rear of tender on sides; 6″ from sides and bottom on back).
Letters	"L N E R" 7 1/2″ Gold, shaded in red, spaced at 3′ 8″ intervals; base of letters 1′ 1 1/4″ above numbers. *"L N E R" 12″ Gold, shaded in red, spaced at 3′ 4″ intervals; base of letters 2′ 8″ from footplate.
Numerals	12″ Gold, shaded in red, spaced at 6″ intervals; base of numbers 1′ 4 1/2″ from footplate.
Frame	Black, with 3/16″ red line 1/2″ from bottom edge.
Rear buffer-beam	Red.

§Officially described as "G.N. Standard light green" (unofficially known as grass green).

LINED BLACK LIVERY—CLASS N2—1924

Boiler	Black.
Clothing bands & angle-iron to cab	Black, edged with ¼″ red line.
Handrails	Black.
Smokebox	Black.
Handrails, handles and hinges	Black.
Cab	Black, with ¼″ red line ¾″ from front and rear beading, tank and bunker beading, and cut-out.
Roof	Black, with ¼″ red line carried over top, front and rear.
Doors	Black.
Front spectacle plate	Black, with ¼″ red line, 1″ from roof and sides, and on edge of firebox angle-iron.
Spectacles	Lined round with ¼″ red, ¾″ from outside of spectacles.
Splashers	Black, with ¼″ red line 2″ from footplate, ¾″ from top and front of sandbox, on either side of coupling rod splashers, and following inside of beading on both splasher and sandbox.
Footplate angle-iron and footsteps	Black, with ¼″ red line ¾″ from bottom edge and ends.
Frames. Portion above footplate	Black.
Fallplate	Black.
Main portion of frames below footplate.	Black with ¼″ red line ¾″ from bottom edge and from cut-outs.
Horn blocks, spring gear, brake gear	Black.
Inside of frames, cross-stays, axles	Red.
Wheels	Black.
Front buffer-beam	Red, with ¾″ black border and ¼″ white line inside.
" No." and figures (on either side of drawhook)	4½″ Gold, with brown and black shading
Tanks	Black, with ¼″ red line 2″ from top and bottom and 7″ from front and rear.
Letters	" L N E R " 7½″ yellow, at 2′ 8″ centres, shaded red and brown.
Numerals	12″ yellow, shaded red and brown, spaced at 6″ intervals ; 1′ 4″ from bottom red line and 7½″ from base of letters.
Bunker	Black, with ¼″ red line 7″ from front and 2″ from horizontal cab beading and footplate ; continuous from sides to back (i.e. not panelled).
Rear buffer-beam	Red (no number shown on rear).

NAMING

NAMED ENGINES AT GROUPING

Only one of the major constituent companies showed any consistency in its naming policy, but this, combined with one other factor, seems to have had far-reaching effects on L.N.E.R. engine naming. The North British Railway alone pursued a regular policy of embellishing all its most prominent locomotives with names, and, just as consistently, never provided a single one of them with a nameplate. Fortunately for all who are locomotive enthusiasts, the chairman of the N.B.R. directors, William Whitelaw, became the first chairman of the ·L.N.E.R. board, and clearly his guiding hand impressed itself on subsequent group policy that engines should carry names. It is doubtful if, in later years, he would have been altogether happy about some of the results being as good as the intentions.

In the notes that follow, dealing with naming policy and the origins of some of the names, readers are also referred to the complete list of names carried by L.N.E.R. engines from 1923 onwards which will be found on pages 98-104.

When the L.N.E.R. began its existence, there were 180 engines bearing names, three from the G.N.R., 45 from the G.C.R., one from the G.E.R., one from the N.E.R., 122 from the N.B.R. and eight from the G.N.S.R. Clearly there was no tradition for naming the products

of Doncaster Works ; the original Atlantic built in 1898 certainly carried the name Henry Oakley (he was General Manager up to the year in which this engine was built), but when his name was applied to the engine in 1900, the job was done somewhat sketchily. Separate plates bearing one word only were fixed to each splasher, but were of insignificant size and completely without any pretensions to style or character, as can be seen today in York Museum (fig. 56). On that single example the Great Northern case rested until only eight months before it went out of existence, and at no time did even one of the ninety-two large-boilered Atlantics acquire the dignity of a name. In April 1922 when Doncaster completed its first Pacific, it was already known that the Company would soon lose its individuality and this, in conjunction with the tremendous interest which it was realised the engine would attract, led to it being named Great Northern. Even so, when the second engine came out in July it was un-named and so it remained for some months, but before Grouping it was named Sir Frederick Banbury to honour the last chairman of the G.N.R. directors. These two engines did, however, set the style of cast brass curved nameplate which became the L.N.E.R.'s first standard type (fig. 57).

Quite a substantial batch of named engines came from the G.C.R. Many of their leading passenger and some mixed traffic

47

engines were named, but there had been little consistency in policy. The four compound Atlantics bore names but not one of the twenty-seven simple Atlantics ever did so and they were in the very forefront of main line passenger work for at least twenty years. Of the eleven mixed traffic engines which became class B8, there were four with names and seven without, whilst three only of the forty 4-4-0's of class D9 had names at Grouping although one other had been named prior to 1913. All the forty-five names used by the G.C.R. had either a patriotic basis or marked important people or places connected with the Company. Dealing with them in L.N.E.R. class order, the naming went according to the following plan :—

B2 CLASS.—Six engines, with the prototype named after the General Manager, *Sir Sam Fay*, and the rest after the main cities served by the Company. Sheffield was a notable exception, especially as it had been included in the Company's title from the very beginning and Manchester and Lincoln both had their names on this class. One engine later had its name removed (see page 53).

B3 CLASS.—Six engines, again with the prototype on a different basis from the remainder. The first carried the Company chairman's name, *Lord Faringdon*, and this caused changes in other directions (see classes D10 and D9). One other was also named after a director, *Lord Stuart of Wortley* (fig. 58) and this too involved a change on a D10. The other four were patriotic to the core, being chosen just after the country had emerged victorious, but at tremendous sacrifice of human life, from the war of 1914-18. Two were named after the leaders of the Navy and Army, *Earl Beatty* and *Earl Haig*, and a third after the Prime Minister, *Lloyd George*. The remaining engine was called *Valour* in memory of G.C.R. employees who gave their lives for their country, as the large brass nameplates clearly stated (fig. 59). On Remembrance Day (November 11th) in each succeeding year until 1938, Gorton Works encircled the nameplates on *Valour* with laurel wreaths and the engine then went to Manchester London Road station where a wreath of poppies was placed on the front. It then worked the 8-20 a.m. to Sheffield Victoria carrying parties of railwaymen from Gorton to the Remembrance Service held at the Company's War Memorial on Sheffield Victoria station. After this engine was withdrawn in December 1947, one of the nameplates went to the Railway Museum at York, but the other was mounted on a wall in Gorton Works where it still serves its memorial purpose and remains most carefully tended. Under totally different circumstances and at an interval of twenty years, two engines of this class subsequently lost their names : they are detailed on page 53.

B4 CLASS.—One engine only out of the batch of ten was named. This was *Immingham*, to emphasise the importance to the G.C.R. of its deep water dock and port on the south bank of the Humber which it completed in 1912 to rival any East Coast port other than London. This engine worked the special train conveying Directors and Company officials to Immingham for the cutting of the first sod for the new dock site.

B8 CLASS.—Eleven engines, of which seven were never named. Of the other four, two received the names of British Army leaders at the beginning of the 1914-18 war, when the engines were new, and the other two had Company names ; *Sutton Nelthorpe* was the name of a director, and *Glenalmond* was the name of the Chairman's Scottish home.

C5 CLASS.—Four engines, one with the name of the reigning monarch when they were new, two named after directors (fig. 60) and the other, *Lady Faringdon*, after the wife of the Chairman. From 1908 to 1917 this engine had been *Lady Henderson* but her husband became Lord Faringdon in the latter year and the engine's name was altered accordingly.

D9 CLASS.—Three only were named at the Grouping, after the King and Queen, and the Queen-Mother. Another (G.C. No. 1014) was named *Sir Alexander* from 1902 to 1913 after the Chairman. In that year his full name *Sir Alexander Henderson* was used for the first of the more powerful Director class engines and No. 1014's name was removed.

D10 CLASS.—Ten engines, all carrying names of G.C.R. directors at the time they were built. Two had their names changed (one of them twice) before Grouping. In 1917, Sir Alexander Henderson became Lord Faringdon and this name was put on a new, and bigger, engine of class B3. The D10 engine then became *Sir Douglas Haig*, who was in charge of the British armies in France at that time, but in 1920, *Earl Haig* (as he had then become) was the name given to another new B3 engine. This time the D10 took the name *Prince Henry* after the third son of the reigning monarch, and the later opportunity to change it once again (in 1928) to Duke of Gloucester was either missed, or discarded. Another D10 engine carried *Charles Stuart-Wortley* until 1920 when that director became Lord Stuart of Wortley and this latter name was used on yet another new B3 engine. The D10 became *Prince George* after the King's fourth son.

D11 CLASS.—Eleven engines at Grouping, of which the five built during 1919-20 carried the names of two more directors who had joined the board since the names were selected for the D10 class, and the other three the names of the King's elder children. The six engines built in 1922 were all named after important battles of the 1914-18 war.

Stratford only contributed a single named engine, the first of their main 4-4-0 passenger class. The Chairman of directors was honoured by the choice of the name *Claud Hamilton*, but the decision to name the engine was also influenced by the intention to send it to the Paris Exhibition of 1900, the year in which it was built. The nameplate was in a style very much akin to L.N.W.R. practice (fig. 61) but it remained an isolated example, and indeed a change to L.N.E.R. style, but with non-standard lettering, was made in 1933 when the engine was rebuilt (fig. 62). Subsequently the name was transferred to another engine of the same class (see page 55). From the G.E. province later came three engines which became class F9. In their early days on the Colne Valley & Halstead Railway they had borne local place names in lieu of running numbers, but the plates had been removed and numbers substituted long before the L.N.E.R. took them over.

Naming of engines formed no part of the otherwise beautifully painted and embellished products of the N.E.R. Its only example was on a small tank engine with the rather curious wheel type of 2-2-4 used almost entirely for hauling inspection saloons. Engine No. 66 ostensibly dated back to 1851, but apart from its name *Aerolite*, meaning meteorite, there could be little else left of its original construction. Even the name had been dropped when the engine was rebuilt in 1886, but was restored at another rebuilding in 1907. Neither the name nor the style of the nameplate had any subsequent influence, but they are still available for visual inspection as this engine also reposes in the museum at York (fig. 63).

On the N.B.R. there was both regularity and consistency ; all the main passenger classes were named and there was both character and euphony in the choice. Twenty-two of Britain's most impressive looking Atlantics led the way, all carrying well-chosen names representative of the districts through which these engines worked and in geographical sequence from Aberdeen to Carlisle for the two main batches. The second engine ran as *Dundonian* from building until April 1912 when the name was changed to *Bonnie Dundee* and in the original list of names *Cumberland* and *Teviotdale* were included but *Auld Reekie* and *Liddesdale* were substituted before the engines actually appeared.

These Atlantics were supported by forty-three main line 4-4-0's, one carrying Sir Walter Scott's name and with all the others named after characters in his novels. Then came thirty-two very similar engines but with smaller coupled wheels, all named after Glens near the West Highland line for which these engines were specifically designed.

Like most British railway companies during the 1914-18 war, the N.B.R. was called on to supply a number of goods engines for service in France and Belgium. They sent twenty-five of the class which became J36, and when these returned to Scotland in 1919, their war service was marked by their being named. Eleven received names of British army commanders and three more honoured French army leaders ; ten were named after Belgian and French towns and rivers which had been in the midst of some of the most bitter fighting, whilst the remaining one *Ole Bill* (fig. 64) commemorated the characterisation by Bruce Bairnsfather (a popular cartoonist) of the rank and file who bore the brunt of that fighting. Thus it came about that the L.N.E.R. acquired two engines each carrying the names *Ypres*, *Marne*, *Mons* and *Somme* but they decided, quite sensibly, that alterations were unnecessary.

After Grouping changes were made in the names of certain members of classes C11, D29, D30, D34 and J36 (see pages 54-56).

The L.N.E.R. continued to employ shaded lettering for the names of N.B. engines until 1947 when a change was made to unshaded Gill Sans lettering. Originally gilt transfers were used (fig. 65), but from about 1935 these were confined to green engines and the yellow lettering (shaded or unshaded) on black engines was neatly painted on by hand (fig. 66).

Some of the N.B.R. engines which became L.N.E.R. classes D51 and E7 and all those in classes D27, D28, D50, G8 and J82 had carried Scottish place names in the early 1880's, but after Holmes took over in 1882, he had them all removed. Nor did these engines get their names restored when naming again became N.B.R. practice just over twenty years later, although the name *Abbotsford* was used for one of the Atlantics.

In 1887 the G.N.S.R. had with considerable ingenuity constructed two engines in its own works, then at Kittybrewster, and, quite exceptionally, conferred names on them. One carried the name of the Chairman's home and the other the Deputy Chairman's own name. But in 1894 a new locomotive engineer arrived from the Great Eastern, where names were just not used, and he soon had these two removed. They are mentioned because these engines survived (still nameless) to become L.N.E.R. class D46, and also because of the pattern which they set for the only other excursion into naming on which the G.N.S.R. embarked. This was as late as 1920 when six superheated 4-4-0's were built by contractors and two more of the same type were built by Inverurie in the following year. They were all fitted with neat cast brass plates curved round the top of the leading splashers (fig. 67), and these they retained until after the L.N.E.R. itself had ceased to exist. During the middle 1950's the nameplates on these engines were removed, and the same names were painted on in small unshaded lettering (fig. 91). The choice of names, and their background, was as follows :—

G.N.S. 45 *George Davidson*, General Manager when these engines were built ;

G.N.S. 46 *Benachie*, the mountain dominating much of Aberdeenshire ;

G.N.S. 47 *Sir David Stewart*, Chairman until the year before they were built ;

G.N.S. 48 *Andrew Bain*, Chairman when they were built ;

G.N.S. 49 *Gordon Highlander*, the famous regiment with headquarters in Aberdeen ;

G.N.S. 50 *Hatton Castle*, residence of G. A. Duff, director and deputy chairman ;

G.N.S. 52 *Glen Grant*, residence of James Grant, another director ;

G.N.S. 54 *Southesk*, the Earl of Southesk was also a director.

L.N.E.R. NAMING POLICY

During its first year the L.N.E.R. did not name a single engine. Doncaster produced ten more Pacifics, but with them reverted to its age-old policy of anonymity. The year 1924 saw but seven names added to the list, despite a plethora of suitable recipients, as thirty-five Pacifics and twenty-four D11's were built, but two of the seven which were named held out just a faint hope for future improvement. In February, Pacific No. 4472 was being prepared for the British Empire Exhibition at Wembley and it went there bearing *Flying Scotsman* nameplates (fig. 71). This connected it directly with the L.N.E.R.'s oldest and most famous train which had recently been recognised officially as the " Flying Scotsman " express and which these Pacific engines had been designed to work. The first twelve had already proved themselves sufficiently for two further batches each of twenty to be ordered, one lot from Doncaster and the other from the North British Locomotive Co. By the end of 1924, twelve from Doncaster and all the outside-built engines were in service but one only, the first of the Scottish-built engines, was named. It honoured William Whitelaw, former N.B.R. Chairman and by this time Chairman of the L.N.E.R. directors. Obviously the policy of engines carrying names had the blessing (and it would seem the encouragement) of top-level management, but it was well into 1925 before results really became evident. From then on, all the more important classes were given names and in the majority of cases these followed a well-defined pattern. They can now be described in class order instead of chronologically, but mention must first be made of the five other engines named in 1924. These were the Raven Pacifics (L.N.E.R. class A2), two of which had been hurried to completion before the N.E.R. lost its identity,

three more being built in March 1924. The first two ran nameless for more than a year but received names when the other three appeared with them : all were named after cities on the N.E.R. (fig. 68).

Notes on Naming

A1 (A10) AND A3 CLASSES

ORIGINAL NAMES.—Ultimately there were seventy-nine engines in these two classes and all except five bore the names of racehorses at one time or another, the majority of them being winners of the classic races, although this was not an essential qualification for inclusion in the list. Three of the five exceptions have already been mentioned—another was No. 2555 *Centenary*, put on the first Pacific built at Doncaster in 1925, the centenary of the opening of the Stockton & Darlington Railway. The application of the racehorse names began with Nos. 4475 *Flying Fox* in April 1925 and 4479 *Robert the Devil* in May, but no more were dealt with until the following August. Naming of the other forty-five engines then existing was spread over the next six months, the last to receive its name being No. 2566 *Ladas* in February 1926. This latter name was originally put on No. 4480 and was at first thought to be too short for the plates and so they were taken off, only to be used later. In a list published for the first ten names, the winner of the 1880 Derby, *Bend Or*, was included but this name was never used. Doubt could be expressed as to the origin of No. 2579's name *Dick Turpin*, because no horse of this name ever contested any of the classic races. It was, however, appropriate as marking the famous ride from London to York, although if this was the intention, the name could more fittingly have been *Black Bess*, the name of the horse instead of its rider. Two further names allocated to A1's were *Rock Sand* and *Common* but these were replaced by *St. Simon* and *Manna* before the plates were made.

All the A1 class had cast brass curved nameplates over the centre coupled wheels, those for the larger names extending over the full curve of the splashers, whilst shorter plates were used for the less lengthy names. Very soon all these plates were found to be prone to cracking (probably due to Doncaster's inexperience in the matter of nameplates) and in 1926 new plates with bigger flanges and ribs at the back were cast and fitted in replacement. Not only were the fixing bolts increased from four to eleven but the splasher top plate was increased in thickness from $\frac{3}{16}$ to $\frac{5}{16}$ inch. All the replacement plates were to the long pattern : the difference between the original and replacement plates can be clearly seen by comparing photographs of those on *Flying Fox* and *Centenary* in particular, both of which were originally amongst those fitted with the short variety (figs. 123 and 69). The A3's, constructed between 1928 and 1935, had the stronger pattern of plates from the beginning. The last nine A3's to be built, Nos. 2500-8, also differed in having Medium Gill Sans lettering on their nameplates, following the pattern set by the first P2, *Cock o' the North*. However, when No. 2563's name was changed to *Tagalie* in 1941 (see below), the old style of lettering was used. In recent years, *Blink Bonny* has had new plates made with Gill Sans lettering.

Several A3's appeared with names other than those originally intended for them. No. 2746 was to have been *Coronach*, but received the name *Fairway* because this horse won the St. Leger less than a month before it entered traffic. The names allotted to Nos. 2746-51 were accordingly moved on to Nos. 2747-52 and the name allocated to No. 2752, *Gainsborough*, was deleted from the list. This name was however used later on No. 2597. Similarly No. 2598 was to have been named after the 1903 Derby winner *Rock Sand* (a name which had been allocated to an A1, as mentioned above) but received *Blenheim* as this horse won the Derby only two weeks before the engine came out new ; its original name was never used. No. 2503 was to have been *April the Fifth*, but this name was deleted and the names allotted to Nos. 2504/5/6 were transferred to Nos. 2503/4/5. No. 2508, the last A3 to be built, had been allotted the name *Caligula* (the winner of the 1920 St. Leger) but came out instead as *Brown Jack*. This latter horse was selected as it had captured public fancy by winning the Queen Alexandra Stakes for six years running from 1929 to 1934, a most exceptional performance.

SUBSEQUENT CHANGES.—No. 2553 lost its racehorse name *Manna* on 11th November 1926 because this engine happened to be the one inspected by the Prince of Wales when visiting Doncaster Works a few days earlier. Its name was changed to *Prince of Wales* (the fifth exception to the racehorse names) despite the fact that this duplicated the name already on D11 No. 5508, which continued unchanged. No. 2553's original name was reused on new A3 No. 2596 which came out in February 1930.

No. 2564 was named *Knight of the Thistle* until it went to Doncaster for overhaul in November 1932. On 30th December 1932 it returned to traffic, but two days earlier it had been fitted with new nameplates reading *Knight of Thistle* only and these are still carried. The original nameplates were correct, not only for the name of the racehorse, but for the Order of the Thistle. No reason for this change has yet been found.

No. 2563 was renamed *Tagalie*, after the winner of the 1912 Derby, at the end of July

1941 because its original name, *William Whitelaw*, was required for use on an A4. No. 2563 returned to traffic with its racehorse name on 4th August 1941.

A2 CLASS

The N.E.R. Pacifics with "City" names were all withdrawn by May 1937 and the A2 classification remained vacant until Thompson used it for his 4-6-2 type rebuilds from class P2. No change was made to the names of these engines on rebuilding : they became class A2/2 from August 1945. Between May 1944 and January 1945, four engines originally intended to be of the V2 2-6-2 type were completed as 4-6-2's and classified A2/1. In 1946 it was decided to name them, following a suggestion from one of the authors, Peter Proud, which appealed to Sir Charles Newton, then General Manager. Names with a Scottish flavour were found, two of which had actually been used before on N.B. Atlantics, whilst a third became *Highland Chieftain* whereas Atlantic No. 9902 had only been *Highland Chief*. The fourth received a name not previously used, *Robert the Bruce*, but did not have the plates fitted until April 1948 (four months after the L.N.E.R. had ceased to exist) and at the same time this engine got its British Railways number 60510. As No. 509 had become *Waverley* in October 1946, it took well over eighteen months to get these four names on to the engines.

In May 1946 the first of a further fifteen Pacifics to Thompson's design appeared and became class A2/3. As he was due to retire at the end of the following month, his name *Edward Thompson* was allotted to the first of the batch and the other fourteen all took racehorse names.

Thompson was succeeded by Arthur H. Peppercorn and he too caused a batch of fifteen mixed traffic Pacifics to be designed and built. The first one appeared just a week before the end of the L.N.E.R. and although the original nameplates carried his name as quoted, they proved too long to mount on the smoke deflecting plates and shorter ones carrying *A. H. Peppercorn* were substituted. Again the following fourteen engines were all given names of racehorses.

A4 CLASS

ORIGINAL NAMES.—The first batch of four engines was built for working the high-speed, streamlined train the "Silver Jubilee" and they all had names carrying on the 'silver' theme. When *Silver Link* first emerged from Doncaster paint shop its name was on straight plates fixed to the sides of the smokebox casing. After only a few days, and whilst still running trials, the plates were removed and the name was then painted in a central position on the streamlined casing. The other three had similarly painted names at first (fig. 71), but between November 1937 and May 1938 plates were fitted to all four, in the forward position. In addition, No. 2512 *Silver Fox* also carried stainless steel replicas of a fox.

Two more groups, one of seventeen and one of fourteen engines, were built. The names originally selected for them were of British birds noted for powerful and swift flight and intended to typify the power and speed of these engines (fig. 70). Before even the first group was completed, two further high speed trains were planned, the " Coronation " and " West Riding Limited," and the engines to run them were given names to correspond. Those for the former, Nos. 4488 to 4492, carried the names of the leading components of the then British Empire, and for the Yorkshire trains Nos. 4495/6 bore names suggestive of the woollen trade. Nos. 4488-92 also carried the arms of the countries concerned on the cab sides (fig. 3).

The decision to depart from bird names for these A4's involved changes from the original list, as follows :—

New engine No. 4488 entered Doncaster Paint Shop early in April 1937 bearing the name *Osprey* but these plates were quickly removed. It remained in the Paint Shop for some weeks as the subject of various experiments in arriving at a suitable blue livery and eventually emerged on 18th June with nameplates covered until the official naming ceremony on 28th June 1937, when it became *Union of South Africa*.

No. 4489 went into the Paint Shop late in April 1937 named *Buzzard* and was renamed *Woodcock* almost immediately. On 4th May it went into traffic painted shop grey but with green-painted coupled wheels. By 17th May it had returned to Doncaster, and one week later emerged painted Garter blue with dark red wheels and with nameplates covered until the ceremony on June 15th, when it became officially *Dominion of Canada*.

Nos. 4490/1/2 were originally intended to be *Woodcock*, *Great Snipe* and *Bittern* but never carried these plates, although these names were all used subsequently on A4 class engines.

No. 4495 was painted green and named *Great Snipe* when it came out new on 28th August 1937. It went back into the Paint Shop on 12th September and reappeared six days later painted blue and nameless. During the following week *Golden Fleece* nameplates were put on without any ceremony.

No. 4496 was to have been *Sparrow Hawk*, but these plates were never fitted to it ; they were used subsequently on another new engine.

One more exception to the bird names was made on No. 4498, where the L.N.E.R. accepted a suggestion from K. Risdon Prentice, a member of the R.C.T.S. and joint author of the former publication " Locomotives of the L.N.E.R. 1923-37," that, as this was the hundredth Gresley Pacific, it should carry the name of their designer and it thus became *Sir Nigel Gresley*. Twenty-three of this class therefore originally carried bird names, but these have been regarded as fair game for changes to be made and ultimately only thirteen retained names of birds.

SUBSEQUENT CHANGES.—From the early part of 1939 it became usual to honour the higher officials of the L.N.E.R. by placing their names on A4 class engines and this policy persisted for almost ten years. On 3rd March 1939 No. 4469 was officially renamed *Sir Ralph Wedgwood* to mark his retirement the previous day from the post of Chief General Manager which he had held since Grouping. This engine had to be scrapped following air raid damage at York in April 1942, but although the plates escaped serious damage, new ones were provided when No. 4466 took over the name in January 1944. It came out that month and was officially renamed at King's Cross station on 22nd January 1944.

No. 4500 came from Plant on 31st March 1939 renamed *Sir Ronald Matthews* ; he had become Chairman just six months before on the resignation of William Whitelaw.

No. 4499 followed during the first week of April renamed *Sir Murrough Wilson*, then deputy Chairman, but in neither case does an official naming ceremony appear to have been held.

No. 4462 was the next to be changed, being altered to *William Whitelaw* at a meeting of the directors held at York on 24th July 1941. He had been Chairman from Grouping until 30th September 1938 and his name had been carried by an A1 from July 1924. The promotion to the more powerful engine was belated, but no doubt sincere, and as already related, the A1 then took over a name in the racehorse series.

No. 4901 was selected in August 1942 to honour Charles H. Newton, the Chief General Manager who succeeded Sir Ralph Wedgwood. It came from Plant so named during week ended 29th August with nameplates covered until the official ceremony was held at King's Cross on 25th September 1942. It emerged from Doncaster again on 8th June 1943 with the name changed to *Sir Charles Newton* to mark the knighthood conferred in the Birthday Honours list of the previous week.

No. 4494 was also altered simultaneously with 4901's first change, to carry the name *Andrew K. McCosh* who was a director and chairman of the Locomotive Committee of the board. It ran with plates covered from the end of August until the renaming ceremony at King's Cross on 29th October 1942.

No. 4496 ranged further afield in the man its new name sought to honour, none other than the Supreme Commander of the Allied Expeditionary Forces 1944-45. It was renamed officially *Dwight D. Eisenhower* on 27th September 1945 at Marylebone station but then ran with plates covered until a date in February 1946 for reasons which have not been established. Possibly it was hoped that Eisenhower would come over to participate in a renaming ceremony.

No further changes on this class were made until almost the end of the L.N.E.R. by which time all the engines had been renumbered; two further executive officers were then honoured. In October 1947 the name of No. 28 was changed to *Walter K. Whigham* who was the last deputy Chairman of the L.N.E.R. board, and the following month No. 26's name became *Miles Beevor* who was the L.N.E.R.'s last Chief General Manager.

In October 1947 it was announced that No. 11's name *Empire of India* was to be changed to *Dominion of India*, and the engine did carry the latter plates for about a week whilst in the Paint Shop, but it returned to traffic with its original name unchanged. Simultaneously No. 20 was to have become *Dominion of Pakistan* but this never took effect.

With the scrapping of B3 No. 1494 in the last month of the L.N.E.R.'s existence the name of Lord Faringdon was no longer in use. He had been the Great Central Chairman until Grouping and one of the original L.N.E.R. directors, but had died in 1934. In March 1948 his name reappeared on an A4 which also assumed its British Railways number 60034 at the same time. Since then, stability has descended on A4 naming.

B1 CLASS

Following Gresley's death, his successor Edward Thompson designed a general purpose mixed-traffic 4-6-0 but, due to war conditions, the appearance of the first ten engines extended from December 1942 to June 1944. Straight nameplates on the sides of the smokebox were used carrying names of animals in the Antelope family, although *Antelope* itself (an old Stockton & Darlington name) was never used. It was only intended that the engines built in the Company's workshops should be named, together with the first engine of an order for one hundred from the North British Locomotive Co. A batch of thirty built by Darlington between November 1946 and December 1947 did manage, with one exception, to carry on the original intention by appearing with antelope names, but further batches built by Gorton and Darlington appeared unnamed. The exception mentioned, No. 1036, even got so far as having plates cast with *Korrigum* on them but they were never used as this engine was selected to carry one of the L.N.E.R. directors' names, as mentioned below. When the L.N.E.R. ceased to exist on 31st December 1947,

there were 274 engines of this class in running stock and a further 66 being delivered against an existing order. As history was repeating itself, one of the final satisfactions of the L.N.E.R. directors was to see their names placed on engines of this class and, at various dates in December 1947, such nameplates were affixed to eighteen B1's, mostly of very recent construction. Owing to the length of some of these names, all eighteen sets of nameplates had smaller lettering than normal (fig. 75).

After nationalisation, further construction and orders on outside builders increased this class to 410 engines but only one more was named. This was 61379 *Mayflower* on 13th July 1951 at the request of a society interested in furthering Anglo-American friendship. The choice of this engine lay in that it was one of the class shedded at that time at Immingham and thus regularly worked through Boston on trains to and from King's Cross.

B2 (B19) CLASS

With the introduction of the "East Anglian" train between London and Norwich in September 1937, appropriate names selected were conferred on the two B17 class engines selected to haul it. One of these was *City of London* hitherto borne by No. 5427 and this engine had its G.C.-type nameplates removed in that month and ran nameless until withdrawn in 1947.

B3 CLASS

No. 6167 named *Lloyd George* at Grouping did not remain long in favour. This politician had ceased to be as popular as he was a few years earlier and on 30th August 1923 the nameplates were removed and the engine then ran nameless for some twenty-four years.

No. 6166 was the subject of some very comprehensive rebuilding in October 1943 as part of Thompson's standardisation scheme in the course of which it lost its name and this was never restored.

B17 AND B2 CLASSES

ORIGINAL NAMES.—By royal permission, the first of ten 4-6-0's built in December 1928 to work express passenger trains in the Eastern Counties was named *Sandringham*. The remaining nine carried names of other large houses in Norfolk and Suffolk belonging to various members of the peerage. Thirty-eight more of this type followed and names were given to all but one of them on the same basis, but coverage extended beyond East Anglia to include L.N.E.R. territory up to the Scottish border. In a handful of cases, house owners other than peers were included. Amongst them, the railway historian A. C. W. Lowe (a large Essex landowner) was asked if his home Gosfield Hall could be used but he was too modest to agree. Names for the final three engines, Nos. 2845/6/7, were to have been *Gilwell Park, Helmingham Hall* and *Kimberley House* but the intention was changed. On 22nd June 1935 new engine No. 2845 was ceremonially named *The Suffolk Regiment* to celebrate that regiment's 250th anniversary. The names *Gilwell Park* and *Helmingham Hall* were passed to Nos. 2846/7, but *Kimberley House* was never used.

A further twenty-five engines of class B17, but with larger capacity tenders, were built in 1936-37 and all of them were named after Association football clubs in the towns served by the L.N.E.R. Curved nameplates of the usual style were used but under them was an 8½-inch metal replica of half a football, flanked by enamelled plates depicting the club's colours (fig. 73). The names on the fourteen engines of this class built by Darlington in 1936 were not affixed as first planned, the names of the 1935-36 F.A. Cup semi-finalists being taken first whilst North Road Works could not resist honouring the team of their town, though only in the Third Division. The introduction of *Darlington* into this series squeezed out *Manchester City*, but this name was used later on No. 2871. The names allotted to the first series of fourteen " Footballs " and those actually carried were as follows :—

Engine No.	Allotted Name	Ex-works as
2848	Huddersfield Town	Arsenal
2849	Derby County	Sheffield United
2850	Sunderland	Grimsby Town
2851	Middlesbrough	Derby County
2852	Sheffield Wednesday	Darlington
2853	Arsenal	Huddersfield Town
2854	Manchester City	Sunderland
2855	Leeds United	Middlesbrough
2856	Grimsby Town	Leeds United
2857	Doncaster Rovers	Doncaster Rovers
2858	Newcastle United	Newcastle United
2859	Sheffield United	Norwich City
2860	Norwich City	Hull City
2861	Hull City	Sheffield Wednesday

SUBSEQUENT CHANGES.—The two engines 2859 and 2870 which were fitted with streamlined casings for working the " East Anglian " train had hitherto carried football club names *Norwich City* and *Tottenham Hotspur* respectively, which was the reason these two engines were selected as these clubs were at each end of the train's journey. As the plates were of the curved type, they were quite out of keeping with the new exterior lines of the engines. New straight plates bearing these names, but without club colours or football replicas, were fitted to the sides of the smokebox and on 13th September 1937 both engines ran trials from Doncaster so adorned. By 21st September No. 2859 had carried two further sets of straight nameplates, *City of Norwich*, which it bore for one day only, and *East Anglian*, which were retained, thus honouring both Norwich and Ipswich and avoiding offence to the latter town, which was not a city. Concurrently the *Tottenham Hotspur* straight plates were replaced on No. 2870 by *City of London* plates. When the streamlined casings were removed from these two engines in 1951, new curved nameplates were again fitted over the middle coupled wheels.

No. 2870 was already accustomed to a change of identity because when new it had been named *Manchester City* and, as such, went into service on 13th May 1937. The following engine was to have been *Tottenham Hotspur* but was not ready in time to be named during an exhibition of rolling stock held at Hoe Street, Walthamstow on 29th May. So 2870 took its place, together with the *Tottenham Hotspur* nameplates. The displaced *Manchester City* plates then appeared on No. 2871 when it entered traffic on 11th June 1937. In August 1945 engine 2871 became the first Thompson rebuild to class B2 and in February 1946 was renumbered 1671, still as *Manchester City*. It was then chosen to be the Great Eastern line's regular engine for royal train workings and on 20th April 1946, its name became *Royal Sovereign* on new curved plates. When this engine was withdrawn in September 1958 the plates were transferred to No. 61632 (formerly *Belvoir Castle*) the following month, but No. 61632 soon joined No. 61671 on the scrap heap, in February 1959.

As recorded above, the name *Tottenham Hotspur* disappeared with the renaming of No. 2870 in September 1937. A few months later *Tottenham Hotspur*, so ceremoniously named in June 1937, was wanted for an " away " match and so in January 1938 No. 2830, formerly *Thoresby Park*, became *Tottenham Hotspur*, whilst *Norwich City* reappeared on No. 2839, formerly *Rendlesham Hall*.

No. 2858 was in service for less than a fortnight with its football club name of *Newcastle United* and on 6th June 1936, at an official ceremony held during an exhibiton of rolling stock at Romford, it became *The Essex Regiment*.

No. 2805 too was the subject of change to a regimental name. On 23rd April 1938 Doncaster Works put new plates *Lincolnshire Regiment* on it and an official naming ceremony took place at Lincoln station on 30th April 1938.

C11 CLASS

No. 9903 was renamed *Aberdonian* by Cowlairs Works on 3rd May 1934 as its own name was required for the first P2 2-8-2 then building ; No. 9868 *Aberdonian* had already been scrapped.

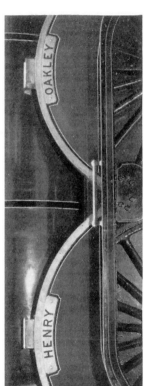

Fig. 56   Class C2 4-4-2 (G.N.R.)

Fig. 58   Class B3 4-6-0 (G.C.R.)

Fig. 60   Class C5 4-4-2 (G.C.R.)

Fig. 57   Class A1 4-6-2 (G.N.R.)

Fig. 59   Class B3 4-6-0 (G.C.R.)

Fig. 62   Class D16/3 4-4-0

Fig. 64   Class J36 0-6-0 (N.B.R.)
Hand painted shaded letters

Fig. 66   Class D30 4-4-0 (N.B.R.)
Hand painted shaded letters

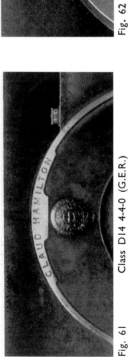

Fig. 61   Class D14 4-4-0 (G.E.R.)

Fig. 63   Class X1 2-2-4T (N.E.R.)

Fig. 65   Class C11 4-4-2 (N.B.R.)
Gilt transfer shaded letters

Fig. 68   Class A2 4-6-2 (N.E.R.)

Fig. 70   Class A4 4-6-2

Fig. 72   Class A4 4-6-2
Shaded transfer letters

Fig. 67   Class D40 4-4-0 (G.N.S.R.)

Fig. 69   Class A1 4-6-2

Fig. 71   Class A1 4-6-2

Fig. 74

Class D34 4-4-0 (N.B.R.)
Hand painted Gill Sans letters

Fig. 76

Class D49/I 4-4-0

Fig. 78

Class K2 2-6-0

Fig. 73

Class B17 4-6-0

Fig. 75

Class BI 4-6-0

Fig. 77

Class D49/2 4-4-0

Fig. 80   Class K4 (K1/1) 2-6-0

Fig. 82   Class V2 2-6-2

Fig. 84   Totem on Q1 0-8-0T

Fig. 79   Class P2 2-8-2

Fig. 81   Class M2 0-6-4T (Met. Rly.)

Fig. 83   Class V2 2-6-2

Fig. 86   Class J35 0-6-0. Showing B.R. 60,000 series number together with E prefix, also Route Availability group

Fig. 88   Class EM2 electric locomotive

Fig. 85   Class A1 (Peppercorn) 4-6-2

Fig. 87   Class A1/1 (Thompson) 4-6-2

Fig. 89   Clayton steam railcar No. 287 *Royal Sailor* at Heaton shed, July 1928. In red and cream livery

Fig. 90   Class J39 No. 1471 at Darlington Bank Top shed. L.N.E.R. Group Standard 4200-gallon tender with stepped out topsides

Fig. 91   Class D40 No. 62279 *Glen Grant* at Elgin shed, September 1954. In B.R. lined black livery. Nameplates removed and name painted on. G.N.S.R. 3000-gallon tender

Fig. 92   Class B2 No. 61671 *Royal Sovereign* at King's Cross, about 1949.   In
L.N.E.R. green but with B.R. lettering and number.   For working Royal trains

Fig. 93   Class A2 No. 60532 *Blue Peter* at Haymarket shed, October 1955.   In
B.R. green livery.   L.N.E.R.-type eight-wheel high-sided tender with
snap-head rivets

Fig. 94   Class WI No. I0000 on a Leeds express near York, 1930

ig. 95   Class D49/I No. 270 *Argyllshire* and D30 No. 9423 *Quentin Durward*
on an Aberdeen-Edinburgh express near Cove Bay, July 1938.   Pilot
engine next to train in accordance with N.B.R. practice

Fig. 96   Class V1 No. 2910 leaving Portobello on Gorebridge-Edinburgh
train, 1935

Fig. 97   Class J39 No. 2712 on a down Southend train at Stratford, about 1935.
L.N.E.R. Group Standard 3500-gallon tender with flush sides

D11 CLASS

In 1924, orders were placed for twenty-four further engines to this Great Central design, but with slight modifications, and virtually the whole of their career was spent on passenger workings from N.B. Section sheds. At first they ran nameless but during 1925-26 all were named after characters in the poems and novels of Sir Walter Scott. Despite this, they were invariably known as the Scottish Directors. In line with former N.B.R. practice, which Cowlairs continued, nameplates were not provided and the names were originally applied by shaded transfers, and later painted without shading, in a straight line along the splashers. No changes were made to the names of this class.

D16 CLASS

No. 8900 *Claud Hamilton* was withdrawn (as No. 2500) in May 1947 but in August the nameplates were transferred to No. 2546 of the same class. When this engine was withdrawn in June 1957, the name went out of use.

D29 CLASS

For about ten days in January 1947 No. 2403 was carrying the name *Jeanie Deans* by mistake, and it could be seen almost daily in Edinburgh Waverley along with No. 2404 *Jeanie Deans*, but 2403's correct name *Sir Walter Scott* was soon restored.

D30 CLASS

No. 9419 was named *The Talisman* until repainted in December 1931, and it then ran as *Talisman* only until February 1938. From thence until the next repainting in May 1940 it was again *The Talisman* and then *Talisman* had to suffice once more. As such it ran until March 1947 when it again became *The Talisman* and this was the final version.

D34 CLASS

Some difficulty arose with the name of No. 9492 and the Railway Company was involved in a certain amount of correspondence with people who could not trace a *Glen Gau* on their maps. Eventually the L.N.E.R. renamed this engine *Glen Gour* in July 1925 but this was not necessarily the Glen originally intended.

No. 9287 left Cowlairs in November 1941 as *Glen Lyon* and ran for about three weeks before resuming its correct name of *Glen Gyle*. In passing it may be noted that *Glenfinnan* (fig. 74) was spelt as one word, the other Glens being invariably two.

D49 CLASS

ORIGINAL NAMES.—The original series of twenty-eight engines were named after English and Scottish counties and all the name-plates included the 'shire' suffix (fig. 76). All the names selected were of counties in which the L.N.E.R. had its own lines. Engine No. 246 was originally to have been *Fifeshire*, but this was changed to *Morayshire* about six weeks before the engine appeared. A further eight engines soon followed, again with county names, but this time including *Northumberland*, *Cumberland* and *Westmorland*. A surprising inclusion was *Berkshire* which contained no L.N.E.R. line, but an equally surprising omission was Durham, especially as all thirty-six engines were built at Darlington in that county.

The engines named *Leicestershire* and *Buckinghamshire* differed from the others in that they were equipped with rotary cam operated poppet valves and from 1932 a further forty engines were built with this type of valve gear. All were given the names of Hunts, four only being in territory not served directly by the L.N.E.R. Standard curved nameplates were used surmounted by a cast brass fox in full flight (fig. 77).

Late in 1931 the names for the first fifteen Hunt class were announced, but those actually carried differed in six instances. The original intentions for these were 201 *The York and Ainsty*, 211 *The Zetland*, 220 *The Bramham Moor*, 247 *The Bilsdale*, 292 *The Sinnington* and 297 *The Staintondale*, the other nine being as they actually appeared. On 7th April 1932 engine 201 *The York and Ainsty*, painted in standard green livery, commenced running in the Darlington district, but on 12th April another 201 appeared painted grey and named *The Bramham Moor* for official photography. It was later painted green, renumbered 211 and renamed *The York and Ainsty*; its discarded plates were then put on the original 201 and all the others followed with the names they bore throughout their existence. This somewhat involved explanation has been included in case someone had the good fortune to photograph a fully painted Hunt as 201 but with the name *The York and Ainsty* during the early days of April 1932.

SUBSEQUENT CHANGES.—In accordance with the decision that rotary cam operated poppet valve engines should carry the names of Hunts, the first two engines then carrying Shire names were brought into line. No. 336 was renamed *The Quorn* on 2nd May 1932 and No. 352 became *The Meynell* on 7th June 1932.

J36 CLASS

After Grouping, works other than Cowlairs were required to overhaul engines of this class and it proved beyond them to restore their names in a number of cases. Nos. 9615 *Verdun* and 9676 *Reims* were repaired at Gateshead in April 1924 and both lost their names, nor were they ever restored on these two. Incidentally, the spelling *Reims* was the official version, but contemporary observers recorded the name as *Rheims*. No photograph to support either version has so far been traced. No. 9176 *French* had its name removed at Inverurie in July 1928 but it was restored during an overhaul at Cowlairs in March 1939 only for Inverurie to take it off again in March 1946. No. 9648 *Mons* was affected by a fire at Peebles shed, and at its subsequent rehabilitation in November 1934 at Inverurie the name was not put on again, until Cowlairs restored it in December 1938.

By the outbreak of war in September 1939, scrapping had reduced the original twenty-five named engines to fourteen and during the next five years they too lost their names. With the scrapping of three more, by the end of September 1947 only eleven of these survived. One of the final decisions of the L.N.E.R., however, was to restore the names, No. 5226 (ex-9650) getting its name *Haig* back at Cowlairs in December 1947. Between April 1948 and June 1949 the other ten received their names once more, three at Cowlairs and seven at Inverurie. The old style of naming with shaded painted letters was used for *Horne*, but all the other names were painted in a new plain Gill Sans style. At the end of 1962, four of these veterans were still in service and yet again some of them had suffered the removal of their names.

The name *Haig* was unofficially painted on No. 65311 at Craigentinny during the summer of 1953. It ran thus for two years and then entered Inverurie Works for general overhaul. Surprisingly, it reappeared with its newly acquired name in June 1955 and has carried it ever since.

K2 CLASS

To augment Scottish motive power, fourteen engines of this G.N. class were transferred in 1924-25 and a further six went north in 1931-32. Thirteen entered regular service on the West Highland line and, between February 1933 and June 1934, curved nameplates were fitted to them : these bore the names of Lochs near to that line (fig. 78). The remaining seven, which worked mainly around Edinburgh, never received names.

K4 CLASS

ORIGINAL NAMES.—These six Darlington-built engines were designed specially for working the West Highland line and the name of the first one was merely an extension of the Loch names of the K2 class. The other five were given names of chiefs of great Scottish clans in the districts served by the line. Darlington brass foundry obviously did not have the Gaelic, and engine 3442 arrived at Eastfield shed on 12th July 1938 with nameplates reading

MacCailein Mor whereas they should have been *MacCailin Mór*. This engine was tucked away inside the shed until 25th July 1938 when it came out renamed *The Great Marquess*, and correctly spelled plates were later used on No. 3445 (fig. 80). The last engine No. 3446, also received an alternative version of its original name of which details are given below.

The nameplates on these K4 class engines were not of the curved type as used on the K2 class but were of the straight type fixed to the sides of the smokebox following the pattern begun in 1934 on class P2.

SUBSEQUENT CHANGE.—Although Lord of Dunvegan is an accepted title for the chief of Clan MacLeod, a member of that family requested that a more Scottish version be used and so, on 29th March 1939 new nameplates bearing *MacLeod of MacLeod* were fitted to No. 3446.

M2 CLASS

These four engines were taken over from London Transport ; they had been built for the Metropolitan Railway. The first three bore the names of the Metropolitan Chairman, General Manager (fig. 81) and locomotive engineer when they were built, but the fourth simply carried the name of a small country town at the farthest extremity of the Metropolitan line.

P2 CLASS

The power of publicity was just beginning to be recognised when Gresley brought out the first British eight-coupled express passenger engine in 1934, to solve the problems posed by the difficult line between Edinburgh, Dundee and Aberdeen. Not only was the engine number, 2001, chosen with some care but Gresley himself picked the name *Cock o' the North* as a clear expression of his confidence in what the engine would achieve, in addition to honouring the chiefs of Clan Gordon. The style of nameplate made another break with tradition, being a long straight plate fixed to the side of the smokebox casing (fig. 79). As the running board was clear of the coupled wheels, there were no splashers and a curved plate would have been incongruous.

The majority of subsequent namings took this form. In addition, *Cock o' the North* was the first L.N.E.R. engine to use Gill Sans lettering on its nameplates and this style was thereafter adopted as standard, except for the rest of the B17's and D49's and several V2's. For the second engine, the choice, *Earl Marischal*, was the title borne by the President of the Scottish College of Heralds. Two years later four more engines were built and they received names in which power and Scottish associations were nicely blended. *Lord President* is the presiding judge of the Court of Session in Scotland ; *Mons Meg* is a large ancient piece of cannon which is one of the showpieces of Edinburgh Castle ; *Thane of Fife* was Lord of the old Scottish kingdom of Fife, and *Wolf of Badenoch* was the Earl of Buchan who had ravaged the Bishopric of Moray. Two of these six names had been borne by N.B.R. Atlantics and as No. 9903 was still in existence, its name had to be changed to allow *Cock o' the North* to be used on the 2-8-2.

After Gresley died, his successor rebuilt the P2 class to the 4-6-2 type. When the first, No. 2005, was so treated it was nameless when it reappeared in January 1943. The next to receive attention was No. 2006 and this, too, came out nameless in April 1944. The discarded front portions of the engines on the scrap road at Doncaster Works still had the nameplates attached and during the week ended 13th May 1944 they were retrieved and repolished. The two pairs of plates were then sent to Haymarket shed at Edinburgh and by 8th June 1944 both engines had their names restored. As and when the other four were rebuilt to Pacifics, they retained their original names without any such hiatus.

V2 Class

There can have been few more deserving, and less rewarded, classes of engines than this one when bestowal of names is considered, Essentially main line engines on account of their high axle loading, and favoured with fully lined passenger livery (apart from the war period) no more than seven out of the 184 were named by the L.N.E.R. This is all the more surprising when six out of the seven were the subject of elaborately staged naming ceremonies.

The first of the class was named *Green Arrow*, which was the symbol and name of a newly-introduced registered goods service. For an extra fee of 2/6d., close supervision of transit, progress, and prompt delivery was provided, and it was likely that this new class of engine would be used on the express parcels trains concerned. The nameplates first cast were a reversion to the curved type, but exposed driving wheels needing no splashers made this type of plate an obvious misfit. Before the engine left Doncaster Works, the curved plates were discarded and straight plates were fitted to the smokebox sides.

Between 11th September 1937 and 20th June 1939, a further six engines were named, four honouring army regiments and the other two public schools. In all cases curved nameplates were cast, but these surmounted panels painted in the regimental or school colours and carrying the appropriate badge (figs. 82 & 83). These panels offset the difficulty found with the first engine's original form of nameplate. The L.N.E.R. carried out no more naming of V2's, but in April 1958 British Railways added one more regimental name using the style already described.

V4 Class

Of the two engines built one only was named, using straight plates on the smokebox. The name *Bantam Cock* was chosen to typify speed, power and activity in small space and light weight.

Petrol Shunter

In September 1925 the shunt horse "Peggy" at Brentwood was replaced by petrol shunter No. 8430 and for some years that engine had the name *Peggy* painted on it. Whilst this was no doubt a local appellation, the name did find its place on the engine record cards kept both at Liverpool Street and at Doncaster ; it also appeared in a list of engine names published in the August 1930 issue of *The L.N.E.R. Magazine*. By May 1937 the name had definitely disappeared from No. 8430 but the date when it did so is not known.

Railcars

The eleven Clayton-built steam railcars, purchased in 1927-28, were all given names of horse-drawn mail coaches, and all except three of the Sentinel railcars drew their names from the same source. These three exceptions were never named : they were the two experimental cars bought in July 1925 and the one taken over in November 1933 from the Isle of Axholme Joint Railway. All the named cars had a descriptive notice inside detailing what was known about the running of the mail-coach from which the car took its name and offering a monetary reward for additional information.

In 1933-34 three Armstrong-Whitworth diesel-electric railcars were taken into stock although the L.N.E.R. had been operating them since 1931-32. The names of two, *Tyneside Venturer* and *Northumbrian* were clearly connected with their place of origin but no satisfactory explanation has yet come to light for the name of the middle one of this trio, *Lady Hamilton*.

The names on all these railcars, steam and diesel-electric, were applied by transfer lettering on the sides of the coaches (fig. 89) and no changes were made to any of them.

Conclusion

When the L.N.E.R. began it took over 180 named engines ; to British Railways it handed over 499 plus 25 for which instructions had been given. These latter were fourteen A2 class in course of construction, the plates cast (but still to be fitted) for No. 510 of class A2/1, and ten J36 class on which the names were to be restored. The engines with names comprised :
A1-1, A2-1, A2/1-3, A2/2-6, A2/3-15, A3-77, A4-34, A10-1, B1-58, B2-9, B4-1, B8-2, B17-

64, D9-1, D10-10, D11-35, D16/3-1, D29-12, D30-25, D34-30, D40-7, D49-76, J36-1, K1-1, K2-13, K4-5, M2-2, V2-7, V4-1.

Postscript

Between August 1948 and December 1949, Doncaster and Darlington built forty-nine Pacifics which were of pure L.N.E.R. design. Two months after the first one, No. 60114, entered service it was named *W. P. Allen*, this gentleman being the locomotive trade union member of the Railway Executive and, incidentally, a former King's Cross driver. The other forty-eight ran without names until by 1950 the authorities had become persuaded that to incur the expense of nameplates could well be good for public relations. Names from widely differing origins were chosen, but all were within the traditions of the L.N.E.R. and its constituents. The names of the four major component companies (other than *Great Northern* which was already in use) together with three G.N.R. and three N.E.R. locomotive superintendents formed one group, whilst another comprised thirteen named after racehorses. The company nameplates incorporated coats of arms (figs. 85 & 87). Scotland came into the picture with seventeen names borne by Atlantic or Scott class engines. One of these did not follow exactly, as the C11 had been *St. Johnstoun* and the A1 became *Saint Johnstoun* whilst, in addition, the name *Marmion* was introduced. This had not been used previously by the Scott class, but it had been on an N.B.R. Clyde paddle steamer. Similarly the B17 names had included only English country houses but now on the A1 class *Balmoral* was used. The remaining six took the names of birds, four of which had previously appeared on A4's, the others being *Curlew* and *Kittiwake*. Fitting of these name-plates began with No. 60133 *Pommern* in April 1950 and was completed with No. 60156 *Great Central* in July 1952. No. 60124, named *Kenilworth* in July 1950, duplicated the name borne by D30 No. 2431 until the withdrawal of the latter engine in October 1958. The other Scotts whose names were re-used were all condemned before the A1's concerned had their nameplates fitted.

No further changes of name have taken place and the only additions, apart from *Mayflower* already mentioned under B1 class, the V2 which was given a regimental name and the unofficial J36 naming, were made on electric locomotives. The pioneer electric locomotive built as No. 6701 in 1941 for the Manchester-Sheffield line had to wait eleven years before it could do the work for which it was designed. In the meantime it was loaned to the Netherlands Railways from June 1947 to March 1952, and on its return was named *Tommy* to perpetuate the name affectionately bestowed on it by Dutch railwaymen : there was an official naming ceremony at Liverpool Street station on 30th June 1952.

After full electric working between Guide Bridge and Sheffield began, it was decided to name the seven express passenger locomotives and twelve of the mixed traffic type. Names from Greek mythology were chosen, those of goddesses for the former and those of gods for the latter. Apart from the first passenger engine being named *Electra* (for obvious reasons), all the other eighteen were names borne by engines working the same stretch of line a century before. The cast brass nameplates and style of lettering used were those which had been standard on the Great Central Railway (fig. 88). Fixing of these nameplates began in May 1959, but it was not until August 1961 that the task was completed.

BRAKES

One of the most difficult problems facing the L.N.E.R. directors at Grouping was the choice of a standard continuous brake, because out of the five major constituent companies two used vacuum, two used Westinghouse and the fifth was changing over from Westinghouse to vacuum. Thus the new Company was confronted with the expense of fitting large numbers of engines and coaching stock with the standard brake and the prospect of having a considerable quantity of redundant equipment left on its hands. It is understandable therefore that it was not until 1928 that a decision in favour of vacuum was finally reached and even then reservations were made to allow the following Sections to retain the air-brake :

(1) Great Eastern (London suburban services and some country branch lines).

(2) North Eastern (Tyneside electric trains).

(3) Great North of Scotland.

The multiple-unit Tyneside electric stock was never converted but the G.E. country branches and the G.N.S. Section (apart from the Fraserburgh-St. Combs branch since changed by British Railways) became vacuum operated. The retention of Westinghouse on the G.E. London suburban services gave rise to the apparent anomalies of new L1 2-6-4T's being put into traffic dual fitted as late as 1948 and some of the older N7 0-6-2T's remaining Westinghouse only until withdrawn.

The G.N.R. and G.C.R. used vacuum and the former was the most straightforward of all because the vacuum equipment provided the brake on the engine as well as on the train, the only variation being that one or two engines had a Westinghouse pump for testing the brakes of East Coast Joint Stock at Doncaster Works. The older G.C. engines were vacuum only but the Robinson classes had steam brakes on the engine and vacuum ejectors for the train, whilst some shunting engines had steam or hand brake only. For handling G.E. stock in the Lincoln area a few G.C. passenger engines had Westinghouse equipment.

On railways employing the Westinghouse brake the position was usually more complicated because vacuum equipment had to be provided on some passenger engines for dealing with "foreign" coaching stock, and on some goods engines for working fitted goods trains. For reasons of economy it was usual for certain goods and shunting engines to have steam brake instead of Westinghouse. These considerations applied on the G.E.R., N.E.R., N.B.R. and G.N.S.R., but on the North Eastern another variety was encountered on small shunting engines—hand brake only. Furthermore, the N.E.R. had already absorbed the Hull & Barnsley which had been a vacuum line but with some steam brake shunting engines. The N.B.R. was at one time a Westinghouse railway, but since 1906 all new passenger tender engines had been dual-fitted (i.e. Westinghouse for engine and train, plus vacuum ejector for use when hauling vacuum braked stock), and from 1911 onwards coaching stock was being converted to vacuum (simultaneously with the East Coast Joint Stock). Like the N.E.R., the N.B.R. had a number of small shunting engines with hand brake only.

From 1923 to 1928 on the L.N.E.R. the brakes fitted to new engines were governed mainly by two factors, (a) place of construction, and (b) section of line on which employed. Doncaster favoured vacuum for engine and train whereas Darlington preferred steam brake on the engine with vacuum for train ; passenger engines for the G.E., N.E., and N.B. Sections were usually dual-fitted. Most of the O4's added to stock in 1924-29 had steam brake only.

From 1929 to 1934 steam and vacuum became standard but Pacifics had vacuum only and shunting engines steam only. The final Gresley development was a complete return to the G.N.R. system of vacuum only but under the Thompson regime steam and vacuum combination brakes were re-introduced.

Alterations to brake equipment on pre- and post-Grouping engines were numerous and these will be fully detailed in the class articles concerned, but the main trends may be summarised as follows :—

(a) Addition of Westinghouse brake to vacuum engines on transfer to sections using the air brake. This could take either of two forms, viz. mere addition of Westinghouse for the train (as, for example, on some B17's, K2's and N2's) or fitting of Westinghouse for engine and train retaining vacuum for train only (e.g. D1 class).

(b) Addition of vacuum equipment to all surviving Westinghouse main line passenger engines, many smaller passenger engines and also some goods engines.

(c) Replacement of Westinghouse brake by steam on dual-fitted passenger engines after the fitting of vacuum brake to carriages on the N.E. and N.B. Sections was deemed to be sufficiently complete in 1930.

(d) Some goods engines were dealt with at the same time as the passenger engines mentioned under (c) but many were left Westinghouse- or dual-fitted and another similar conversion programme was initiated during the 1939-45 War presumably to simplify maintenance. Nevertheless some classes escaped both (c) and (d) such as C15 and C16 which were dual-fitted until withdrawn.

Two types of steam and vacuum combination existed, viz. the older pattern with the plain steam brake valve and the later graduable pattern ; a third type came in with the M. & G.N. engines in 1937 as most of these had the Midland type with a single application handle for both brakes. The Metropolitan engines absorbed in 1937 had steam and vacuum brakes.

There were two isolated examples of unusual brake fittings to be found on small shunting engines. On the G.E. Section a Y5 had Westinghouse and vacuum equipment for train testing in addition to the engine steam brake, whilst on the N.E. Section a J79 had hand brake only on the engine with vacuum equipment for the train.

An entirely new braking system introduced in L.N.E.R. days was the counter-pressure type employed on some of the four-wheeled Sentinel shunting locomotives.

DRIVING POSITION

Generally speaking the English constistuents of the L.N.E.R. favoured right-hand drive whereas on the Scottish lines the driver was placed on the left-hand side of the cab (exceptions are noted in the class articles). In due course English engines were stationed in Scotland in addition to the N.E. engines already allocated to Haymarket and these all now came to be handled by N.B. men who did not take kindly to the change in driving position, so much so that they made strong representations to have left-hand drive adopted as standard for the whole system. In this they were successful and whereas all new engines built in 1923-24 (except the N15's, an N.B.R. design) had right-hand drive, from 1925 onwards all new engines had left-hand drive apart from A1 2555-62 ; J72 500/12/6/24/42/ 66/71/4/6/81 ; K3 126/7/34/5/40/1/3/6/53/6/8/ 9/63/7/70/8/80/4/6/8/91/5, 200 ; P1 2393/4 ; T1 1656-60 (all built in 1925) and B12 8571-80 (built in 1928). The ex-R.O.D. O4's added to stock up to 1929, however, retained right-hand drive as did the M. & G.N. and Metropolitan engines absorbed in 1937. Although left-hand drive was thus adopted for new construction, engines already being driven from the right-hand side were not usually altered and the relatively few exceptions to this rule will be dealt with under the individual classes. Worthy of mention here, however, is that certain of the 1924-25 Darlington-built K3's were so altered, also all the surviving 1922-25 Gresley Pacifics, these latter being dealt with during 1952-54 under B.R. auspices.

TENDERS

Most of the tenders inherited by the L.N.E.R. were six-wheeled vehicles, but there were a handful of interesting exceptions. The Scottish companies supplied a number of four-wheelers, those from the G.N.S.R. being particularly antiquated. A few eight-wheeled tenders also existed at Grouping : the G.N.S.R. still possessed two of Manson's peculiar " bogie tenders," in which the two leading axles were mounted in a bogie but the rear axles were rigid, and the G.C.R. had one double-bogie tender, built for experimental purposes. The two G.N. Pacifics had eight-wheeled tenders with all axles rigid, and these became the prototype of a design which, with successive modifications, was multiplied throughout the life of the L.N.E.R.

G.N.R. Tenders

The G.N.R. handed over to the L.N.E.R. 897 tenders but only 852 tender engines, the former generally outlasting the engines for which they had been built. As a result of this longevity, considerable changing of tenders from one engine to another used to occur and in its last fifteen years the G.N.R. built tenders only for stock and (apart from the two Pacifics) not for individual engines. During this period only 220 new tenders were constructed, against 366 new tender engines. The balance was made up by utilising tenders from older engines then being withdrawn. Normal procedure was to have the most modern tenders attached to the engines performing the most arduous duties, these being latterly the 2-6-0, 2-8-0 and large boilered 4-4-2 types. It is not generally appreciated that in 1918-21 the engines only of the O1, O2 and K2 classes built by the North British Locomotive Co. and Kitsons were supplied, Doncaster providing the tenders for them, either from new building or by a process of substituting older tenders on the engines whose duties were being taken over.

Ivatt introduced the G.N. tender classification using the letters A to G to distinguish the various types. The original class G had become extinct before Grouping but Gresley re-used this letter in 1922 for the new eight-wheeled Pacific tenders. Sixty-nine class E and eighty-seven class F tenders were taken over by the L.N.E.R., fitted mainly to the J3 and J4 classes. These were the early Stirling tenders with the springs hidden between the frames (fig. 106). When first built they were devoid of coal rails, these having been added later by Stirling. Class F tenders had wells between the frames, increasing the water capacity to between 2500 and 2954 gallons. The flat-bottom version, class E, carried under 2500 gallons. The later Stirling tenders had their springs outside the frames and were represented at Grouping by the seventy-nine class C (flat-bottom) tenders and the 146 class D (well-bottom) tenders. These all had three coal rails except for the sixteen class D tenders built in 1894-96. These latter were the largest G.N. six-wheeled tenders, with a capacity of 3850 gallons of water and 5 tons of coal and were distinguishable from all other Stirling tenders by having only two coal rails. After Grouping the class C and D tenders were mainly attached to engines of the E1, J3, J4, J7, Q1, Q2 and Q3 classes (fig. 20).

During the first few years of Ivatt's superintendency several changes were made in the tender design. The shape of the frame cut-outs was altered, the top edge being straight instead of curved as in all Stirling designs. Wheels were standardised at 4ft. 0in. nominal diameter to which should be added 1½in. to 2in. for tyre thickness. Two coal rails were fitted as against Stirling's three. The inside of the tender was redesigned and the " water bunker " style gave place to the " horseshoe tank " style, with the water space surrounding three sides of the coal space, slightly decreasing the water capacity. Ivatt tenders also had steel buffer plates instead of wooden buffer beams, whilst the straight guard-iron fixed to the buffer beam on all Stirling tenders gave way to an irregular shaped guard-iron bolted to the frame. The rear corners of Ivatt tenders were rounded instead of squared. Not all the changes took place simultaneously so that there are a few examples of hybrids e.g. a batch of six tenders with Ivatt-style frame cutouts and two coal rails but Stirling-style 3ft. 6in. nominal diameter wheels and wooden buffer beams built as late as 1898. It is interesting to observe that these six hybrids were originally class A but that in 1922 after they had been carefully re-examined they were pronounced to be class C ! Before these six hybrids appeared, Ivatt had already introduced his standard class A 3170-gallon tender with a coal capacity of 5 tons, to be followed in 1898 by his well-bottom version, class B, increasing the water capacity by 500 gallons. These latter first appeared on the " Klondykes " (L.N.E.R. class C2). Sixty-seven of these 3670-gallon tenders were built (fig. 119) plus a batch of ten in 1899 with slightly higher sides increasing the water capacity to 3720 gallons. Also in 1899 appeared the 3140 gallon version of the class A tender, the slight reduction in water capacity being accounted for by the provision of a water-scoop. Forty-one were built by 1901 when another important change was made in tender design.

Between 1901 and 1906 fifty new-pattern class A tenders were constructed with self-trimming coal bunkers. The sloping bunker sides increased the coal capacity to 6½ tons and decreased the water capacity to 3000 gallons. The last forty of these 3000-gallon tenders had unequal wheel bases, 6ft. 1½in. plus 6ft. 10½in., another departure from previous G.N.R. practice. In 1908 appeared the well-bottom class B version carrying 3500 gallons. The wheelbase was again altered, the axle spacing now being 6ft. 0in. plus 7ft. 0in. The weight in full working order of this, the last, G.N.R. six-wheeled tender design was 43 tons 2 cwt. and 190 of these tenders were constructed prior to Grouping. Altogether the L.N.E.R. took over 247 class A tenders with water capacities varying between 3000 and 3280 gallons mainly attached to classes C2, D1, D2, D3, D4, J1, J2, J5 and J6. The 267 class B tenders were mainly attached to classes C1, C2, K1, K2, K3, O1 and O2. The final G.N.R. tender design, class G, will be described more fully in the section dealing with the L.N.E.R. eight-wheeled tenders.

After Grouping an additional thirty class B tenders of the 3500-gallon type were built and these were attached mainly to new O2 engines (fig. 121) and to some C1 class where they replaced tenders of the earlier 3670-gallon design. Fifty more eight-wheeled tenders of class G were built for A1's 4472-81 and 2543-82. The last tenders of pure G.N.

design (in classes B and G) were completed by mid-1925.

G.C.R. Tenders

During Robinson's time at Gorton, policy regarding tenders was very different from that at Doncaster. Changing of tenders was carried out to only a limited extent and standardisation of tender design had been settled for twenty years. There were two types, an early one with 3250 gallons water capacity (fig. 55), soon discarded for a development carrying 4000 gallons (fig. 127) ; both carried a nominal 6 tons of coal. Those built prior to 1905, also the tenders attached to the R.O.D. 2-8-0's, were without water scoops, otherwise these were fitted as standard to tenders of both capacities. New tenders were built for individual engines, and in corresponding numbers, so that there was no considerable surplus as on the G.N.R. Two major movements of tenders were carried out. The thirty-six Q4's which had originally been fitted with 3250-gallon tenders received the 4000-gallon type in exchange. Although begun just before Grouping, this move was not completed until 1930 : it was done at the expense of the J11's. A similar exchange had been carried out many years before Grouping : 3250-gallon tenders had been fitted originally to the first two G.C. Atlantics and the corresponding pair of 4-6-0's, also the B5 class, and these tenders were changed for the 4000-gallon variety then running with J11's and Q4's. For some unknown reason, two of the B5's were not dealt with at that time, but were brought into line just after Grouping.

The G.C.R. contributed to L.N.E.R. stock the only example of a double-bogie tender. This came out with O5 No. 5422 in June 1919 and was an experimental design holding 4000 gallons of water, and 450 cubic feet of coal dust, according to G.C. records (on the L.N.E.R. diagram these capacities were given as 4150 gallons and 7 tons respectively). The purpose of this tender was to provide a comparison between pulverised coal and oil fuel firing and, after running with the O5 until May 1922, it was coupled to O4 No. 5966 which was then carrying a boiler six feet in diameter as part of the trials. It remained with No. 5966 (with both of them still in Great Central livery) until the experiments were concluded in February 1924. It then stood spare in Gorton Works until June 1925 when the two bogies were sent to Dukinfield to be used in a well trolley wagon and the body became an oil storage tank at Gorton.

The older G.C. engines possessed several different types of tender. All the Sacré tenders which survived the Grouping had springs above the platforms, narrow bodies, and coal rails. Except for the earliest Parker tenders, those built by Parker and Pollitt were originally devoid of coal rails or copings, but about 1910 the fitting of copings to these tenders was begun. At first the style employed was similar to that of the standard Robinson tenders. After Grouping, however, a more austere pattern with squared ends was used on the remainder. According to records at Gorton, the task was completed in 1933.

The general tender position on the G.C.R. at Grouping was as follows :—

Water Capacity	Coal Capacity	Water Pickup	Attached to Classes
1800 galls.	2t 15c	No	D12, G.C. "18" and "12A"
2500 galls.	2t 15c	No	D12 (1 only), J8/1, J12
2600 galls.	2t 15c	No	D8, D2 (1 only)
3000 galls.	3t 16c	No	J8/2 (2 only), E2 (2 only)
3080 galls.	5t 0c	No	J10 (58 engines), J9, J13, D7
3250 galls.	6t 0c	No	J11 (33 engines), Q4 (3 engines)
3250 galls.	6t 0c	Yes	J11 (72 engines), Q4 (33 engines), B5 (2 only)
4000 galls.	6t 0c	No	D5, D6, X4, J10 (66 engines), O4 (R.O.D. type)
4000 galls.	6t 0c	Yes	Q4 (53), J11 (69), B1, B2, B3, B4, B5, B6, B7, B8, B9, C4, C5, D9, D10, D11, O4 (except R.O.D. type), O5

In the immediate post-Grouping period further new tenders of the 4000-gallon type with scoop were built for the completion of the order for class B7, and also for the twenty-four D11/2's for Scotland. They were all completed before the end of 1924. These post-Grouping tenders were of the self-trimming type which had been introduced on the G.C.R. in 1922 with the last six D11 4-4-0's. They were distinguishable by the fact that the body was slightly wider resulting in a reduction in the amount of flare to the coal copings, also a driver's locker was provided on the tender front above the coal door (fig. 126).

G.E.R. Tenders

Stratford-designed tenders were notable for the smallness not only of their physical size but also in the number of types employed : at Grouping five kinds covered the requirements of the G.E.R. Whilst it was not uncommon for G.E. engines to have their tenders changed (800 were handed over to the L.N.E.R. with 779 engines), replacements were usually of the same type, at least in L.N.E.R. days.

The most individual type of G.E. tender was that with the sides curved inwards at the top and known variously as "water carts," "tarpots" or "Bohemian tenders" (fig. 21). They were designed to hold 2790 gallons of water, 1½ tons of coal and 720 gallons of fuel oil. They first appeared with James Holden's 4-2-2 engines (G.E.R. Nos. 10 to 19) built in 1898 and similar tenders came out behind the first twenty-one "Clauds" built in 1900-01. It was soon found that the working range of

these "Clauds" was being handicapped by the limited water capacity and, shortly after Nos. 8880-9 were built, their "water cart" tenders were changed for others of more orthodox external shape with the water capacity increased to 3300 gallons. The tenders thus displaced were used for ten new 2-4-0's which ultimately became E4 class Nos. 7407-16 on the L.N.E.R. The changing of the tenders on the other eleven "Clauds" was never completely effected. Nos. 8897 and 8900 lost their "water carts" before Grouping and Nos. 8890/8 afterwards, whilst No. 8894 received an ordinary tender in 1932. The remaining six engines ran with these curiously shaped tenders until withdrawal.

The 4-2-2's referred to above had a very short life, all being withdrawn between 1907 and 1910 but their "water cart" tenders found further employment behind D13's 8020-9. After oil firing was abandoned by the G.E.R. about 1911, the fuel capacity of the "water carts" was altered to 5 tons of coal in place of the previous 1½ tons and 720 gallons of oil. In later L.N.E.R. days the water pick-up apparatus was removed.

As mentioned above, "Clauds" 8880-9 soon received tenders holding 3300 gallons of water and the next twenty engines, Nos. 8860-79, were built with this type of tender. All thirty had their coal capacity increased from 1½ to 5 tons when they ceased to carry oil. L.N.E.R. engine diagrams ignored these 3300-gallon tenders and included them all with the standard type holding 3450 gallons which accompanied all the engines built as L.N.E.R. classes D15 and D16. Similar tenders came out with the B12 class 4-6-0's (fig. 50) except that these had the water capacity increased to 3700 gallons at the expense of the coal capacity which went down to 4 tons. For a 4-6-0 these tenders had a singularly short length, but this was necessary to keep the total wheelbase down to 48ft. 3in. as there were many turntables on the G.E.R. only 50ft. in diameter. At Grouping the tender position on the G.E.R. was as follows :—

Water Capacity	Coal Capacity	Water Pickup	Attached to Classes
3700 galls.	4 tons	Yes	B12
2640 galls.	5 tons	Yes	D13 (except 8020-9)
2640 galls.	5 tons	No	E4, J14, J15, J16/17 (8150-69 only)
2790 galls.	5 tons	Yes	D13 (8020-9 batch), D15 (8890-9 batch), E4 (7407-16 batch)
3450 galls.	5 tons	Yes	D14, D15, D16 (from March 1923)
3500 galls.	5 tons	No	J16/17 (except 8150-69), J18, J19, J20

After Grouping, the G.E.R. design of tender not surprisingly appeared on D16 class 8780-9, constructed in 1923, and even on the B12/2 engines built by Beyer, Peacock in 1928. The Beyer, Peacock tenders weighed one ton more than Stratford-built B12 tenders although curiously the water capacity went down from

3700 to 3670 gallons. By that year, increased engine power became an absolute necessity on the G.E. Section and the solution was sought by the introduction of the B17 class. Even so, the turntable restriction on length still persisted and engines 2800-47 all had short G.E.-type tenders, holding 4 tons of coal and 3700 gallons of water, which kept their total wheelbase down to no more than 48ft. 4in. Thus tenders of pure G.E. design were built as late as 1935.

From 1926, as they were repaired, G.E. tenders were fitted with extra side copings to minimise coal spillage.

M. & G.N. Tenders

This was the only company absorbed by the L.N.E.R. subsequent to Grouping to contribute any tenders. Those taken over were very definitely in keeping with the M. & G.N.'s title. Twelve were of purely G.N. design and the remainder, with their panelled side sheets (unique on the L.N.E.R.), were just as strongly Midland in their appearance. These latter consisted of two types. One, weighing 33 tons 11 cwt., held 3 tons of coal and 2950 gallons of water and was fitted with coal rails. This design was attached to the classes which became D52, D53, D54 (except one engine), J40 and J41 (fig. 34). The other was a straight-sided tender with coping but no coal rails. It held 3 tons of coal and 3000 gallons of water and weighed 36 tons 9 cwt. The old Beyer, Peacock outside-cylindered 4-4-0's (Class A Rebuild) were running with this type of tender, also D54 No. 054. The G.N.-pattern tenders were attached to engines which had originally been diverted to the M. & G.N. from an order placed by the G.N.R. with outside builders. Not surprisingly, they were G.N. Class A, holding 6 tons of coal and 3170 gallons of water, and their engines were absorbed into L.N.E.R. classes J3 and J4. No M. & G.N. tenders appear to have been fitted with water pick-up apparatus.

N.E.R. Tenders

The tender contribution of the N.E.R. (the same in total as the engines) could best be likened to the hymns described as 'ancient and modern'. They ranged from the antiquities attached to classes " 398 " and " 1001 " (fig. 32) to the up-to-date self-trimming type holding 4125 gallons (fig. 51). There had been little interchanging of types, but it was not unknown for tenders to be interchanged within the same type. As the following table shows, three main patterns covered the majority of engine classes. However, in one respect class D20 did not conform : alone of all tenders built from 1885 onwards, their tender wheels were 4ft. 0in. diameter, no others deviating from the standard 3ft. 9¼in.

The allocation of N.E.R. tenders was as follows :—

Water Capacity	Coal Capacity	Water Pickup	Attached to Classes
4125 galls.	5½ tons	Yes	A2, B16, C7, D21, Q6, Q7
3940 galls.	5 tons	Yes	B13, B14, B15, D17, D18, D19, Q5*
4125 galls.	5 tons	Yes	C6
3800 galls.	5 tons	Yes	C8
3940 or 3537 galls.	5 tons	Yes	D20
3038 galls.	5 tons	Yes	D22, D23, J21, J24, J25, J26, J27
2651 galls.	5 tons	No	E5
2500 galls.	3½ & 4 tons	No	J22, "901", "1440"
2200 galls.	3 tons	No	"398"
1600 galls.	3 tons	No	"1001"

*Some of the tenders behind the Q5 class only carried 3701 gallons of water.

After Grouping the building of further A2's and B16's brought additions to the stock of 4125-gallon 5½-ton self-trimming tenders and this same type was also built for the ten new Q7's in 1924, these being the last constructed to North Eastern design.

H. & B.R. Tenders

Although all the H. & B. tenders were of roughly similar capacity, the tenders behind each class of engine differed, the only constant dimension being the 3ft. 9in. wheel diameter (fig. 24). None of them ever had water pick-up apparatus fitted, and all were built by contractors.

Water Capacity	Coal Capacity	Attached to Classes
3500 galls.	5½ tons	D24
3000 galls.	6 tons	J23 (except engines 2513-22)
3300 galls.	6 tons	J23 (engines 2513-22 only)
3500 galls.	5 tons	J28
3300 galls.	4 tons	Q10

No changing of tender types occurred and no tenders to H. & B. design were built after 1915, when the last J28 engine appeared.

N.B.R. Tenders

Apart from the two G.N. Pacific tenders, the N.B.R. brought into the L.N.E.R. the largest tenders as regards both coal and water capacity. Water troughs were non-existent on the N.B.R. and the standard passenger engine tender was designed to carry enough water for non-stop running over the difficult 98-mile route between Edinburgh and Carlisle. There was an insignificant difference of water capacity between the Atlantics and the more modern 4-4-0's, the former holding 4240 and the latter 4235 gallons (fig. 44). Similarly the J37 tenders carried 3500 gallons but the same design attached to classes D26 and D32 was rated at 3525 gallons. Other 3500-gallon tenders were attached to the J35's but their coal capacity was only 4½ tons. Most of these tenders were to Reid's design and were much bigger than those of his predecessors as the

63

following position at Grouping shows :—

Water Capacity	Coal Capacity	Attached to Classes
4240 or 4235 galls.	7 tons	C10, C11, D29, D30, D33, D34
3525 or 3500 galls.	7 tons	D26, D32, J37
3500 galls.	6 tons	Some D27, D28 & D31
3500 galls.	4½ tons	J35
2500 galls.	6 tons	D27, D28, D31, D35, D36, J33, J36
2500 galls.	4 tons	D25, J32, J34
1800 galls.	4 tons	J31
1652 galls.	3 tons	E7
1800 galls.	2½ tons	Y10 (4-wheeled tender)

In addition to the four-wheeled tender attached to the N.B. 0-4-0 No. 1011, four-wheeled wooden coal carriers were often coupled to the Y9 0-4-0T's (fig. 162). These latter were not included in annual returns of tenders and were in fact numbered in the wagon series.

After Grouping, no more tenders of N.B.R. design were built. In 1923-24 water pick-up apparatus was fitted to the tenders of C11's Nos. 9510, 9877/8 for through working between Edinburgh and Newcastle, otherwise N.B. tenders were devoid of this facility.

G.N.S.R. Tenders

From 1893, when Johnson introduced his 4-4-0's which became class D41, tender design had been standardised on the G.N.S.R. Earlier examples of this design carried only 3 tons of coal, but the later addition of coal rails increased this to 5 tons, and all the main passenger classes were so fitted by 1923 (fig. 91). This was the type of tender which replaced the curious eight-wheeled tenders Manson had originally fitted to six engines built in 1890. As mentioned earlier, the front of these tenders was carried on a bogie whilst the rear two axles were rigidly fixed to the tender frame. They were originally attached to the engines which became D43 class Nos. 6812/3/4 and D38 Nos. 6875/6/7 on the L.N.E.R. When these six engines were rebuilt in 1914-20 some had their tenders replaced by the six-wheeled type, but Nos. 6813/76 still had the " bogie " tenders at Grouping. So far as can be established they received six-wheeled tenders in November 1924 and April 1925 respectively.

Older tenders to Cowan and Manson designs were a varied collection and there were even a few four-wheelers still running at Grouping. At each end of the Kintore-Alford branch, the turntables were only 40ft. 3in. diameter and the only tender engines able to use them were those in classes D44, D47 and D48, providing they were fitted with four-wheeled tenders. After Grouping, engines known to have run with four-wheeled tenders were G.N.S. Nos. 45A, 54A, 66 and 67 and this type of tender was still in use up to August 1925 at least. It is unlikely that any were still used

after December 1926 as three of the above-mentioned engines had been scrapped by then, whilst the fourth, No. 6867, reappeared from shops in that month with a six-wheeled tender.

Water troughs were never laid on the G.N.S.R., consequently none of the tenders was fitted with pick-up apparatus. At Grouping, exactly 100 tender engines and the same number of tenders were handed over, their distribution being as follows :—

Water Capacity	Coal Capacity	Attached to Classes
3000 galls.	5 tons	D38, D40, D41, D43
3000 galls.	4 tons	One D38, one D43 (8-wheeled tender)
2100 galls.	4½ tons	D42, D46
2000 galls.	4½ tons	D44, D48
1950 galls.	4 tons	D39, D45
1800 galls.	4 tons	D47
1050 galls.	2 tons	Some D44 & D47 (4-wheeled tender)

No tenders to G.N.S.R. design were built after Grouping.

L.N.E.R. Tenders—Eight-Wheeled Types

As mentioned above, the tenders attached to the first fifty-two Gresley Pacifics were of G.N. design (fig. 9), but a most interesting variant appeared in 1928. For the non-stop workings between London and Edinburgh it was imperative to use two sets of enginemen and the changeover had to be made somewhere in the vicinity of York. The trains *could* have halted momentarily opposite Clifton engine sheds, just north of York station (an arrangement which satisfied such scruples as a rival line possessed), but this would have been totally out of keeping with Gresley's character. To him, a non-stop *was* a non-stop, and providing the means to make it so was not beyond his ingenuity. From Doncaster came a batch of ten eight-wheeled tenders with the same underframe design as before and the same water capacity of 5000 gallons (fig. 49). In place of the coal rails, the sidesheets were extended upwards and the coal capacity was increased from 8 to 9 tons. But, in addition, space was found along the right-hand side of the tender for an access corridor 5 feet high and 18 inches wide. A vestibuled connection at the rear end gave access to the train itself (figs. 6 and 7). This effective method of changing engine crews continued in use until steam locomotives were no longer rostered to the non-stop workings ; diesels took their place in 1962. Admittedly the tender weight was increased by slightly more than 5 tons, and each pair of enginemen travelled almost 200 miles " on the cushions," but the changeover was effected without any delay in running time and the ' non-stop ' claim was valid. The decision to build as many as ten corridor tenders was probably influenced by the placing of an order about the same time for Doncaster to construct ten more Pacifics, with the boiler pressure increased from 180 to 220 lb. per sq. in. On the completion of these first ten class A3 engines, Nos. 2743-52, the surplus tenders were all absorbed. The corridor tenders were, of course, attached to engines which were, or were likely to be, concerned with the non-stop workings. Some engines were consistent performers over many years, whilst others had corridor tenders attached for only brief periods.

In 1930, eight more A3's were built and with them appeared a new type non-corridor tender. The framing and wheels followed the original G.N. design but the tank sides were high and there were no coal rails. The capacity was again 5000 gallons of water with 8 tons of coal, but as corridors were not provided the weight in working order came down to 57 tons 18 cwt. against 62 tons 8 cwt. of the corridor type, and was little more than the 56 tons 6 cwt. of the original G.N. design. At the same time, one more corridor tender was built to run with the experimental high-pressure water-tube boilered engine No. 10000 which did manage to put in a few runs on the non-stop trains. This tender remained with No. 10000 until as late as April 1948 when it was replaced by one of the high-sided non-corridor type.

The next eight-wheeled tender to be built (in 1934) was something of an experiment ; of the high-sided non-corridor type it had spoked instead of disc wheels and the body was of all-welded construction. These modifications reduced the weight in working order by 2 tons 12 cwt., but no further tenders were built exactly in this form. The spoked wheels were later replaced by the disc type. This tender came out with *Cock o' the North* and remained with that engine throughout. It was followed by nineteen high-sided non-corridor tenders of the 1930 design, fourteen of which came out new with the remaining five engines of the P2 class and the final nine A3's, Nos. 2500-8. The other five tenders were sent to the North Eastern Area for use with the Raven Pacifics Nos. 2400-4 but, after less than four years, the scrapping of these engines released the tenders for use elsewhere. They were then all coupled to A3's, in turn releasing tenders for new A4 class engines, as recorded below.

With the appearance of the first A4's, Nos. 2509-12, to which streamlining was applied, new corridor tenders were built for them (fig. 47). Whilst the coal and water capacities remained at 9 tons and 5000 gallons, additional top hamper connected with the streamlining increased the total weight to 64 tons 3 cwt. The tender originally attached to the second A4, No. 2510, was notable in having Timken roller bearing axleboxes, but within six months Nos. 2509 and 2510 ex-

changed tenders. The roller bearing tender remained with *Silver Link* for almost twenty years.

When a further seventeen A4's, Nos. 4482-98, were constructed, Doncaster built a corresponding number of eight-wheeled tenders. Only the last seven were of the corridor type and these were fitted to Nos. 4491-7. The other ten engines came out with the original 1928 batch of corridor tenders which had been collected from various A3's and modified to the streamlined design. The ten new tenders, of the non-corridor type, were coupled to A1 and A3 class engines, but not necessarily those from which the corridor type had been taken.

For the final series of fourteen A4's, Doncaster only needed to build nine new tenders, because by then the five Raven Pacifics had gone and their high-sided eight-wheeled tenders made up the balance. Thus the total number of eight-wheeled tenders then corresponded to the engines in the classes (A1, A3, A4, P2 and W1) using them. Of these 121 tenders, 52 were of the original design with coal rails, 22 were of the corridor type, and 47 were of the high-sided non-corridor type. Whilst changing of tenders between individual engines frequently occurred, use of the coal rail type was confined to A1 and A3 engines, whilst the P2 class had only the high-sided non-corridor type. Although engines of classes A1 and A3 were once regular users of the corridor type, this ceased completely after the A4's came into service. From 1937, with the sole exception of No. 10000, corridor tenders ran only with A4 class engines and this position still obtains*. Of the corridor tenders built in 1937, one was fitted with Hoffman, and another with Skefko roller bearing axleboxes.

One of the eight-wheeled high-sided non-corridor tenders was attached to A4 No. 4469 when it was bombed in York shed on 29th April 1942. Whilst the engine was scrapped, the tender was repaired, but remained spare at Doncaster Works until 22nd December 1945. It then replaced a six-wheeled tender behind A2/1 No. 3696.

The eight-wheeled tender, of non-corridor type, was a Gresley feature that his successor Thompson was apparently able to accept. Between 1946 and 1949 a further 82 new eight-wheeled tenders were built, 59 at Doncaster and 23 at Darlington. They were to exactly the same design as the final tenders built for the A4's in 1938, but with detail differences. The most important was that these tenders did not have vacuum brakes, hence they never subsequently ran with A3's or A4's. The Darlington products had the customary countersunk rivets for the tank sides, but, most exceptionally, Doncaster used the snap-head

---

* The privately preserved A3, No. 4472 *Flying Scotsman*, has been fittted with a corridor tender.

variety (fig. 93). These tenders were coupled to the fifteen Thompson A2/3 class, the fifteen Peppercorn A2 class and the 49 Peppercorn A1 class engines, the remaining three replacing six-wheeled tenders on the other three engines of class A2/1, similar to No. 3696. Five of these tenders, those attached to A1's 60153-7, had Timken roller bearing axleboxes. In 1946-47, the L.N.E.R. purchased two hundred W.D. Austerity 2-8-0's and whilst strictly ' in,' they were never ' of ' L.N.E.R. stock. Their tenders were of the non-bogie eight-wheeled type holding 9 tons of coal and 5000 gallons of water.

L.N.E.R. Tenders—Six-Wheeled Types

After the L.N.E.R. was formed, the first order for new construction placed at Darlington Works was for fifty G.N.-type 2-6-0's of class K3. From the outset, there was some doubt as to the type of tender to be fitted, with the result that construction of the engines outpaced the tenders. Eventually it was decided that a new type of tender should be designed for these engines, to hold 7½ tons of coal and 4200 gallons of water, and to be known as a Group Standard type. When the first two engines, Nos. 17 and 28, were completed, no Group Standard tenders were ready for them, and so Doncaster sent two G.N. standard 3500-gallon tenders to Darlington with which Nos. 17 and 28 first went into traffic : No. 32 was thus the first engine to receive a Group Standard tender. The design dispensed with coal rails but had stepped-out copings (fig. 100). The wheelbase was 13ft. 6in., unequally spaced at 7ft. 3in. plus 6ft. 3in. The weight in working order varied in different batches from 51 tons 10 cwt. to as much as 52 tons 13 cwt. with 52 tons 0 cwt. quoted for the majority.

Apart from detail alterations, the 4200-gallon tender continued to be built for almost thirty years, from engine No. 32, which appeared with it on 29th August 1924, until the very last engine of L.N.E.R. design, British Railways No. 61399, came out similarly fitted on 22nd April 1952. Between those dates 1063 tenders were built to this design and the classes of engine normally fitted with them were B1 (Thompson), B17 (Nos. 2848-72), D49, J38 (prior to 1931), J39/2, K1 (Peppercorn), K3, O2/3 and V2. The most apparent detail alteration was that the stepped-out sides were discontinued from 1928 as in April 1929 a change was made to flush sides with engine No. 1300 of class K3. Also, late in 1937, the front-end shield was made considerably higher (fig. 40), not only to provide additional protection for the enginemen, but also to give the fireman an access door to the coal space, enabling him to get at the fuel in the back of the bunker towards the end of long runs. V2 No. 4791's tender was the first with the high front-end. Between individual engines there were many exchanges of tenders of the same type. Details are given in a following paragraph concerning changes to, or from, a different type, of which some examples were quite interesting.

Between September 1951 and April 1952, four of the 4200-gallon Group Standard tenders from B1 class engines were modified and fitted with coal weighing apparatus. One was used in the North Eastern Region and another in the Scottish Region, both behind various B1's. The other two tenders worked in the Eastern Region, mostly with B1's but also, for short periods, with K1's.

The next L.N.E.R. tender design to appear was a special one and only two examples were built. Although appearing in 1925, they were flush sided, thus anticipating the standardisation of this feature by some three years. Holding 7 tons of coal and 4700 gallons of water, they were the tenders attached to P1's Nos. 2393/4 throughout the twenty years of their existence (fig. 102). When these engines were scrapped in 1945, the tenders were sent to Darlington and there put behind B2 rebuilds Nos. 2815 and 1632 ; they were withdrawn from service together with these engines in February 1959.

Only one more six-wheel tender design was constructed, a smaller version of the 4200-gallon Group Standard type. It held 5½ tons of coal and 3500 gallons of water and its weight in working order was 44 tons 4 cwt. The wheelbase was 13ft. 0in., again unequally spaced at 7ft. 0in. plus 6ft. 0in. The type was normally used with classes J38 (from 1931), J39/1 and K4. It first appeared in September 1926 with the original J39 No. 1448, and the last one came out with K4 No. 3446 in December 1938. Stepped-out sides were used at first (fig. 90), but a change to flush sides was made in August 1928 with the tender coupled to new J39 No. 2691 (fig. 97). Only the last eighteen (those entering traffic in May to December 1938) had the high front-end shield (fig. 120). In all, 197 Group Standard 3500-gallon tenders were constructed.

Finally, two more 3500-gallon tenders were built for use with the V4's, Nos. 3401/2, and whilst they were substantially to the Group Standard design with high front end, the tender behind No. 3401 is shown on the diagram as only weighing 42 tons 15 cwt. although with an increase in coal capacity to 6 tons. The same reduced total weight is given for No. 3402's tender, but with the usual 5½ tons of coal. When the engines were withdrawn and cut up in 1957, this fate did not extend to the tenders. The first to be uncoupled was made ' spare ' and L.M.S. tender No. 3846 was cut up in lieu. The other was sent from Inverurie to Cowlairs for use as a water carrier by the Electric Traction Section.

During the war, both Doncaster and Darlington built engines and tenders of the L.M.S. class 8F 2-8-0 type to some of which the L.N.E.R. applied their livery and classification O6, but both the engines and tenders soon went to the L.M.S.

Principal Changes of Tender Type

Here it is not intended to deal with movements whereby classes J11 and Q4 exchanged tenders of 4000 and 3250 gallons capacity and vice versa, nor with the transference of more modern self-trimming tenders from the Q6's to the C7's. These will be dealt with in the individual engine class descriptions, but there were other movements with more interesting features.

The first ten engines of class K3, Nos. 4000-9, had tenders of G.N. standard design which they kept until the latter part of 1925. Then, over a very short period, all except No. 4007 received 4200-gallon Group Standard tenders in replacement. Seven of these tenders came from the later built K3's which had been allocated to the Scottish Area (Nos. 32, 184/6/8/91/5 and 200) and for the rest of their career these seven engines were coupled to G.N.-type tenders. It is believed this was done to suit the turntables on the West Highland line but the change proved fruitless as the Civil Engineer declined to pass them for this section on weight grounds. In addition to No. 4007, two other Southern Area K3's, Nos. 80 and 91, ran with G.N. tenders until 1942 when all three received 4200-gallon Group Standard tenders released from Scottish D49 engines. For short periods K3's Nos. 134 and 140 also had G.N. type tenders coupled to them, but this was very probably the same tender and the one that later settled with engine No. 91.

During 1931 it was decided to substitute smaller tenders for the Group Standard 4200-gallon type which had been built with the thirty-five class J38's in 1926. Their duties did not call for such large capacity and the water pick-up apparatus was superfluous as there were no troughs in the area in which they worked. So Doncaster built twelve 3500-gallon Group Standard tenders, sent these to Scotland, and in return received the same number of 4200-gallon tenders, which were then used behind new O2's Nos. 2954-61 and 2430-3. Similarly Darlington built twenty-three of the smaller tenders for the remainder of class J38. The first exchanges were effected by bringing the J38's south to Darlington Works. Darlington coupled the larger tenders so gained to a variety of new engines. Four were put behind J39's Nos. 2977-80 built in 1932, actually for the Scottish Area, so the higher capacity must have been the paramount feature in their case and not the facility for picking up water. Fifteen more were put behind the D49's which Darlington

built in 1932-33. The remaining four ex-J38 tenders were coupled to new J39's Nos. 1453/69/71/80 built at Darlington in 1932. In 1938, these same four tenders were moved on again, this time to run with new V2's Nos. 4804/5/13/4. They were replaced on the J39's by tenders of North Eastern design, then space, as recorded below.

In connection with the eight-wheeled tenders, it has been mentioned that the five N.E.R. Raven Pacifics were fitted with this type in 1934. The released tenders, of the N.E. 4125-gallon self-trimming type, were quickly coupled to new J39's Nos. 1475-9, thus introducing class J39 Part 3. To this class part, four more were added in 1937 when a pair of tenders from scrapped B13's were attached to J39 class Nos. 1469/71, and two surplus C7 tenders began to run with Nos. 1453/80. In 1941, when eighteen new J39's, Nos. 3081-98, were built, they too were added to class J39/3. Instead of building new tenders for them, Darlington utilised second-hand tenders of North Eastern design, eight from scrapped D17's and the other ten from the D21 class on which they were replaced by surplus G.N. tenders supplied from Doncaster.

D49 was another class of engine appreciably affected by change of tender type. All except one of the thirty-six engines built as Shires lost the Group Standard 4200-gallon tenders with which they were originally fitted. The first to go were seven from engines 256, 318/20/2/7/35/6 in 1938, these being used for new V2's Nos. 4806-12; they were replaced on the D49's by North Eastern tenders from class Q6. On the latter, the replacements were earlier N.E. tenders, two from B13 and five from B15 engines which had been withdrawn. Wartime economy was responsible for the next changes, for in May 1941 five more Group Standard tenders were taken from D49's Nos. 234/6/45/51/3 and used with new O2's built at Doncaster from May 1942 onwards. As this was a batch of twenty-five, to be numbered 3833-57, more tenders were needed to obviate new building which would use steel badly needed in other directions, so a similar exchange was effected on the Scottish-based Shires. Between June 1941 and October 1942, all twenty-three Scottish D49's had their Group Standard tenders replaced (as were those of the five North Eastern Area engines) by 4000-gallon Great Central-type tenders which had become spare. Thus twenty-eight Group Standard tenders became available, twenty-five of which filled the needs of Nos. 3833-57 whilst the remaining three were used to replace G.N.-type tenders running with K3's Nos. 80, 91 and 4007 thus bringing all the Southern Area K3's into line in this respect after a lapse of seventeen years. It will be noted that whilst the tenders were taken from Nos. 234/6/45/51/3 in May 1941, the new O2

67

engines for which they were intended did not materialise until twelve months later. For two of these tenders this interval was occupied by use behind new V2 engines Nos. 3656/7 from June and July 1941 until April 1942, respectively, by which time Doncaster had built new tenders of the flush-sided type for them.

In 1931, when the experiment was made of fitting booster equipment to C7 class engines Nos. 727 and 2171, it was necessary to articulate the engines and tenders. Two tenders were built for this purpose with their front end carried by the power bogie and the rear on a separate bogie. Although the tender side sheets were the same design as the Group Standard 4200-gallon type, the capacities of these two tenders remained at the N.E.R. figures of 5½ tons and 4125 gallons. When Nos. 727 and 2171 were withdrawn in 1943 and 1942 respectively, their tenders were put aside until 1945 when Darlington rebuilt them into orthodox six-wheelers. Even then, they remained spare for at least two more years, but in December 1947 one of them was used with new B1 No. 1039, and sometime between August 1948 and June 1949 the other was put behind No. 1038. When the latter first came out early in December 1947 it was accompanied by an N.E.-type tender from withdrawn C7/2 No. 732.

When Thompson ordered the rebuilding of ten B17's to the two-cylinder B2 class, nine then had the small G.E.-type of tender ; all were replaced by tenders of greater capacity. Two (as mentioned earlier) took the tenders from the P1 class engines, but the other seven, Nos. 2814/6/39, 1603/7/17 and 61644, all received tenders of N.E. design from withdrawn C7's. It was the original intention to use the surplus G.E.-type tenders with new B1's destined for the G.N.S. Section, and indeed, in June 1948, four of these tenders were lying unattached in Inverurie Works yard. By then, however, practical experience of working B1's north of Aberdeen had proved they could operate with their Group Standard 4200-gallon tenders. Between September 1948 and February 1950 Inverurie attached these four tenders to B12's Nos. 61508/32/9/63 and they remained in use with this class of engine until withdrawn in 1952-54.

Tenders Used as Service Vehicles

Regular use was made of tenders for other purposes after the engines which they had served were withdrawn. Numerous examples could be found employed as water carriers, mobile drinking water tanks for gatehouses at remote level crossings, receptacles for removal of sludge from line-side water softening plants, or solid backing for snow ploughs. It has thus been possible to be directly reminded of happy days of railway observation of a full generation earlier, and a few examples will serve to round off this tender section. Cut up at Kilmarnock in 1954 was a tender still in lined N.B.R. livery with a number plate showing it had been built by Wheatley in 1872 for use with a goods engine scrapped in 1902. It had then served with, and survived, an engine of the J31 type which was sold in 1919, after which it went into service stock. Then in March 1939 in Great Eastern service stock at Cambridge, was recorded the tender built originally for one of James Holden's 2-2-2 express passenger engines, the engine concerned having been withdrawn by 1904. Also from a single-driver, the tender from North Eastern No. 1530 in that company's full passenger livery (with crest) was photographed at Hull Dairycoates in June 1931, although the engine had been cut up in April 1921. Tenders in service stock could well roam far from their original home and one in L.N.E.R. green livery with the number 9870 clearly showing was providing drinking water for pigeon traffic at Grantham in 1955. What memories it revived of the North British Atlantic *Bon-Accord* ! And finally, a Hull & Barnsley tender noted in September 1954 was providing the sole supply of drinking water for a crossing keeper and his family on the remote Alnwick-Coldstream branch which closed to passengers in September 1930.

Water Pick-up Apparatus

At Grouping, water troughs were in use on the four principal English constituent companies, their locations being as under :—

Section	Line	Name of Troughs	Nearest Milepost	Between	And
G.N.	King's Cross-York	Langley	26	Hatfield	Hitchin
		Werrington	80	Peterborough	Grantham
		Muskham	123	Grantham	Retford
		Scrooby	146	Retford	Doncaster
N.E.	York-Newcastle	Wiske Moor	32	Northallerton	Darlington
	Newcastle-Berwick	Lucker	48	Almnouth	Tweedmouth
G.E.	Liverpool St.-Norwich	Halifax Junction	67	Colchester	Ipswich
		Tivetshall	100	Ipswich	Norwich
G.C.	Manchester (London Road)-Marylebone	Eckington	51	Sheffield	Staveley
		Charwelton	135	Leicester	Woodford

Water troughs were also situated at Ruislip (milepost 2) on the G.W. & G.C. Joint Line from Northolt Junction to Princes Risborough.

Main-line engines belonging to these four companies were usually equipped with water pick-up apparatus, the scoops being air-operated on the G.E. but manually on the other three lines. As no troughs were installed on the H. & B., N.B. or G.N.S. Railways, scoops were not provided on their tenders. Just after Grouping, three N.B.R. C11 Atlantics had scoops fitted so that they could operate to Newcastle, and at the same time it was proposed to fit D30's for the same working. This was dropped, however, as the liberal water capacity of their tenders enabled them to run from Edinburgh to Newcastle without replenishment.

Manually operated scoops became standard on the L.N.E.R., but three engines, C1 4414 and A1 4471/3, had steam operated scoops. The two A1's were so equipped in 1929 and the C1 in 1932, but the gear was removed from all three in 1938. At the end of that year the G.C. Section decided that water pick-up apparatus was unnecessary on goods engines and in 1939 it was removed from 29 J11's, 12 Q4's and 35 Q4's. War conditions reduced the rate of removal, but in March 1946 it was agreed with the C.M.E. to dispense with the pick-up apparatus on classes C6, C7, D1, D2, D3 (except No. 2000), D9, D20, D21, J1, J2, J3, J4, J5, J6, J11, J39, K2 (internal fittings to remain), O1, O2, O3, O4 and Q4. Other classes affected were A5, where twelve engines had it removed between September 1948 and March 1949, whilst between December 1951 and May 1955 no less than 87 D16's lost their scoops.

LOCOMOTIVE DIAGRAMS

It was customary on most railways to have some form of engine diagram book available, not only for use by the mechanical, but also by the civil engineering and locomotive accounts departments. To the first mentioned it provided the main dimensions and usually gave some idea of haulage capacity, and to the civil engineers it was the reference book for axle loadings, total weights and clearance dimensions, whilst the accountants also used it for reference purposes. The main weights and measurements were features common to these diagrams, but how far the information provided extended beyond this varied widely, and there was certainly no common scale to which the diagrams were drawn. The G.N.R. used $\frac{3}{16}$in. to a foot, but the G.C., N.E. and N.B. Railways used $\frac{1}{4}$in. whilst the G.E., H. & B. and G.N.S.R. were content with $\frac{1}{8}$in. to a foot. With engines seventy feet in length coming into use, the $\frac{1}{4}$in. scale had clearly become too cumbersome, and even the $\frac{3}{16}$in. scale gave a

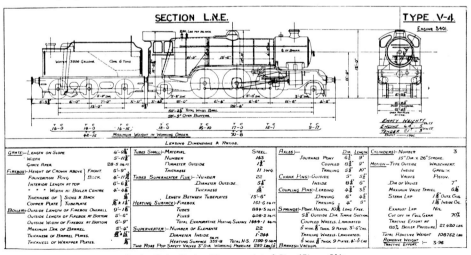

Gresley-Series Engine Diagram—Actual Size 17in. x 8¼in.

69

line drawing of the engine and tender over thirteen inches long ; it was also very desirable to portray the end view to show the ever-diminishing clearances. With the early possibility of engines being required to run over other sections of the grouped lines, there was an urgent need for a common diagram book, but with some 230 classes of engine having been absorbed, the compilation of such a book was something which could not be quickly or easily completed.

The L.N.E.R. Diagram Book

Much of 1923 was occupied in taking stock of the absorbed engines and in working out a classification system for them. The preparations for the diagram book, like the classifying, were centred on the Doncaster Drawing Office, and it is not surprising that their usual scale of $\frac{3}{16}$ in. to a foot was adopted as standard. In addition to the amply dimensioned line drawing of the side and front elevations, occupying the top half of the sheet, a similar area beneath was devoted to Leading Dimensions & Ratios, on a much more detailed basis than any of the constituent companies had ever attempted. This information was set out in the following standard sequence :—

Grate : Length, width, and area.

Firebox : Height of crown, interior length and width, thickness of plates.

Boiler : Length and width of firebox, diameter and length of barrel, plate thicknesses, diameter and length of smokebox.

Tubes : Material, number, diameter and thickness of both small and flue tubes, and their length.

Heating Surfaces : Firebox, tubes, flues, total evaporative, superheating, and full total.

Safety Valves : Number, type, diameter and working pressure, also boiler horsepower.

Axles : Diameter and length of all journals, crank pins and coupling pins.

Springs : Type, length, and sectional dimensions.

Cylinders : Number, diameter, stroke and horsepower.

Motion : Type, type and size of valves, valve movements and cut-off in full gear.

Power : Tractive effort, total adhesive weight and ratio between them.

The boiler horsepower was calculated on a formula based on Total Evaporation of Boiler divided by Steam Rate per Horsepower. Evaporation of tubes and flues was based on heating surface multiplied by a figure computed from their length and spacing. A separate figure was calculated for the firebox heating surface. Steam rate per horsepower

was taken at 27.0 for saturated steam and 20.8 for superheated steam.

The cylinder horsepower was based on 85% boiler pressure and a piston speed of 1,000 feet per minute at which speed horsepower was assumed to be at its maximum. This ultimately gave for 2-cylinder saturated engines a formula of $.0212 \times P \times A$ with P = boiler pressure and A = area of one cylinder in square inches and for 2-cylinder superheated engines a formula of $.0229 \times P \times A$.

Particularly with varying degrees of superheating, these formulae did not in practice give a true guide ; hence they were soon abandoned.

To accompany the Diagram Book, it was decided to provide an Index of engines according to number and classification, the sheets to be the same size as the diagrams themselves and to be bound with them. It was found that one book would be unduly large and Gresley gave instructions on 3rd January 1924 that it should be divided into two, one for Tender Engines and one for Tank Engines. At that date, the numbers being applied to engines were those carried at Grouping plus a suffix letter to indicate their previous ownership and, to some degree, the works responsible for maintaining them, and the Diagram Book Index was divided into columns with headings corresponding to these suffix letters, in the order N (Doncaster), C (Gorton), E (Stratford), D (Darlington), B (Cowlairs), and S (Inverurie). The diagrams themselves also carried these sectional headings (plus " Section LNE ") and the headings continued to be applied until the smaller scale left-hand facing diagrams appeared in 1943. Although this method of numbering was on the point of being changed, and was in fact changed from February 1924, nevertheless the Diagram Book Index went to the printers in its sectionalised arrangement, and actually survived in this form until the yearly alterations were made to show the stock position at the end of 1925. Meanwhile, each drawing office had prepared its quota of diagrams in the standard form and, during the early months of 1924, a firm of lithographers in Bristol prepared the stones required for printing. With the size of the job and its urgency, they found it necessary to augment their staff of artists. This accounts for the very apparent variation in drawing and lettering styles on the diagram sheets in the original issue and the undoubtedly poor standard of work on some of them. By May 1924 it was possible to issue the Diagram Books, with the sheets between dark green linen-bound stiff covers carrying imposing gold blocked titles and secured at the left hand edge by two brass pillars with screw tops. This facilitated easy amendment at the end of each succeeding year to keep the books up to date.

Fig. 98   Class K3 No. 208 hauling a fast goods on the G.N. main line

Fig. 99   Class B17 No. 2814 *Castle Hedingham* on an up express on Belstead
Bank, Ipswich, 1937

Fig. 100   Class D49/1 No. 265 *Lanarkshire* on an Edinburgh-Carlisle stopping train
at Millerhill, April 1928. L.N.E.R. Group Standard 4200-gallon tender
with stepped-out copings

Fig. 101   Class P2 No. 2006 *Wolf of Badenoch* on an Aberdeen-Edinburgh express
near Cove Bay, July 1938

Fig. 102   Class PI No. 2394 with an up coal train at Langley troughs. L.N.E.R. 4700-gallon tender

Fig. 103   Class A3 No. 2796 *Spearmint* entering King's Cross with the " Flying Scotsman," about 1933

Fig. 104   Class K2 No. 4649 on a down Cromer express at Harringay, August 1929

Fig. 105   Class N2 No. 2676 near Hatfield, 1938

Fig. 106   Class J4 No. 314N heading a down goods near Potters Bar.   With
early Stirling tender

Fig. 107   Class C1 No. 4442 starting from King's Cross with the " Queen
of Scots " Pullman, August 1932

Fig. 108   Class C12 No. 4508 at Essendine on a Stamford branch train, about 1935

Fig. 109   Class C2 No. 3990 *Henry Oakley* near Peascliffe Tunnel on a Grantham-Boston train, July 1937

Fig. 110   Class D2 No. 4375 at Finsbury Park with an up local from Hitchin, 1935

Fig. 111   Class C1 No. 3286 on a down semi-fast at New Southgate, 1937.
Small numerals on cab side

Fig. 112   Class O4 No. 6283 on a Godley-Wath empties at Dinting, August 1935

Fig. 113   Class B3 No. 6169 *Lord Faringdon* leaving Guide Bridge with the 12-40
p.m. Manchester-Cleethorpes, July 1935

Fig. 114   Class J11 No. 6082 on a G.C. Section goods

Fig. 115   Class A5 No. 5158 near Beaconsfield with a Marylebone-High Wycombe local

Fig. 116   Class B4 No. 6101 on an up Relief near Brookmans Park, 1938

Fig. 117   Class D11 No. 6378 *Bailie MacWheeble* on Cowlairs Bank with a
Sunday excursion to Newcastle, about 1929

In the original issue there were 272 separate diagrams to cover 229 individual class designations. The difference is represented by diagrams to cover individual engines—in C1 class there were separate diagrams for G.N. engines 1419 (with booster), 279 (four cylinders), 292 (compound) and 1300 (the Vulcan-built engine) —and also division of individual classes into what, from the beginning, were described as " Class Parts." These divisions varied so widely in their effect and importance that the next section deals with the original interpretation that was put upon them.

The N.E.R. classes which never received any L.N.E.R. classification (such as the " 398 " 0-6-0's) did not figure in either the Diagram Book or the Index ; as far as official records were concerned they did not exist !

The Division of Classes into Parts

Sixteen of the classes included in the original Diagram Books were divided into parts ; four of them were G.N., eight were G.C., one was N.E. and three were N.B. These class parts or subdivisions were normally indicated in written form by a stroke after the class followed by the part number, e.g. K2/1 for K2 Part 1. Looking first at the G.N. classes, J51, J54, K2 and O2 were each divided into parts 1 and 2. In J51 the difference entirely concerned an increased coal and water capacity which made part 2 a slightly longer and heavier engine, but part 1 contained nine saturated and one superheated engines, and this difference received no recognition, nor was any separate diagram issued for this single engine. In J54, the part 2 engines had closed cabs, stronger springs, were slightly heavier, and had chimneys shorter by 6¾in. than on part 1. The two parts of class K2 differed in that the first ten engines built had appreciably smaller journals to the coupled wheels, slightly shorter crank pins, the tender closer coupled by 1¾in. and the engine weight being 14 cwt. less than that of the fifty-five later engines which became known as part 2. But in class O2 the differences concerned only heights from rail level, the part 2 engines having been constructed to the L.N.E.R. Composite Load Gauge which resulted in a 3½in. reduction in the height of the chimney and a modified cab roof. The appreciable difference of the original engine of this class was acknowledged by providing a separate diagram for " Engine 461 only."

The G.C. classes originally divided into parts were B7, F1, J8, J10, J11, N4, O4 and Q4. In class B7 heights from rail level were the only differences, but in F1 and N4 the part 2 engines carried 5 cwt. more coal and 60 gallons more water, were six inches longer at the rear overhang, and in consequence were slightly heavier. On both F1 diagrams details for saturated and superheated engines were in-

cluded without any distinction being made for this difference. In J8, J11, O4 and Q4 the part difference only concerned the size of tender but without consistency of treatment. In three classes the smaller tender was part 1 but in O4 the smaller tender took part 2. The J10 class was divided into three : part 1 included the earliest engines with tenders holding 5 tons of coal and 3,080 gallons of water, part 2 had ½in. bigger journals, were 3in. wider across the cab, 5 cwt. heavier and the tenders held 6 tons and 4,000 gallons, whilst in part 3 the engines were similar to part 2 but the tenders were the smaller type as on part 1.

It had not been the original intention to have any parts in the N.E. classes. The engines which became D17 parts 1 and 2 had originally been allocated D16 and D17 and the change was made to accommodate the G.E. engines which appeared in 1923 with similar characteristics to class D15 but with larger diameter boilers.

Turning to the N.B.R., in the D30 class the part 2 engines had 22-element superheaters, against 18-element in part 1 and there were other differences such as in the journal sizes, the bogie springing and the piston valves. The J35 class was divided into four ; the boiler on part 2 had quite different dimensions from part 1 ; part 3 had the same boiler as part 1 but had slide valves where part 1 had piston valves, and part 4 was a superheated version of part 1. In the N15 class the part 2 engines' tanks held 45 gallons more, making them slightly heavier, and they had Westinghouse brake whereas part 1 had steam brake only.

In the original Diagram Book there was thus no consistency about what the qualification was for a class to be divided into separate parts, and in many other classes there were differences similar to those just described which either went unnoticed or were not regarded as needing to be indicated separately. In B15, D20, C1, D13, etc. both saturated and superheated engines existed ; C1 also had both slide and piston valve engines, whilst the D13 engines had three types of tender as well as two different cylinder strokes. Yet these and many other classes with such differences were not divided into parts.

As this division into parts persisted throughout the L.N.E.R.'s existence, and some parts had quite different meanings, a complete list forms an Appendix to this book ; this gives the dates introduced and discarded, also the main reason for the changes.

Revision of the Diagram Books

As early as possible each year, Doncaster sent to each holder of a Diagram Book a statement of the changes to be made, accompanied by additional or revised diagrams where required, to bring the book into line with the locomotive stock position at the previous 31st

December. Usually these statements were in the form of duplicated foolscap sheets, but in some years they were blue prints from linen tracings. They were issued regularly to show the year's end position until the end of 1944, but there was no issue for 1945. By the time the information for that year had been gathered, the complete engine renumbering scheme was well into its stride and it was no doubt felt that confusion between old and new numberings would inevitably arise. The next statement covered the two years to the end of 1946, but a rather more surprising issue was made twelve months later, because this covered the three years to 31st December 1947, thus duplicating the previous statement, but at least giving the final position on the L.N.E.R.

New and revised diagrams continued to be issued on the ⅜ in. scale and showing the " Leading Dimensions & Ratios " until after Thompson succeeded Gresley. Then, from the end of 1942 onwards, a change was made to ¼ in. to a foot scale. The additional information provided was drastically reduced and was now :—

Boiler : Diameter of barrel, lengths and width of firebox, plate thicknesses.

Tubes : Number and diameter of small and flue tubes, and of superheater elements.

Grate : Area only.

Heating Surfaces : Firebox, tubes, flues, total evaporative, superheater and total.

Axles : Journals, crank pins and coupling pins, diameters and lengths.

Cylinders : Number, diameter and stroke.

Motion : Type, valve details and movements, cut-off in full gear.

Power : Tractive effort, adhesive weight and ratio between them.

Brake : Type.

These smaller diagrams, in which the engine faced to the left instead of to the right as in all previous diagrams, had to be inserted in their appropriate place amongst the large number of the former standard size which were still current, and this position continued until about 1949-50. Then some of the bigger diagrams were re-drawn to the new scale but, with the exception of one N2 diagram, only classes which had been introduced after Grouping were included in the new small folders which were then issued. The position had become untidy as the large books still had to be kept for reference to pre-Grouping designs : even fourteen years after the end of the L.N.E.R. there were still very substantial numbers of classes J27, J36, J37, Q6 and the whole of the fifteen Q7 class in active use and the diagrams applicable to them were still to the ⅜ in. scale.

Alterations and Corrections to the Original Issue

The L.N.E.R. Diagram Books were first issued in May 1924 and by the following month Darlington was complaining that some Section D diagrams were not correct and that a considerable number of printer's errors had been found. By the end of September, Gresley himself was writing to those in charge at Darlington, Doncaster, Stratford, Gorton and Cowlairs that the Locomotive Running Superintendents were reporting numerous errors (and some omissions) in the diagrams. In addition to the determined but not entirely successful effort made at the end of 1924 to effect the necessary corrections and additions, each diagram was additionally to have the empty weight of the engine (and tender where appropriate), and the type of brake fitted. Whilst reviewing their corrections, Gorton pointed out in November 1924, that the tractive effort figures on all Section C diagrams were not on the same basis as those of all the other sections. It was Gorton practice to take away the diameter of the piston rod from the cylinder diameter in their tractive effort calculation, but they found this had been ignored by the other sections. This affected not only the tractive effort figure, but the ratio of the adhesive weight to it. Although Gorton provided the revised figures in November 1924, these were not circulated for amendment of the diagrams until the corrections for the 1926 year end were issued. Darlington got rather more prompt attention, as the cylinder horsepower figures on all Section D diagrams were notified as needing amendment and when the 1924 year end alterations were sent out the corrected figures were included. On diagrams issued after December 1933 however, the figures for boiler and cylinder horsepowers were no longer included.

Additional Information Provided by Diagram Books

It has been mentioned that, in addition to the diagrams, there was an index according to number and classification of each engine so that, in effect, a complete stock book was provided. There were two sections at the front of each of the Tender and Tank Engine Diagram Books. The first was a straightforward list, in numerical order, simply showing the class opposite the number or giving a reference to the other book. To take an example, opposite 1621 in the tender book was D17 in the type column ; in the tank book appeared the word " Tender " opposite number 1621. The second index set out to be reasonably informative about any engines which were exceptions in some way. It listed each class individually and divided them into Parts where appropriate (apart from one or two oversights), showed which were superheated and which were not (unless all the class were the same in this respect), gave details of any differences in cylinder and boiler diameters, and drew attention to which were slide and which were piston valve engines if a class contained both types. Doncaster were naturally dependent upon the accuracy and extent of the information supplied to them by the other works. This was not always complete or timely so that, from the historian's aspect, the information in the Index, admirable though it is, must not have absolute reliance placed upon it. For instance, in supplying the diagrams for B15, D17 and D20 classes, Darlington only provided the superheated versions and in the lists of engines made no mention (until the December 1929 revised Index) of any still without superheaters. Yet when the first Index was issued, four B15's, thirteen D17's and two D20's had still to be fitted with superheaters and even at the beginning of 1928 there were twelve of these engines using saturated steam and it was June 1931 before the last D17 was converted. Then, as late as March 1936, when sending the list of engines which had changed their classification, Gorton drew special attention to the fact that not all which were included had been changed in 1935, stating "some had been done in previous years and not recorded." It is not therefore enough to take the position set out in the Index as indicating the actual year in which changes were made, and further guidance needs to be sought from the official records of individual engines. This has been done in dealing with each class separately, but the above explanation is given to avoid any difficulty in reconciling this information with the Index position.

Completely new and revised sets of Index sheets were issued showing, in printed form, the position at the end of 1925, 1929, 1934 and 1938 and, at some intermediate year ends, a few odd sheets were revised by issuing drawing office prints. Finally, duplicated foolscap sheets were issued as a revised Index, to show the classification at 31st December 1947 and these of course are the only ones to use the altered engine numbers. The date of issue was also particularly apt as it shows the position obtaining when the L.N.E.R. ceased to exist. Except when a revised Index was sent out, the annual alterations contained instructions not only about the addition, withdrawal or substitution of diagrams, but also the alterations to be made on the various Index sheets concerning new engines, those withdrawn, and any which had been altered in classification or significant detail. By this means, Doncaster endeavoured to keep all concerned up-to-date on the locomotive position.

Revisions after Nationalisation

Alterations to the Diagram Books were issued to correct them to 31st December 1948 and then four years elapsed before the next corrections were sent out. These covered 1949 to 1952 inclusive and with them were issued what proved to be the last batch of diagrams. Alterations were then issued annually for the year ends 1953 to 1961 inclusive but their contents were almost exclusively lists of engines withdrawn and diagrams to delete. The final Index was in printed book form, issued in May 1949, and entitled "Index to Engine Diagram Books—L.N.E.R. Type Engines." This recorded the position at 31st December 1948 and the engine numbers used were the British Railways series.

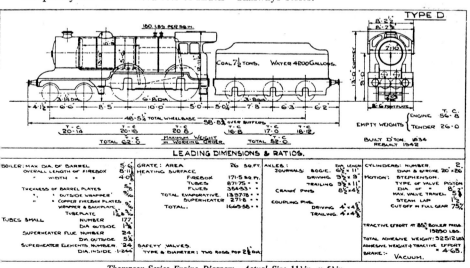

Thompson-Series Engine Diagram—Actual Size 11¼in. x 5¾in.

BOILER CLASSIFICATION AND DIAGRAMS

Although locomotive diagrams were dealt with on an "all-line" basis soon after Grouping, corresponding work on the boilers was not undertaken until 1928, when a diagram book was issued in the same format as the locomotive diagrams, subsequent alterations and additions being issued annually. In July 1928, the various types of boiler were numbered consecutively from 1 upwards, minor variations being indicated by a suffix letter. Like the locomotive diagrams the boiler diagrams were grouped into Sections, N indicating Doncaster origin (or responsibility for maintenance), C Gorton, E Stratford, D Darlington, B Cowlairs and S Inverurie, followed by an L.N.E. Section, which began at Diagram 94.

In each Section the diagram numbers were originally allotted in descending order of total heating surface. Each diagram was marked with a Heating Surface Classification, A applying to boilers exceeding 2,000 square feet, B covering 1,000 to 1,999 square feet and C being applied to boilers with less than 1,000 square feet. An almost identical system of boiler identification had been introduced in the Scottish Area in 1925 for boilers maintained by Cowlairs and Inverurie, the only difference being that the numbers were allotted in ascending instead of descending order of heating surface. Otherwise, pre-Grouping practices of description continued to be used at the other works until 1928.

All the L.N.E.R. boiler diagrams, both in the 1925 Scottish and the 1928 all-line series,

were drawn to a scale of $\frac{1}{4}$in. to one foot (as against $\frac{3}{16}$in. with the engine diagrams) and there were no subsequent departures from this size. The format was similar to that employed for the engine diagrams, the top half showing side and end elevations, together with dimensions. The all-line 1928 drawings faced to the right, but Thompson introduced left-facing drawings, as he also did with the engine diagrams. The upper half of the boiler diagrams contained, in addition, the Heating Surface Classification (referred to above) and the type of engine to which the boiler applied and the number fitted. The lower part contained the leading particulars, as follows :—

Grate : length ; width ; area.

Firebox : interior length at top ; interior width at boiler centre ; thickness of plates ; number, diameter and material of stays.

Boiler : thickness of barrel and wrapper plates.

Working pressure.

Safety valves.

Empty weight (including mountings).

Tubes (and flues, where applicable) : material ; number ; diameter outside ; thickness.

Superheater elements (where applicable) : number ; diameter inside.

Heating surface figures.

At Doncaster, the boiler types had been numbered from 1 upwards in the same order as the G.N. engine classifications to which the boilers were applicable. The list was extended

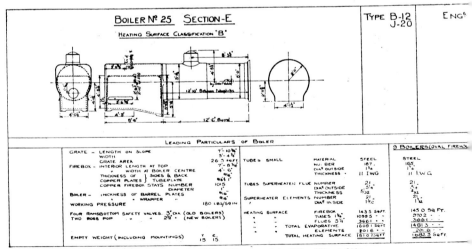

1928 All-Line Series Boiler Diagram—Actual Size 17in. x 8½in.

after Grouping to include the boiler of the U1 Garratt-type engine in 1925 and also, from May 1927, two G.C. (ex-L.D. & E.C.) classes, M1 and N6, for which Doncaster took over the maintenance when Tuxford Works were closed. The following table shows the position obtaining at Doncaster until 1928, together with the equivalent later L.N.E.R. boiler classification numbers :—

Doncaster Diag. No.	L.N.E.R. Diag. No.	L.N.E.R. Classes to which fitted
1	94	A1
2	4	C2, Q1, Q2, R1
3	1	C1
4	11	C12, D4, E1, G1, J4, J7, J50, J55, J57
4A	—	G2, J54, J56, J57
5	8	D3, J3, J7
6	7	D1, D2, J1, J2, J5, J6, N1, N2
7	6	K1
8	3	K2, Q3
9	96	K3
10	9	J52
10A	—	J53
11	12	J51
12	—	R1
13	2	O1, O2
14	95	U1
15	10 (21A later)	N6
16	5 (19A later)	M1

The boilers on the E. & W.Y.U.R. engines were neither included in the above list nor the 1928 classification.

At Gorton, Robinson introduced a standardisation scheme for boilers about 1909. This represented a big step forward from the multiplicity of boiler types then in use. At Grouping, in addition to eight standard boiler designs, a further eighteen types were still being used, though on a relatively small proportion of the total G.C.R. locomotive stock. The list of boilers in use at Grouping as supplied by Gorton to Doncaster, together with the later L.N.E.R. diagram numbers, was as follows :—

Gorton Type	L.N.E.R. Diag. No.	L.N.E.R. Classes to which fitted
No. 1 Standard	21	D7, D8, E2, J8, J9, J10, J12, J13, N4, N5
No. 2 ,,	20	F1, F2
,, 3 ,,	22	C13, C14, D5, D6
,, 4 ,,	18	A5, D9
,, 5 ,,	14	D10, D11, L1
,, 6 ,,	15	C4, C5, O4, S1
,, 7 ,,	13	B2, B3, B7, B8
,, 8 ,,	15B	B6, O5
9J	19 & 19B	J11, J10 (one engine only)
8A	17	Q4
18T	—	J59
5	24	J62, J63
A	10 (later 21A)	N6
8	17	B5
18conv	—	G.C. " 18," J58
8F	16	B1, B4
8G	17	B9
6B	—	D12
B & C	23	G3, J60
D	5 (later 19A)	M1
13	—	X4
12AM	—	E8
7	—	G.C. " 7 "
4	—	J61, Y2
12A	—	G.C. " 12A "
WM & CQ	—	W.M. & C.Q. 0-8-0T

Before L.N.E.R. diagram numbers were adopted, replacement boilers for classes B5, B9 and Q4 had been called No. 9 Standard and those for class J11 No. 10 Standard. In July 1928, one D12, four J58, four J59, two J61 and two Y2 class engines still remained but none of their boilers received L.N.E.R. diagram numbers : all these classes had disappeared by June 1931. Classes M1 and N6 were transferred from Doncaster to Gorton maintenance in September 1931 and in 1932 their L.N.E.R. boiler diagram numbers were changed from 5 and 10 to 19A and 21A, respectively.

Stratford's practice was to allot Works order numbers equally to engines, tenders and boilers and these gave no indication of classification. It is believed this method continued until the change to L.N.E.R. diagram numbers in 1928.

Darlington used the same classification for their boilers as for their engines ; for example S3 and T3 applied equally to the engines which became L.N.E.R. classes B16 and Q7 as they did to the boilers which were fitted to them. It is therefore unnecessary to set out the pre-1928 position. Former Hull & Barnsley classes were treated in the same way ; for instance replacement boilers built in 1927 carried the designation A (H & B) and J (H & B), as Darlington did not commence using L.N.E.R. locomotive classifications until 1929. For the original boiler diagram books of 1928, Darlington actually prepared diagrams in the L.N.E.R. style for classes " 398 " and " 1463 " (ex-N.E. " 1463 ") but no diagram numbers were allotted to them, nor were they issued generally. By July 1928 (the date of introduction of the all-line boiler classification) all the " 398 " class had been withdrawn and the last E5 had gone by February 1929.

Cowlairs had no boiler classification system before Grouping, but introduced one in 1925 using the numbers 1B to 17B, in ascending order of total heating surface, with 18B and 19B tacked on to the end for classes D28 and D26 which were obsolete but of which there were still survivors. The series was continued from 20B to 35B for engines from other Sections and Group Standard types, by then working on the N.B. Section, and was completed in 1926 by allotting 36B to the J38 boilers. The diagrams themselves showed no tube arrangements and did not quote figures for heating surfaces. Where differences existed in the front tube plates of boilers embraced within one diagram number, the various front elevations were distinguished by letters A, B, C and D (for example, 10B had four variants) and instructions were included as to which pattern was to be followed when ordering tubeplates. A list of all engines carrying each particular type of boiler was given, quoting the appropriate pattern. There was also a

75

general classification according to heating surface—A for 2,000 square feet and over, B for 1,000 but less than 2,000 square feet and C for less than 1,000 square feet. When the all-line classification was introduced in 1928 the N.B. Section boilers took numbers 76 to 87, but now in descending order of heating surface, except that 83 was never used. This number had been clearly intended for the previous 7B boiler but engines in the classes carrying it, E7 and J34, were all withdrawn by January 1928. The details of the 1925 Cowlairs classification were :—

1925 Cowlairs Diag. No.	1928 L.N.E.R. Diag. No.	Classes to which fitted
1B	85	Y9
2B	—	Y10
3B	86	D51, J82
4B	87	J88
5B	84	G7, J31, J33, J83
6B	—	D50, G8
7B	—	E7, J34
8B	82	D25
9B	79	D32/2
10B	81	C15, C16, G9, J36, N14, N15
11B	80	D31, D36
12B	78	D29, D30, D33, D34
13B	—	D32/1
14B	—	J35/2
15B	77	J35/1, J35/3
16B	77	J35/1, J35/2, J35/3, J35/4, J35/5, J37
17B	76	C11
18B	—	D28
19B	—	D26
20B	94	A1
21B	48	C7
22B	7	D1, N2
23B	14	D11
24B	65	D17
25B	70	D22
26B	21	J9
27B	67	J21, N8
28B	69	J22
29B	69	J24
30B	57	J27
31B	73	J71
32B	3	K2
33B	96	K3
34B	15	O4
35B	50	Q6
36B	97A	J38

Until 1925, Inverurie used the same classification for boilers as for engines, but then re-classified their boilers on a similar basis to Cowlairs.

1925 Inverurie Diag. No.	1928 L.N.E.R. Diag. No.	Classes to which fitted
1S	90	D44, D48
2S	91	J90, J91
3S	—	D39, D45
4S	89	D46
5S	88A	D38, D42, D43
6S	88	D40, D41, G10
7S	93	Z4
8S	92	Z5

When the all-line classification was adopted in 1928, no diagram was included for the D45 class, although the last engine was not withdrawn until June 1932.

Post-1928 Boiler Diagrams

When the London Transport engines were taken over in November 1937, their diagrams were allocated to Section C, despite the fact that maintenance was undertaken by Stratford. There were two types of boiler, one fitted to class L2, and the other serving both classes H2 and M2. They were given Diagram Nos. 12 and 12A respectively (Diagram 12 had been vacant since March 1935 and 12A had never been used).

The engines taken over from the M. & G.N. however were allocated a separate section in the Diagram Books. As with the locomotives themselves, it was not until 1942 that the surviving boilers were incorporated within the L.N.E.R. classification system, the boilers then being given numbers at the end of the former Great Eastern types, taking 46A to 46D inclusive.

When the Boiler Diagram books were first issued, the highest diagram number was 101. As new boiler designs appeared, so they were added to the list of numbers, and by the end of the L.N.E.R.'s existence, number 120 had been reached. In certain instances, later versions of boilers designed to work at a higher pressure than the original (usually embodying thicker barrel plates) retained the same diagram number but with the suffix HP meaning "high pressure." For example Diagram 102, working at 180 lb. per sq. in. was used on class V1 and Diagram 102 HP (200 lb. per sq. in.) on class V3.

List of L.N.E.R. Boiler Diagrams from July 1928

Diagram No.	Engine Classes to which applicable	Diag. No.	Engine Classes to which applicable
1	C1	12	J51 (to March 1935) ; L2 (from November 1937)
2	O1 (O3 later), O2, O4/4		
3	K2, Q3	12A	H2, M2
4	C2, Q1, Q2, R1	13	B2 (B19 later), B3, B7, B8
5 (19A from 1932)	M1	14	D10, D11, L1 (L3 later)
6	K1	15	B5/2 (engine 5184 only), C4, C5, O4/2, O4/3, O4/6, S1
7	D1, D2, J1, J2, J5, J6, N1, N2		
8	D3, J3, J7 (five only)	15A	O4/5
9	J52, J53 (4' 2½" domed boiler)	15B	B6, O5
10 (21A from 1932)	N6	15C	S1/1 (engine 6170 only)
11	C12, D4, J4, J7, J50, J55, J56 (two 4' 2½" diam. only), J57 (domed boilers)	15D	O4/7
		16	B1 (B18 later), B4
		17	B5, B9, Q4

76

Diag. No.	Engine Classes to which applicable	Diag. No.	Engine Classes to which applicable
17A	Q1 (0-8-0T)	67A	J21, J25, N8, N9, N10 (boilers built from July 1938)
18	A5, D9		
19	J11 superheated	67B	J21, J25, N8 (five only, boilers built in December 1936 and January 1937)
19A	M1		
19B	J11 saturated	68	G6, J76, J77, X2, X3
20	F1, F2	69	D23, F8, G5, J22, J24, J73, J74
21	D7, J8, J9, J10, J12, J13, N4, N5	69A	G5, J24, J73 (boilers built from September 1938)
21A	N6		
22	C13, C14, D5, D6	70	D22, J21 (three engines only)
23	G3, J60	71	Not allocated
24	J62, J63	71A	J75, N12, N13 domeless
25	B12/1, J20 Belpaire firebox	71B	J75, J80, N12, N13 domed
25A	B12/4, J20/1 round top firebox	72	X1
26	D16/1, D16/2	73	J71, J72
27	D15, J17, J18, J19/1	74	J78, J79, Y7
28	D14, J16	75	Y8
28A	D14/2 (to May 1936), D16/3, J19/2	76	C11
29	D13	77	J35, J37
30	N7 (original twenty-two built to G.E. order)	78	D29, D30, D33, D34
		79	D32 5' 0" diam. front ring
31	J15 flat bottom firebox	79A	D32 4' 10¾" diam. front ring
32	E4, F3, J15	80	D31, D36
33	F4	81	C15, C16, G9, J36, N14, N15
34	F4, F5, F6	82	D25
35	G4	83	Intended for E7, J34
36	F9	84	G7, J31, J33, J83
37	J68, J69	85	Y9
38	J92	86	D51
39	J65, J66, J67	87	J88
40	Y4	88	D38, D40, D41, D42, D43, G10
41	N18	88A	D42
42	F7	88B	D41
43	Y5	89	D46
44	J64	90	D44, D48
45	Y6	91	J90, J91
46	J70, Y6	92	Z5
46A	C17, D52, J40	93	Z4
46B	D53	94	A1 (A10 later), A2 (engine 2404 only), P1 round domes
46C	D54, J41		
46D	J93	94HP	A3, P1 round domes
47	A2	94A	A3, P1 steam collector domes
48	C6, C7	95	U1
49	B16, Q7	96	K3
49A	B16, Q7 (boilers built from April 1939)	96A	K5 (225lb.), 35 K3 (working at 180lb.)
		97	D49, J38/2, J39
50	B15, Q6	97A	J38/1
50A	Q6 (boilers built from October 1938)	98	N7/1, N7/2
51	Q10 domed	99	B12/2 (included with Diag. 25 from 1938)
52	C8		
53	B14	99A	B12/3
54	B13	100	B17 Parts 1 to 5
55	A7	100A	B1, B2, B3/3, B17/6, O1 (225lb.) and O2/4, O4/8 (both 180lb.)
56	Q5/1		
56A (51 re-no.)	Q5/2	101	N7/3, N7/4, N7/5
56B	Q5/1 (boilers built from July 1936)	102	V1
57	J26, J27	102HP	V3
57A	J26, J27 (boilers built from September 1939)	103	W1 water-tube boiler
		104	C9
58	Not allocated	105	S1/2 (engine 6171 only), S1/3, O4 (one engine only)
58A	D24, J28 domeless		
58B	D24, J28 domed	106	P2/1, P2/2
59	D20	106A	A2/2 (five engines)
59A	D20 (boilers built from November 1935)	107	A1/1, A4 (both 250lb.), also A3 (from January 1954, at 220lb.)
60	D21		
61	A6, T1	108	P2/3 (engine 2006 only)
62	D19	108A	A2/2 (one engine only, 2002 from June 1944 to November 1945)
63	H1, A8 Schmidt superheater and barrel in three rings		
		109	A2/1, V2
63A	A8 Robinson superheater and single-plate barrel	110	K4
		111	W1 rebuilt
63B	A6, A7, A8, T1 (boilers built from May 1939)	112	V4
		113	V4 with thermic syphon
63C	A6, A8 (five only, boilers built in September and October 1936)	114	O6
		115	L1
64	Not allocated	116	K1, K1/1
64A	J23/1 domeless	117	A2/3, also A1 (from April 1955), A2 (from May 1957), A2/2 (from September 1957)
64B	J23/2 domed superheated		
64C	J23/3 domed saturated		
65	D17, D18	118	A1, A2, also A2/2 (from February 1951), A2/3 (from August 1950)
66	N11		
67	J21, J25, N8, N9, N10	119	O7
		120	J94

77

ENGINE ROUTE RESTRICTIONS

Restrictions exist on most railway systems as to the use of certain locomotive classes on some of the routes. This may be due to a variety of reasons, for instance lightly-laid track or bridges of limited capacity may prohibit the use of heavy engines; similarly, sharp curvature frequently precludes the use of eight-coupled, or even in some cases six-coupled, engines. The physical size of a locomotive has also to be taken into account: height and width can debar an engine from working over a line with restricted clearances, so can overall length where for example the outside cylinder casing of a long engine could foul the edges of platforms when traversing crossover roads in stations.

Each railway company evolved its own set of standards for track, bridges and structure clearances and when the L.N.E.R. was formed it naturally inherited all these variations in the practice of its constituents.

LOAD GAUGE AND ROLLING STOCK GAUGE

Of the constituent companies of the L.N.E.R., the G.N.R., N.E.R. and H. & B.R. all had generous load gauges which permitted the construction of engines up to 13ft. 6in. in height above rail level in most cases, though the absolute limit in this respect was not exercised; at 13ft. 5in., whilst the G.C.R. gauge was an inch less at 13ft. 5in., whilst the G.E.R. gauge was only 13ft. 1in. The G.N.S.R. was limited to the passage of 13ft. 0in. engines and the N.B.R. load gauge was as little as 12ft. 11in. though the gauge to which their rolling stock was constructed was 13ft. 0in.

Before going further it must be explained that down the years the term load gauge has been used loosely in many quarters, including official ones, to embrace also rolling stock gauge (the dimensions to which stock could be built). On some railways these two gauges were identical, but on others the rolling stock gauge was slightly greater than the load gauge: generally this allowed an extra inch or two in height, particularly in the vicinity of the centre line. Local dispensations existed also; for instance N.E.R. engines, which in many cases were 13ft. 3in. tall, were permitted over N.B.R. metals between Berwick and Edinburgh.

The differences in gauge resulted in the majority of the G.N., G.C., N.E. and H. & B. locomotive stock being unable to work without restriction on to the G.E. and Scottish lines. Naturally this position was unacceptable on the newly formed L.N.E.R. if full

use was to be made of the available locomotives and over the course of years the L.N.E.R. was put to much expense altering the taller ones by reducing the height of boiler mountings and cabs in order to permit greater availability.

A further difficulty arose in the case of G.C. engines of Robinson's design which in most cases had been built to the limit of the width gauge on that line, running plates being up to 9ft. 3in. in width, whilst the outside cylinder engines were up to 8ft. 10½in. over cylinders. These dimensions were enough to bar them from many routes off their native system.

One of the first tasks of the new L.N.E.R. administration was to arrive at a standard load gauge to which all new designs of locomotives and vehicles could be constructed and to which existing stock could where necessary be modified. This was known as the L.N.E.R. Composite Load Gauge and was of necessity based on the North British, that being the smallest gauge of the amalgamated companies. In 1947 however there was introduced the L.N.E.R. Standard Rolling Stock Gauge for exclusive use in locomotive and vehicle design as distinct from the dual purpose composite gauge used hitherto. Both the Composite Load Gauge and the Rolling Stock Gauge had an outset of 1ft. 0in. to each side of the vertical centre line at 13ft. 1in. above rail level thus allowing the Pacifics and other big locomotives to have their boiler mountings and cab ventilators built up to this height. In a few instances, such as with classes A1 (later A10), A3, P1, and P2, dispensation was given for dome covers and safety valves to exceed the figure of 13ft. 1in. by up to an inch. Chimneys however were never allowed to exceed 13ft. 1in. due to throw effect at the extremities of locomotives on curved track.

All the new L.N.E.R. locomotive classes conformed to this Composite Load Gauge, as did most of the pre-Grouping designs that continued to be added to by the L.N.E.R. A summary is given below of the principal alterations made to pre-Grouping engines to increase their availability, also of certain engines modified or built for particular restricted routes.

Great Northern Engines

Most of the G.N. tender engines were outside the limits of the new L.N.E.R. Composite Load Gauge, consequently modifications to chimneys, domes, safety valves, whistles and cabs were introduced on classes A1 (later A10), K3 and O2 perpetuated for new construction after Grouping. Of these classes, the last engine (No. 1481N) of the batch of ten Gresley Pacifics turned out from Doncaster Works in 1923 had its overall height reduced somewhat. It was still however slightly outside the new gauge and caused some concern when it ran through to Edinburgh in November 1923. Subsequent additions to the class were constructed to the L.N.E.R. gauge and in due course Nos. 4470-81 were altered to conform. All the K3's and O2's built after Grouping were to the new gauge (figs. 121 and 122), but it was not until 1939-40 that the G.N.-built members of these classes (K3 4000-9 and O2 3461/77-86) were brought into line; at the same time the opportunity was taken to replace the G.N. style cabs by the more modern side-window type on these particular engines.

The original K1 class engines were altered immediately after Grouping to enable them to work on to the G.E. Section, as also were certain K2's which were transferred to the G.E. and N.B. Sections. The conversion of the remainder of the K2 class proceeded slowly and was not completed until the early 'thirties.

Another G.N. class that received early alteration was D1, all fifteen of which were sent to the N.B. Section in 1925. Soon after being fitted with a booster and Pacific-type side window cab in 1923, C1 4419 was altered to suit the Composite Load Gauge and in fact carried out certain trials in Scotland. Another large Atlantic, No. 4447, had its cab and boiler mountings cut down in 1923 (fig. 118) and took part in trials against N.E. Atlantic No. 733 and N.B. Atlantic No. 9878 between Newcastle and Edinburgh in August 1923. Certain members of the D2 class were altered to work on the G.E. Section shortly after Grouping, if required.

It was not until the clouds of war began to gather in 1939 that further steps were taken to increase the availability of G.N. classes. Then, as mentioned above, the G.N.-built K3's and O2's were altered, as also were the surviving D2's and D3's and the whole of class J6. Certain of the O1 (later O3) class also appeared with short chimneys and domes but this was more by accident than design as the boilers were standard with those fitted to the O2 class, the O1's themselves being prohibited from the G.E. Section due to other considerations.

The majority of G.N. tank engines were well within the L.N.E.R. gauge due to the fact that they had generally been constructed to work over the Metropolitan Widened Lines, if required, where the maximum permitted height was only 12ft. 8in. However, some of the older tank engines gained taller chimneys and domes when they left the London area, whilst others had them from the start if intended for the West Riding District. When further N2's were built by the L.N.E.R., slightly taller chimneys were fitted to those

destined for the N.B. Section and the West Riding District but they were of course still within the L.N.E.R. gauge.

Great Central Engines

Robinson's engines made practically full use of the G.C. load gauge, maximum heights being in the majority of cases about 13ft. 3in. whilst generally they were wider than most of the other L.N.E.R. stock. Many of the Parker and Pollitt engines were also taller than the L.N.E.R. gauge.

Following Grouping it very soon became necessary to alter G.C. engines to pass the L.N.E.R. Composite Load Gauge. To meet deficiencies in the motive power position in Scotland, an O4 (No. 6185) received a shortened chimney and flatter dome and had the whistle repositioned. It underwent trials on the N.B. Section between June and July 1923. Following this, other members of the class were similarly altered and transferred north in July and August 1924. The question of new construction also arose after Grouping, further engines of classes A5 and B7 being in course of erection at Gorton. The former were in fact not altered and appeared with full length chimneys, domes, etc., but in the case of B7's a very short chimney was used together with a squat dome and a cab of reduced height, bringing their maximum height down to 12ft. 10⅜in. from 13ft. 3⅜in. (figs. 125 and 126).

During 1924-26 further series of A5's and D11's were built by contractors for the N.E. and N.B. Sections respectively. Both these series received similar treatment to B7's, although the chimneys were of Gresley built-up type. In addition the A5's were narrower over the platform compared with the earlier members of that class.

The altered chimney designs used on the B7's and D11's built after Grouping followed the experimental fitting of new chimneys to a G.C.-built B7 and D11. However the problem of dealing with the existing G.C. stock was not tackled seriously until early in 1924. In March of that year, D7 4-4-0 No. 5710 was fitted with a built-up tapered chimney (fig. 136) which became known as the "flowerpot" type for obvious reasons; this disfigurement of G.C. engines evolved from that date. The style of chimney fitted to No. 5710 was adopted as standard for all the smaller G.C. engines with few exceptions, and for some of the larger Robinson designs which began to be altered a few months later. It was based on the G.N. pattern. On classes J11 and Q4 however a plain cast chimney with a slight taper to the rim was used, as it was also on classes C4, C5, D9 and O4 at first (fig. 128).

Some difficulty arose with class J9, twenty-five of which were transferred to the N.B.

79

Section in 1924-25. The 1924 L.N.E.R. Diagram showed a chimney height of 12ft. 8¼in. but when they began to arrive in Scotland it was found that they were 13ft. 3in. tall and therefore outside the N.B. loading gauge. There were instances of these engines running with N.B. chimneys as used on class N15 (fig. 124), but most of them were fitted with the flowerpot type, in many cases at Gorton before they left for Scotland.

Before going further it is convenient here to discuss more fully the chimney styles used on G.C. engines. In G.C. days, engines fitted with boilers of 5ft. 0in. diameter or less generally had the shapely Robinson cast chimney with its characteristic wide flare at the base (fig. 127). Following the introduction of the 5ft. 3in. boiler a shorter chimney became necessary and this was of more conventional design, being very similar to the G.C./L.N.E.R. chimney finally standardised for the larger G.C. engines in the mid-1930's. In addition to the large-boilered engines this new style of chimney was also fitted to the A5 4-6-2T's because of the height of the boiler centre line. It is believed that the earlier style of chimney was prone to cracking and there is evidence to support this in that Robinson introduced another design of long chimney on the J63 0-6-0T's in 1906. This was much plainer and the taper was in the reverse direction, i.e. outwards from base to top (fig. 131). After the First World War several locomotives of other classes were fitted with this type of chimney, such as C13, C14, D8, J10, J11, J12, J62, N5 and Q4, the actual lengths of the chimneys varying according to the class.

The use of the flowerpot type as outlined above continued until the mid-'thirties when the larger Robinson engines (including classes C4, C5, D9 and O4) began to appear with a new pattern of chimney of G.C. style, reminiscent of their original type except that they tapered outwards towards the top rather than towards the base (fig. 129). Despite being already within the L.N.E.R. gauge certain engines of classes G3, J60, and N6 that survived for any length of time after Grouping were fitted with new chimneys of the flowerpot type, no doubt due to standardisation of the latter pattern.

In addition to reduction in the height of chimneys to suit the L.N.E.R. gauge, it was necessary to cut down the height of domes on many of the classes, and also in some cases to transfer the whistle from a position on the cab roof to the top of the firebox. From about 1924 most, if not all, new boilers constructed for G.C. engines incorporated where necessary domes of reduced height to suit the L.N.E.R. gauge, whilst existing boilers were similarly altered where possible.

Of Robinson's bigger engines, classes A5 (Gorton-built engines), B2 (later B19), B3, B6, B7/1, B8, D11/1 and O5 all possessed cabs which exceeded the L.N.E.R. gauge. Plans had been made soon after Grouping to modify these in conjunction with the boiler mountings, but in most cases nothing came of it. The only exceptions were the rebuilds to O4/6 from O5, plus the few then unrebuilt members of the latter class which had their cab roofs cut down at the beginning of the war. In addition, three A5's (Nos. 69824/6/9) were altered in 1952 by British Railways for use on the G.E. Section. It should perhaps be mentioned that most of the boilers carried by the above classes in their later days had low domes due to the fact that nearly all the boilers were of post-1923 construction, the designs being standard with those used on other classes which had all been cut down to the L.N.E.R. gauge by 1939 (e.g. A5 had boilers standard with D9).

It was not until 1939 that the task of converting the G.C. locomotive stock (with the exception of the classes mentioned) to suit the L.N.E.R. gauge was completed. During the interim period additional class parts were adopted to distinguish which engines of a class had been so altered, this information being of vital importance to the Running Department. Confusion reigned during the period of conversion and there were many cases of engines reverting from L.N.E.R. gauge to G.C. gauge, this being brought about principally by reboiling with old boilers possessing tall domes, although the chimneys on the engines concerned had already been cut down.

The three classes absorbed in 1937 from London Transport (H2, M2 and L2) had been built to a load gauge similar to that in use by the G.C.R. and consequently required the full modification of new chimneys, domes and cabs. The chimneys used were of the later Gresley-G.C. pattern.

Great Eastern Engines

None of the Great Eastern's stock of locomotives exceeded 12ft. 11in. in height, so no alterations were necessary as they were already within the limits of the L.N.E.R. gauge. Although the G.E. load gauge remained unaltered, engines with chimneys up to 13ft. 3in. high, provided their central width did not exceed 18in. at this height, were allowed to work over most parts of the G.E. system.

Severe height restrictions existed in the low level goods yard at Devonshire Street (later known as Mile End). Only the 0-4-0T's of the Y5 class ("Coffee Pots") and Hill's large Y4 class were able to work in this yard, although of the latter class No. 7227 had until July 1931 a tall chimney, dome and cab which prevented its use with the other members of the class there.

It may perhaps be mentioned here that a number of F4 and F5 2-4-2T's had their chimneys cut down at the beginning of the last war but this was for use in case of emergency by London Transport on their Metropolitan and District lines.

Midland & Great Northern Joint Engines

Of the M.&G.N. classes, only the " C Rebuild " 4-4-0's, or D54 class as they eventually became on the L.N.E.R., were outside their new owner's rolling stock gauge with their chimney height of 13ft. 3in. No alterations were made to these engines, doubtless due to the fact that the L.N.E.R. regarded the whole M. & G.N. stock as life expired from the word go.

North Eastern Engines

Although the larger N.E. engines were constructed to a height of 13ft. 3in. few alterations were made by the L.N.E.R. to permit their usage generally throughout the system The last fifteen B16's constructed after Grouping, Nos. 1371-85, were fitted with reduced chimneys bringing them within the L.N.E.R. Composite Load Gauge and the earlier members of the class were later modified similarly. Shortly after Grouping a number of J27's received shorter chimneys prior to transfer to the Southern Area, where some of them took up workings from March shed : later the remainder of the class were similarly altered. Many of the smaller N.E. engines were however within the L.N.E.R. Composite Load Gauge and in consequence found ready use outside the N.E. Area.

In June 1948, British Railways fitted J72's Nos. 68671, 68701/14/27 with chimneys ten inches shorter than hitherto, thus reducing their overall height to a mere 11ft. 0½in. (fig. 130) in order that they might be available at Wrexham on a duty previously undertaken by a J62.

Hull & Barnsley Engines

No alterations were carried out to the H. & B. locomotive stock despite the fact that most of the tender engines were 13ft. 2in. high.

North British Engines

As already mentioned, the N.B. load gauge was the smallest of any of the constituent companies of the L.N.E.R., and consequently no alteration was required to the N.B. locomotive stock.

However a pair of 0-6-0 tender engines with greatly cut down boiler mountings were always required at Kipps shed for working the Gartverrie branch with its severe 11ft. 1in. height restriction. At Grouping J31's 1164 and 1208 shared this duty, but due to with-

drawals J31's 10180, 10206 and J33's 9021, 9249 were their successors, all having had their boiler mountings appropriately reduced of course. Early in 1937 J36's 9714/6 became the branch engines. Being bigger, the alterations required were in consequence more drastic and the cab roofs had to be lowered whilst the domes and chimneys became so small as to be nearly non-existent (figs. 133/4). The pair, now numbered 65285/7 respectively, still share the duty, though currently stationed at St. Rollox shed.

Kipps also required a small engine for the Souterhouse branch, which had a bridge on it with headroom of only 12ft. 3in. For this the Y9 " Pug " 0-4-0ST's were normally used.

Great North of Scotland Engines

No alterations were necessary to the G.N.S.R. locomotive stock.

ROUTE AVAILABILITY

In the early years of Grouping, with the multiplicity of locomotive designs which formed the L.N.E.R. stock at that period, many engines were required for one reason or another to work in areas outside their originally intended sphere of operation. An important factor that the Civil Engineer's Department had to consider, assuming the engines concerned were within gauge, was that of weight. At first each class was assessed for new routes as and when required by the Locomotive Running Department. On the approach of the Second World War the probable need to make extensive use of engines in unfamiliar areas was anticipated. The existing stock was then comprehensively assessed for suitability over all L.N.E.R. routes and availability lists were published, purely for emergency purposes, in which every class permitted over each stretch of running line was tabulated.

As can be imagined, due to the large number of locomotive classes even then still running, the above system was somewhat cumbersome. Consequently in 1940 the Southern Area Civil Engineer's Department adopted a system of grading routes into groups by number, the lowest, R.A. (Route Availability) 1, being the most restricted and the highest, R.A.8, being suitable for the heaviest engines.

Each class of engine had its R.A. number and, in brief, this was calculated by determining the bending moment produced (measured in British Standard Units) on bridge spans of ten feet and upwards in increments of five feet. The worst, or highest, figure thus produced decided the R.A. number for the particular class. Only static weight was taken into account, no consideration being given to dynamic forces, i.e. speed, hammer blow, lurching and rail joint effect or other limitations due to height, width or length of an engine.

Generally speaking any locomotive class having an R.A. number equal to or less than a route could work over that route subject to it not being banned by gauge considerations. Certain exceptions applied such as restrictions on the use of engines with long rigid wheelbases on routes with sharp curvature. Conversely if a particular route had no bridge spans exceeding a certain length, additional engine classes of a higher R.A. number than the route itself could be permitted if their B.S.U. rating did not exceed the allowable figure for the actual spans on the route. To reduce the dynamic effects a speed restriction was sometimes imposed in order to accommodate the locomotive class concerned. Double heading of permitted engines was normally permissible unless expressly forbidden in certain locations.

In due course the Running Department became interested in the R.A. scheme and after some discussion it was adopted in revised form in late 1947 for general use throughout the L.N.E.R. The revision consisted of the expansion of the number of R.A. categories from eight to nine, this being due to the large number of engines previously falling in the R.A.5 group. The same method of calculation, as outlined above, was used, but it can be appreciated that the maximum axle load of an engine could be a guide to the R.A. number allotted, viewed in conjunction with weight per foot run, i.e. the effect of close axle spacing. For instance the six-coupled J70 class tram engines with their light maximum axle loading 11 tons 7 cwt. might be expected to be in R.A.1, but their extremely short wheelbase of 6ft. 8in. meant that the weight was concentrated and in consequence when assessed they came out as R.A.2.

The R.A. groups are shown in the table below with their B.S.U. values together with the approximate equivalent maximum axle loading; in table 2 will be found the R.A. numbers allotted to the individual locomotive classes.

As mentioned above, the scheme came into general use on the L.N.E.R. in 1947 and from September of that year the letters R.A. followed by the appropriate number were painted in 2in. yellow characters on the cab sides (fig. 86). It will be noted in the table opposite that some classes were included that had been rendered extinct prior to the implementation of the scheme. Parts of classes are in general indicated only where differences in grouping occurred.

The R.A. system is still in use on the Eastern and North Eastern Regions of British Railways, R.A. numbers having been allotted to B.R. standard locomotive classes, including diesel locomotives, as well as to engines of other companies' origin, principally L.M.S., where they work regularly over E.R. and N.E.R. lines. In Scotland the R.A. system is also still used but only on L.N.E.R. lines; the L.M.S. section still adheres to that company's system of route prohibition.

In order to give some idea of the R.A. restrictions as they applied in practice to the various sections of the L.N.E.R. system, the section which follows shows the position at the time the R.A. scheme was first generally applied towards the end of 1947. For convenience this section has been divided into the pre-Grouping constituents of the L.N.E.R. Only the more important main and branch lines have been shown, as a complete list of all running lines would be both lengthy and boring. At the same time an attempt has been made to draw attention to the effect that R.A. restrictions had upon the motive power position in certain localities. It must of course be realised that over the intervening years since 1947 a number of changes have taken place not only in the R.A. group numbers of certain routes but also in the locomotives that were in some cases additionally permitted.

Finally it is of interest to mention that a committee was set up shortly after nationalisation to make recommendations as to whether a uniform system of route restriction indication and power classification should be introduced on B.R. So far as route restrictions were concerned the choice lay between a positive system, as used on the L.N.E.R. and G.W.R., or the negative systems followed by the L.M.S. and S.R. The latter school of thought allowed any engine anywhere on the system unless specifically prohibited. The view of the committee was that the L.N.E.R. Route Availability system plus the L.M.S. power class system should be adopted for universal use and that this information together with the class of each engine should appear on a cast metal plate on the cab side. Little came of this, however, other than the application of the L.M.S. power classification to the whole of B.R. stock.

ROUTE AVAILABILITY GROUPS

Group No.	British Standard Units	Maximum Axle Load (Tons)
1	Up to 11	13.75
2	11.01-12	15
3	12.01-13	16.25
4	13.01-14	17.5
5	14.01-14.5	18.125
6	14.51-15	18.75
7	15.01-16	20
8	16.01-17	21.25
9	17.01 and over	21.25 and over

ROUTING GROUPS—1947

Group No.		Classes of Tender Engine		Classes of Tank Engine
1	J	15	F J Y Z	7 (Scottish Area)* 62, 63, 65, 71 1, 3, 5, 6, 7, 8, 10, 11 4
2	E J ES	4 24 1 (Electric Shunting)	F J Y Z	7 (G.E. Section) 67/1, 70, 72, 77, 93 9 5
3	B D J	12, 12/4 3, 41, 42 3, 4, 10, 21, 25, 36, 40	F J N	2 (G.E. Section)*, 3, 4, 5 66, 67/2, 68, 69, 88, 92 9, 10, 11
4	B C D J Q V	9, 12/3 2 2, 6, 13, 31, 43, 53 1, 5, 17, 26 5 4	A F G J N	6 1, 6 5 55, 60, 83 4, 5/2, 8, 12, 13, 14
5	B D J K EB	1, 2, 3/3, 4, 5, 6, 17/1, 17/4, 17/6, 18 1, 9, 15, 16/2, 16/3 2, 6, 11, 19, 20, 27 2 1 (Electric Freight)	A C F G J L M N DES	5, 8 12, 13, 14, 17 2 (G.C. Section) 10 52, 73, 75, 94 2 1, 2 1, 5/3, 7 1 (Diesel-Electric Shunting)
6	D J K O Q	10, 11, 17, 20, 29, 30, 32, 33, 34 35, 39 1, 4 1, 2, 3, 4, 6, 7 4, 6	C J N V Y	15, 16 50 2, 15 1 4
7	A B C P Q EE	10 3, 7, 8, 15, 16/1, 17/5, 19 1, 4, 5 1 7 1 (Electric Passenger)	A H L U V	7 2 1, 3 1 3
8	B C D J K O	16/2, 16/3 6, 7, 7/2 21, 49/1, 49/2, Engine No. 2768 37, 38 3, 5 7 (Oil Burning)	Q S T	1 1 1
9	A P V W EM	1, 2, 2/1, 2/2, 2/3, 3, 4 2 2 1 1 (Electric Mixed Traffic)		

*Weight redistributed resulting in lower maximum axle loading.

THE ROUTES—1947

Great Northern Section

The main line from King's Cross to Doncaster and Leeds had no restrictions other than certain prohibitions on assisting engines over Welwyn Viaduct, Nene Viaduct, Ouse Bridge and Newark Dyke Bridge. On the Hertford loop R.A.9 engines were allowed only in emergency but such engines could use the Hitchin-Cambridge branch at any time, though subject to a speed restriction.

In Lincolnshire, Werrington Junction via Spalding to Boston was barred to Group 9 engines except in emergency; onwards to Grimsby was R.A.7 with classes D49, K3 and K5 also permitted. The G.N. & G.E. Joint Line from March to Doncaster was normally R.A.8 plus class V2 over most of its length though all Group 9 engines were permitted in emergency. A similar state of affairs existed on the Grantham-Lincoln line. Boston to Lincoln was R.A.8. The other G.N. lines in Lincolnshire were more restricted, the worst being the Mablethorpe loop and Louth-Bardney, which were R.A.5, and Essendine-Sleaford and Essendine-Stamford, both of which were R.A.4 plus certain Group 5 types such as D1, J6, J11, K2 and C12.

Grantham to Nottingham was R.A.8 (9 in emergency), also the connection from Newark. The G.N. & L.N.W. Joint Line southwards to Melton Mowbray was R.A.7 plus K3 and K5 but onwards to Leicester (Belgrave Road) was R.A.5 plus J39 though Austerity 2-8-0's were allowed down to Market Harborough. Most of the G.N. lines north and west of Nottingham were R.A.7 with classes K3 and K5 also permitted over the majority.

In the West Riding, Leeds-Bradford and Ardsley-Bradford were R.A.7 routes plus classes D49, K3 and K5, but Wakefield-Bradford via Dewsbury was plain R.A.7. Similar restrictions existed on most of the other G.N. lines in the area. The East & West Yorkshire Union Railways line from Lofthouse to Robin Hood and thence to Stourton Junction on the Midland Railway was R.A.3 plus classes J52, N4 and N5.

Great Central Section

The G.C. main lines were up to R.A.9 standard from Manchester to Sheffield and southwards on the London Extension via the G.W. & G.C. Joint Line into Marylebone. On the Met. & G.C. Joint route via Aylesbury the line was R.A.8 with classes A3 and V2 also permitted. The connection to the G.W.R. from Woodford to Banbury was R.A.9.

The route from Sheffield via Retford and Gainsborough to Cleethorpes was free of restriction, as also was Sheffield to Doncaster, but onwards to Barnetby, also Lincoln to Barnetby and from Brocklesby to New Holland, etc., the lines were R.A.7 with classes D49, K3, K5 and Q1 also allowed. The Torksey loop between Retford and Lincoln was barred to Group 9 engines except in emergency.

The L.D.E.C. line from Lincoln to Chesterfield (Market Place) was R.A.7 plus D49, K3 and Q1, as also was the connection from Killamarsh, south of Sheffield, via Clowne to Langwith Junction but with B16 and V2 additionally allowed. Edwinstowe to Kirkby-in-Ashfield was R.A.8 plus V2.

R.A.9 engines were prohibited between Mexborough and Penistone via both Barnsley and the Worsborough incline, except of course class EM1 electric locomotives.

In the Manchester area the Dinting branch was barred only to the heavier engines. Presumably because they were jointly owned with the L.M.S., the Hayfield and Macclesfield branches did not come under the R.A. system. On these branches only the smaller G.C. tender and tank classes were permitted (in effect up to Group 5), together with class J39 on the former and class D11 on the latter. West of Manchester, the Wigan and St. Helens branches were R.A.7 plus D49, K3, K5 and Q1, also the line from Chester to Bidston (Birkenhead). From Hawarden Bridge to Wrexham was R.A.5 plus J39 and J50. Severe restrictions existed on the Wrexham Mold & Connah's Quay branch from Buckley Junction to Connah's Quay, where only classes J63, J69, J71 and J72 were permitted, also on the Brymbo branch, latterly worked by the J60 class.

Cheshire Lines Committee

The R.A. system was not extended to include the C.L.C. section, and individual permission for classes continued to be the order of the day. This created the curious situation that class D49, which was permitted over the G.C. outpost branches from Glazebrook on the C.L.C. to Wigan and St. Helens and from Chester to Bidston, was apparently not allowed to traverse the intervening C.L.C. lines to reach these branches, probably because permission had never been sought to use the class in the area.

The C.L.C. main lines from Manchester to Liverpool and Southport and to Chester were in effect equal to R.A.7 with classes K3 and Q1 also allowed; no other R.A.8 engines, nor R.A.9, were permitted, except for V2's as far as Padgate via Guide Bridge. Before the War, however, Gresley A1's worked to Aintree. Only classes J10, J11 and N5 were allowed on the Winsford & Over branch from Cuddington. The Helsby branch was similarly

84

restricted but could also take classes J39, O1, O2 and O4.

Great Eastern Section

The majority of the main routes of the G.E. Section were R.A.7 with class K3 additionally permitted. In effect, of the L.N.E.R. classes, this precluded the use only of the various Pacifics, other than the original Gresley A1's, together with D49's and V2's, although the latter class was permitted from Cambridge to Bethnal Green (but not into Liverpool Street station) though never known to operate on that line. After they had first been allowed from 1931 onwards, considerable restriction existed for some years on the use of eight-coupled engines ; O2's were allowed only between March and London and later from Norwich to London (but not into Liverpool Street station) also from Ely via Bury St. Edmunds to Ipswich, whilst the O3's were banned from nearly all G.E. routes. Due to clearance problems the O4's, which were ubiquitous throughout the rest of the Southern Area, could not run from Ely or Goodmayes to Norwich, nor the East Suffolk line. However, the wartime-built Austerity 2-8-0's suffered no special restrictions and were allowed on all R.A.6 routes in East Anglia.

March via Ely to Cambridge was R.A.9 and together with the G.N. & G.E. Joint Line and the Hitchin branch formed a useful diversion route in emergency for the East Coast main line. Peterborough to March was only R.A.8 with class V2 additionally permitted, though subject to severe restriction at Peterborough.

The cross-country route from Cambridge via Haverhill and Long Melford to Marks Tey was R.A.5 which, while allowing Sandringhams for passenger trains, normally kept all eight-coupled engines and K3's off freight work.

The long branches in the Dereham and Swaffham areas could not take Sandringhams, K2's, K3's, or J20's (though other G.E. classes in Group 5 were permitted), nor could the line from Tivetshall to Bungay. The continuation from Bungay to Beccles was even more restricted at R.A.2 with classes F3, J68 and J69 also permitted. Bishop's Stortford to Witham was R.A.6 plus V3 but excluding O2, O3 and O4 classes.

Most of the other G.E. branch lines suffered restrictions. Of those with the severest restrictions, the Maldon, Thaxted, Eye and Mildenhall branches were all R.A.3 (the last mentioned with J17 also permitted) ; most of the Colne Valley & Halstead Railway was R.A.2 ; only classes J65, J67/1 and J70 were allowed on the Kelvedon branch ; and and Mid-Suffolk Light Railway was R.A.1, plus J70. The branch lines in the London area were generally up to the prevailing G.E. R.A.7 level, except that the Blackwall line was R.A.3.

Midland & Great Northern Joint Section

The M. & G.N. system was R.A.6, except for the stretch from Sutton Bridge to South Lynn, which included the bridges over the Rivers Nene and Ouse, which was R.A.4 plus classes D9, D15, D16, J6, J11, J19, J20 and N7 (all of R.A.5).

North Eastern Section

The N.E.R. had provided itself with a substantially laid track system on the majority of its main and secondary lines on which the largest L.N.E.R. locomotives were able to run with but little hindrance, for fewer restrictions existed in the N.E. Section than in any other part of the L.N.E.R.

In the East Riding of Yorkshire the only restrictions of consequence were from Selby via Market Weighton to Beverley, which was R.A.8, and on the Hornsea branch, limited to R.A.7. Most of the N.E.-owned and joint lines in the West Riding were free of restriction, but the routes radiating from Wetherby were R.A.8 (from Cross Gates the down line was, however, R.A.9) with class V2 additionally permitted between Church Fenton and Harrogate (Harrogate via Wetherby to Cross Gates was soon uprated to R.A.9 throughout). The Hull-Doncaster line, although practically free of limitation as far as the end of N.E. ownership at Thorne, was in effect an R.A.7 route, with classes D49, K3 and K5 also allowed, due to the fact that the continuation southwards from Thorne to Doncaster on the G.C. route carried such a restriction. The short Cawood branch from Selby was R.A.2 whilst the Axholme Joint Railway from Marshland Junction, near Goole to Haxey was R.A.3.

Whitby had restriction on access from all directions, the severest being by the coast route from Scarborough which was nominally only R.A.2, although certain classes from groups as high as R.A.8 were also permitted, such as D2, D17, D20, D49, J27, A5, A8 and G5. In the opposite direction, from Loftus the line was R.A.4 with similar additional classes allowed plus also Q5 and Q6. The route over the moors from Pickering took R.A.5 engines with such classes as D20, D49, O1, O2, O4, O7 and Q6 in addition.

Over Stainmore summit between Barnard Castle and Kirkby Stephen the lofty viaducts at Belah and Deepdale imposed a severe weight limitation and in consequence the line was in the R.A.2 category with, among other classes, D3, J4, J10, J21, J25 and J36 also permitted.

The multiplicity of routes in County Durham were nearly all in the top category which made possible a number of diversion routes from the East Coast main line in case of emergency or engineering work. The line from

Ferryhill to Bishop Auckland however was R.A.7, as also was the Wearhead branch. A number of the minor branches to collieries, etc. had more severe restrictions.

In Northumberland the branch from Haltwhistle to Alston was R.A.9, but with Group 8 and 9 engines restricted to 30 m.p.h. The wooden coal staiths for loading steamers at North and South Blyth were R.A.2, which fact accounted for the long life of the J77 class. The staiths at West Blyth were R.A.3.

Hull & Barnsley Section

Most of the H. & B. system was R.A.5 but many locomotives in the R.A.6 category were also permitted, including D17, D20, J39, K1, O1, O2, O3, O4, O7, Q4 and Q6.

North British Section

The full R.A.9 standard prevailed on the main lines from Edinburgh to Berwick, Carlisle, Glasgow (via both Falkirk and Airdrie, but not the Low Level lines), Perth and Aberdeen, except that double heading was much restricted ; southwards to Berwick and also to Carlisle the A, V and W classes could be piloted only by a 4-4-0 whilst westwards to Glasgow a similar prohibition existed except that D49's could not be used for piloting the largest engines. On the Aberdeen line, which crossed the Forth and Tay bridges, there was a complete ban on the double heading of the A, V and W classes, and nothing bigger than a J35 could pilot an O or Q class engine.

Much of the remainder of the N.B. system was R.A.6 with the use of classes J37 and J38 (which were R.A.8) also permitted, though many of the routes were barred completely to eight-coupled goods engines. To the south and east of Edinburgh most of the routes, other than the main lines referred to above, were in this category, except that class K3 could also travel over the Peebles loop and the branch from St. Boswells on the Carlisle line via Duns to Reston on the East Coast main line. In case of emergency, larger engines were permitted over the latter route, and also the continuation of the N.E.R. line from Tweedmouth to St. Boswells via Roxburgh. Class D49 as well as class K3 was allowed on the Border Counties line from Riccarton Junction to Hexham. Reedsmouth to Morpeth together with the Rothbury branch was however limited to Group 3 engines which, as far as N.B. locomotive stock was concerned, meant that only class J36 was permitted other than purely shunting engines. The Eyemouth branch was also R.A.3. Even more severe restriction existed on the Gifford branch which was R.A.2 plus class J67/1, whilst the Lauder Light Railway was limited to a 12-ton axle

loading and was in R.A.1. The Carlisle-Silloth branch was R.A.7 plus classes J37 and J38.

Inverkeithing via Dunfermline to Thornton Junction was R.A.9 but most of the branches and colliery lines in the Fife area were in the usual Group 6 plus range. The Alva branch from Cambus was R.A.3 and the Lochty branch from near Methil was R.A.4 plus J35 and N15. North of Dundee the Carmyllie branch was only R.A.2, as was the Arbroath Harbour branch. Montrose to Inverbervie was R.A.6 plus J37 and J38.

The colliery branches in the Bathgate area were generally more restricted than the Fife branches, being R.A.4 plus the use of J35 and N15, or even R.A.3 in some cases. Most of branches in the Coatbridge district were also in this latter category. Around Glasgow the 6 plus category prevailed but with an additional prohibition on the use of class N2 on several routes ; on others in the area this class was restricted to 35 m.p.h. due to trouble that had occurred with derailments. The line out to Helensburgh was R.A.7 plus J37, J38 and K3 but the West Highland was R.A.6 plus J37, J38, K3 and L1. Classes K3, K4 and eight-coupled goods engines were forbidden to be double headed on this line. The Mallaig extension was similar to the West Highland except that classes K3 and L1 were not permitted. The Fort Augustus branch was R.A.3.

Great North of Scotland Section

The G.N.S. Section was severely handicapped by weight restrictions and set the L.N.E.R. authorities many problems in the provision of suitable motive power to work it. Even the main line from Aberdeen via Craigellachie to Elgin was only R.A.6 (with double-heading of large engines not allowed), which meant that none of the bigger Gresley engines was permissible. At one time the restrictions were even more severe and the largest engines normally found on the section were the G.E. B12's of R.A.3. Certain strengthening work was done and in due course the Thompson B1's, which were R.A.5, appeared, but apart from the main line from Aberdeen to Elgin, they were confined to the alternative route via the coast and the Peterhead, Fraserburgh and Ballater branches. All these routes were in fact R.A.4 with the B1's additionally allowed.

The Alford, Old Meldrum, Macduff and Boat of Garten branches were R.A.3 plus D31 and D40. The Banff branch was also R.A.3 but plus D40 and G5, whilst the Lossiemouth branch was R.A.4. The St. Combs branch ranked as a light railway and was restricted to 14-ton axle loadings though some tolerance was apparently permitted as the G.E. F4 class, which had a maximum axle load of 14 tons 18 cwt., worked the branch for many years.

Fig. 118   Class C1 No. 4447 at Doncaster shed.
Boiler mountings and cab reduced to
L.N.E.R. rolling stock gauge

Fig. 119   Class Q1 No. 3424. G.N.R. class B 3670-gallon tender

Fig. 120   Class K4 No. 1994 *The Great Marquess* at Fort William
shed, August 1947. L.N.E.R. Group Standard 3500-gallon
with flush sides and high front shield

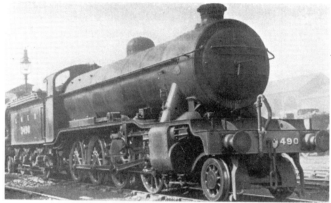

Fig. 121   Class O2 No. 3490 at Hornsey shed. Built
with boiler mountings and cab reduced to
L.N.E.R. rolling stock gauge.   G.N.R. class B
tender with unequal wheelbase.   G.N.R. load
class tablet on vacuum standpipe

Fig. 122   Class O2 No. 485N at Hornsey shed.   To G.N.R.
rolling stock gauge.   1923 sectional suffix to
number.   G.N.R. class B tender with equal wheelbase

Fig. 123   Class A1 No. 4475 Flying Fox.   To G.N.R. rolling stock gauge.
Original short nameplate

Fig. 124   Class J9 No. 5663 at Parkhead shed about 1927.
With N.B.R. chimney

Fig. 125   Class B7/1 No. 5469.   Retaining G.C.R. livery but with L.N.E.R.
number on G.C. plate on cab side.
G.C.R. rolling stock gauge

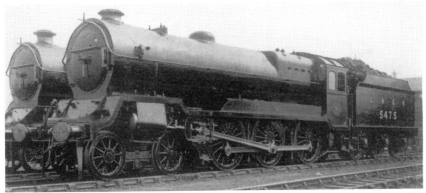

Fig. 126   Class B7/2 No. 5475.   Built with boiler mountings and cab
reduced to L.N.E.R. rolling stock gauge.   G.C.R.-pattern
4000-gallon self trimming tender

Fig. 127   Class D9 No. 5110 *King George V.* G.C.R. chimney
and dome. L.N.E.R. green livery with number on
tender. G.C.R. 4000-gallon tender

Fig. 128   Class D9 No. 6024. L.N.E.R. plain cast chimney.
Black livery with number within beading on splasher

Fig. 129 Class D9 No. 5113. Later style L.N.E.R. chimney and low dome

Fig. 130   Class J72 No. 68701 at Bidston shed, May 1952.
Fitted with short chimney

Fig. 131   Class J63 No. 5089. With G.C.R. plain tapered
chimney

Fig. 132   Class V1 No. 7674 at Eastfield shed, August 1947.
Post-war Gill Sans lettering

Fig. 133   Class J36 No. 65287 passing under
the low bridge on the Gartverrie
branch, April 1962

Fig. 134   Class J36 No. 5285 at Kipps shed, April 1947. With reduced
boiler mountings and cab for working the Gartverrie branch.
Inverurie paint date at leading end of footplate angle-iron

Fig. 135   Class D51 No. 10425 on Lauder branch train at Fountainhall,
August 1927

Fig. 136   Class D7 No. 5710 approaching Sheffield, about 1930.   With L.N.E.R.
" flowerpot " chimney.   Engine painted black with number on
tender—interim livery of 1928-29

Fig. 137   Class C4 No. 5263 on a Marylebone-Manchester express near Saunderton,
August 1932

Fig. 138   Class C13 No. 7415 on a local at Fairfield, June 1948

Fig. 139   Class H2 No. 6416 leaving Nottingham Victoria with a Mansfield
train, June 1946

Fig. 140   Class E4 No. 7466 and J15 No. 7941 at Haverhill, October 1935

Fig. 141   Class D16/2 No. 2590 at Wickham Market with a Framlingham-
Felixstowe special, June 1947

Fig. 142   Class B12/3 No. 8510 ascending Belstead Bank, Ipswich with an up
express

Fig. 143   Class D16/3 No. 8861 on an express in East Anglia

POWER CLASSIFICATION

L.N.E.R. LOAD CLASSES

The constituent companies of the L.N.E.R. had their individual systems of haulage capacity rating for their locomotives whereby maximum loads were laid down for each class on the various routes. In some cases these load classifications applied to both passenger and freight locomotives, but it was more usual for them to be used purely for freight movements. There were several different systems in use, some of a complex nature, the basic arrangement being for locomotives of similar power rating to be combined in groups, often designated by letters or numerals. Only three of the constituent companies, the G.N.R., G.C.R. and N.B.R., generally displayed load classifications on their locomotives.

After Grouping, the three Areas formed by the L.N.E.R. adopted different systems of load classification and will be considered separately.

Southern Area

The G.N.R. displayed load classifications on its locomotives by means of a cast metal tablet attached to the vacuum standpipe at the front end. The G.N. system consisted basically of a letter classification with little order in the allotment of the letters. Details of the load classes in use at the time of Grouping were as follows :—

Load Class	Locomotive Class
A	J5, J6
B	J3 ; J4 & J7 (175 lb.)
C	J4 & J7 (160 lb.)
D	Q1, Q2, Q3
D1	O1, O2
E	J1, J2
E1	K1, K2
E2	K3
F	J53, J54, J56, J57, N1, N2
H	J50, J51, J52, J55 ; R1 (4′ 2″ blr.)
L	G2
M	C12, G1
N	R1 (4′ 8″ blr.)
P	A1
T	D4, E1
W	D1, D2, D3
Z	C1, C2

G.N. load class tablets continued to be fixed to new engines of the A1, J50 and O2 classes built at Doncaster immediately after Grouping.

The G.C.R. had a loading classification system for freight trains whereby freight locomotives were divided into five categories, numbered 1 to 5 in descending order of power. These numbers were sometimes painted on the cabsides or, in certain cases, incorporated in the G.C. number plate as a raised figure beneath the running number. At Grouping, G.C. freight motive power was classified as follows :—

Load Class	Locomotive Class
1	O4, Q4
2	B9, J11 (incl. engine 5134), M1, N6
3	B4, B5, J12 (Belpaire f'box), J13, J60, N4, N5
4	J8, J9, J10, J12 (R.T. f'box), W.M.C.Q. 0-8-0T
5	G.C. " 18 " 0-6-0

G.E.R. goods train loads were divided into eight alphabetical categories, as follows :—

Load Class	Locomotive Class
A	J16, J17, J18, J19, J20
B	B12, D14, D15, G4
C	J14, J15, J66, J67, J68, J69
D	F4, F5, F6
E	F3
F	E4
G	D13
H	J65

The load class letters were not indicated on the locomotives themselves.

In 1924 a new scheme was formulated applying to all Southern Area engines, but for freight workings only. The locomotive classes were placed in one of eight groups numbered 1 to 8 in ascending order of power. In July and August 1924 orders were issued for the casting of the necessary tablets to be fixed to the brake pipes or, in the case of engines with steam brake only, to the bufferbeams near the centre above the engine number.

Some G.N. engines ran for a time with both the G.N.R. and L.N.E.R. tablets displayed ; many G.N. classes continued to be known throughout the remainder of their existence by their G.N. load classification (e.g. J6's were always referred to as " A engines " by the men). The Eastern Section (G.E. lines) at first decided also to bring certain of their passenger engines within the scheme and authority was given for the appropriate tablets to be cast giving load classifications for use when employed on goods duties. However, in only a few cases were these tablets actually affixed to G.E. passenger locomotives.

In addition to new locomotive designs, certain N.E.R. and H. & B.R. classes transferred to the Southern Area or which worked frequently into that Area were later incorporated in the scheme.

Except on the G.E. Section and in South Yorkshire the practice of fixing load class tablets to engines gradually fell into disuse. However, wartime operating conditions, whereby engines often wandered far from their usual haunts, led to the extensive reintroduction of load classification numbers on Southern Area motive power in 1942. Where engines had lost their tablets, or had never carried them, these numbers were painted on the front bufferbeam prefixed by "Ld" or "L" (load). A new group, load class 9, was introduced to cater for the two P1 2-8-2's which had been rebuilt with high pressure A3-type boilers. All locomotive classes, with the exception of specialised shunting types, were now embraced by the scheme which, of course, still applied only to freight movements. Many of the low power passenger locomotive classes, mainly of low power, did not have their loading classification painted on the bufferbeam but were shown in the freight train loading books as conveying a certain number of mineral wagons less than No. 1 load class (the lowest) engines.

From the time of introduction of the Southern Area freight train loading classifications until superseded by the British Railways scheme, a few alterations took place in the grading of certain locomotive classes whilst local variations also occurred. The table opposite shows the ratings generally applicable.

In the Southern Area, no load classifications were published for passenger trains. Timings were however laid down for certain principal express trains (some of which were not permitted to load beyond a certain number of vehicles) on the assumption that these trains would be hauled by customary motive power, but generally drivers were expected to use their best endeavour with the particular locomotive provided them, whatever its type.

North Eastern Area

The North Eastern Area used the complicated freight loading system introduced by the N.E.R. in 1907, and the 1917 (and final) edition of the "Loads of Engines" book ran to 499 pages, with more than 1,600 entries. This system continued in use throughout the whole existence of the L.N.E.R. and was not, in fact, superseded until 1950. Each entry covered a stretch of line and the load was given for various classes of engines when working goods or mineral trains. The more important locomotive classes were quoted as 'standards' for loadings, but with the more modern classes usually given as a percentage increase in load on one or other of the highest powered 'standards,' e.g.

class S2 (B15) 5% more than class S (B13). Similarly the lower 'standard' was for Old Tender Engine (classes "59," "398" and "1001"), and the various 2-4-0's and small tank engines received a percentage derating, e.g. class B.T.P. (G6) 20% less than Old Tender Engine load. At no time did N.E. Area locomotives have the above load classifications marked on them. However, certain of the Area's locomotives were noted carrying Southern Area freight load classes, generally as a result of a visit to Doncaster Works for overhaul.

The N.E. Area Passenger Train Loading Book was arranged in a like fashion to the freight book with the locomotive classes divided into various groups. The load for each group was shown when working express passenger, ordinary passenger or excursion trains over every line in the Area.

Scottish Area

Since the inauguration of its Train Control System in September 1913, the N.B.R. had had a very comprehensive power classification scheme for its engines. This has already been mentioned under the heading of "Classification" (p. 23), the letters A to G being used for goods engines in descending order of power and H to R for passenger engines. Several alterations to the list were made before Grouping, the most notable being the introduction of two previously unused letters, I and S. The former applied to the saturated Atlantics when the superheated version took the H classification, whilst the latter was used for the 19½-in. Reid 0-6-0's (L.N.E.R. J37) with increased boiler pressure. From 1919 onwards small cast metal plates giving the class letters were fixed to the cab or bunker sides and the list as at Grouping was as follows :—

Load Class	Locomotive Class
A	N14, N15
B	J35 ; J37 (165 lb.)
C	J32, J36
D	J33, J34, J83
E	J31, J81, J84, J85, J86
F	J88
G	Y9
H	C11
I	C10
J	D29, D30
K	D26, D32, D33, D34
L	C16, D36
M	C15, D27, D28, D31, G9
N	D25, D35
P	D50, E7, G7, G8
R	D51, J82
S	J37 (175 or 180 lb.)

Unclassified : Y10 and Petrol Shunter (later Y11).

L.N.E.R. SOUTHERN AREA FREIGHT TRAIN LOADING CLASSIFICATION

Load Class	Tender Engines	Tank Engines
9	P1 (220lb.)	
8	O1 (later O3), O1 (Thompson), O2, O7, P1 (180lb.), Q7	
7	A2, O4, O5, O6, V2*, W1	
6	A1, A3, A4, B7, B16, J20, K3, K5, Q2, Q3, Q4, Q5, Q6	L1 (later L3), Q1
5	B1 (Thompson), B6, B8, J18, J19, J26, J27, J39, K2, Q1, Q10	
4	B2 (Thompson), B3, B17, J16, J17, J25, J28	J50, J51, L2
3	B9, B12, B13, B15, J5, J6, J11, J15, K1 (Gresley)	J52, J53, J54, J55, J56, J57, J68, J69, J77, J94, M1, M2, U1
2	B2 (later B19), B4, B5, J1, J2, J3, J4, J7, J21, J23, J24, J40, J41	A5, J66, J67, N1, N2, N4, N5, N6, N7
1	J9, J10, J12, J13	J60

To convey eight mineral wagons (or equivalent) less than Class 1 load : Tender Engines—C2, C5, D1, D2, D3, D6, D7, D52, D53, D54 ; Tank Engines—C12, C13, C14, F1, F2, F7, H2, J65.

To convey six mineral wagons less than Class 1 load : Tender Engines—C1, C4, C6, C7, D9, D10, D11, D13, E4 ; Tank Engines—F3, F4, F5, F6, G4.

To convey four mineral wagons less than Class 1 load : Tender Engines—B1 (later B18).

To convey three mineral wagons less than Class 1 load : Tender Engines—D15, D16.

*Class V2 was rated as Load Class 7 for mineral trains, but on braked goods trains the loading was generally 6 plus four or five additional wagons.

There were anomalies in the scheme, the most glaring example being the position of the Scotts higher in the scale than the more powerful Glens, but in actual practice the loads for J and K were invariably the same. With characteristic thoroughness the N.B.R. Maximum Loads of Engines Book gave conversion tables for the ready reckoning of passenger loads when hauled by goods engines and vice versa. After the Grouping N.B.R. load class letters were allotted to certain English classes stationed in the Southern Scottish Area, but the engines never carried the plates :—

Load Class	Locomotive Class
C	J9, J24
J	D11
K	C7
M	D1
S	K2

With the publication of a new load book in 1928 the N.B. scheme fell into disuse because, although the 1928 volume was in the same format as hitherto, the L.N.E.R. locomotive classification was used throughout, classes of like power being grouped at the head of the load tables. The N.B. plates however remained on the engines until the 1939-45 War during and after which many were removed (fig. 171).

On the G.N.S. Section, engines were divided broadly into load classes as under :—

Load Class	Locomotive Class
Special	D40, D41
First	D38, D42, D43, D45, D46, G10
Second	D39, D44, D47/2, D48, J90, J91
Third	D47/1
Harbour engines	Z4, Z5

No indication was carried by the engines and no loads were published for passenger trains, drivers being given wide powers of discretion regarding the loads they took. Separate goods load tables were published for summer and winter, the latter loads being generally 10% less than the summer rating due to the prevalent adverse climatic conditions in the G.N.S. area during winter.

The foregoing arrangements obtained until the publication of the first Northern Scottish Area Appendix in March 1928, when passenger loads were published and standard goods loads set out. At the same time class D31 engines were listed as equivalent to Special Class, J36 were rated to take five wagons more than Special Class, whilst definite loads (unrelated to existing standards) were given for class N14. Similarly a later supplement gave completely independent load tables for the B12 4-6-0's. G.N.S. Section loads continued to be printed in the Northern Scottish Area Appendix until June 1943, after which they were included in the Scottish Area load book.

BRITISH RAILWAYS POWER CLASSIFICATION

Prior to nationalisation officials of the four main line companies met to discuss the provision of a uniform classification system intended to cover the whole of British Railways locomotive stock. Eventually it was decided to adopt the L.M.S. power class system virtually as it stood and to use this in conjunction with the existing locomotive classifications of the companies.

Two power rating categories were used, P (Passenger) and F (Freight), these letters being preceded by a numerical index. Passenger ratings ran from 0P to 7P (later expanded to 8P) in ascending order of power, whilst Freight ratings were from 0F to 8F, with the later addition of 9F. Many locomotive classes received both P and F ratings, in many cases not identical.

In addition to this Loading Classification, a simplified system was adopted for office use, known as the Statistical Classification. This related to the primary use of the locomotive—Passenger, Mixed Traffic or Freight —the subsidiary use being ignored. For example, a Shire class D49 4-4-0 was Load Class 4P2F but, as its primary use was for passenger working, the Statistical Class was 4P. Mixed Traffic locomotives (termed MT under the Statistical Classification) usually had the same load index as the Freight Load Class even where the Passenger Load Class differed. An exception, however, was the N2 0-6-2T where the Statistical Class was the same as the Passenger Load Class, with the the Freight Load Class differing.

The Statistical Classification was divided into six categories, Passenger Tender (P), Passenger Tank (PT), Mixed Traffic Tender (MT), Mixed Traffic Tank (MTT), Freight Tender (F) and Freight Tank (FT), all preceded by the appropriate power index. The full list of L.N.E.R. locomotive classes that received B.R. Statistical Classes is set out in the table opposite. It will be noted that certain locomotive classes that had become extinct during 1948 were included, whilst others for specific duties were excluded from the scheme and remained unclassified. Locomotive class parts have been omitted except where differences in grading occurred.

After a few year's experience with the B.R. power classification system, certain revisions were made. From January 1951 the higher groups in the passenger range were expanded from 6 and 7 to 6, 7 and 8 thus bringing them into line with the freight range. As a result classes A1, A4 and W1 were upgraded from 7P to 8P whilst the A3's remained 7P. Class A10 had by then been rendered extinct by rebuilding.

In May 1953 many of the surviving L.N.E.R. classes were altered in power rating, as follows :—

Power Class	Locomotive Class
4P to 5P	B2, B17/6
4P to 3P	A5, A8
2P to 3P	D16
2P to 1P	C12, D40, F5, F6, G5
6MT to 5MT	B16/1
5MT to 4MT	V4
4MT to 3MT	N14, N15, V1
7F to 8F	Q7
7F to 6F	S1
7F to 5F	T1
6F to 5F	J20
5F to 3F	A7
4F to 5F	J19, J26, J27, J37, J39
4F to 3F	N13
3F to 2F	J68, J69
0F to Unclassified	J71
0F to Dock Tank	Y8

The final list of B.R. Statistical Classes applying to L.N.E.R. stock (i.e. as from May 1953), taking into account locomotive classes that had become extinct in the meantime, is set out in the table on page 92. Diesel and electric locomotives had at first been removed from the scheme but the Manchester-Sheffield-Wath Bo-Bo electrics of class EM1 were subsequently classified 8F.

During the early years of nationalisation comparable changes occurred in the actual Loading Classification, many locomotive classes being uprated or derated and it was not until 1953 that the scheme at last settled down. The list applying to L.N.E.R. locomotive stock from May 1953 onwards is given in the table on page 93.

From January 1949, the Scottish Region painted the Statistical Class on the cab sides of its locomotive stock as they passed through the shops. The Eastern and North Eastern Regions did not follow suit, except that where locomotives belonging to these Regions were overhauled in Scotland these power classes were often applied.

B.R. STATISTICAL POWER CLASSES, JANUARY 1949

Power Class	Passenger (P)		Mixed Traffic (MT)		Freight (F)	
	Tender	Tank	Tender	Tank	Tender	Tank
8					O1, O2, O3, W.D. 2-8-0 (O7)	
7	A1, A3, A4, A10, W1		A2, A2/2, A2/3		O4, Q7	S1, T1
6			A2/1, B7, B16, K1, K3, K4, K5, V2		J20, J38, Q5, Q6	
5			B1, B8, B9, V4		Q4	A7, L3, Q1
4	B2, B3, B4, B12, B17, D49, D(62768)	A5, A6, A8	K2	L1, L2, N14, N15, V1, V3	J17, J19, J26, J27, J37, J39	J50, J94, N12, N13
3	C6, C7, D10, D11, D29, D30, D32, D33, D34		B5	M2, N2, N7, N8, N9	J5, J6, J11, J24, J25, J35	J52, J55, J68, J69, J73, J75, N10
2	C1, C4, D9, D15, D16, D20, D31, D40, D41	C12, C13, C14, C15, C16, F5, F6, G5	J1, J2	N1, N4, N5	J3, J4, J10, J15, J21, J36	J66, J67, J72, J77, J83
1	D1, D2, D3, D17/2	F1, F2, F3, F4, F7	E4			J60, J93
0						J62, J63, J65, J70, J71, J88, J92, Y4, Y6, Y7, Y8, Y9, Z4, Z5
Unclass.						U1, Y1, Y3, Y5, Y10, Y11

B.R. STATISTICAL POWER CLASSES, MAY 1953

Power Class	Passenger (P) Tender	Passenger (P) Tank	Mixed Traffic (MT) Tender	Mixed Traffic (MT) Tank	Freight (F) Tender	Freight (F) Tank
8	A1, A4, W1				O1, O2, Q7, W.D. 2-8-0 (O7)	EM1
7	A3		A2, A2/2, A2/3		O4	
6			A2/1, B16/2, B16/3, K1, K3, K4, K5, V2		J38, Q6	S1
5	B2, B17/6		B1, B16/1		J19, J20, J26, J27, J37, J39	L3, Q1, T1
4	B12, B17, D49		K2, V4	L1, V3	J17	J50, J94
3	D10, D11, D16, D30, D33, D34	A5, A8		N2, N7, N8, N9, N14, N15, V1	J5, J6, J11, J25, J35	A7, J52, J73, N10, N13
2	D20	C13, C14, C15, C16	J1, J2	N1, N4, N5	J3, J10, J15, J21, J36	J66, J67, J68, J69, J72, J77, J83
1	D40	C12, F4, F5, F6, G5	E4			
0						J63, J65, J70, J88, Y4, Y9, Z4, Z5
Unclass.						J71, U1, Y1, Y3, Y8, Y11

B.R. LOADING GROUPS, MAY 1953

Load Group Pass.	Freight	Tender Engines	Tank Engines
8	7(a)	A2, A2/2, A2/3, W1	
8	6 (a)	A1, A1/1, A4	
7	8		EM1
	8	O1, O2, W.D. 2-8-0 (O7), Q7	
7	6 (a)	A2/1, A3, V2	
	7	O4	
5	6	B16/2, B16/3, K1, K3, K4, K5	
	6	J38, Q6	S1
5	5	B1, B16/1 (b)	
5	4	B2, B17/6 (c)	
4	5	J39	
3	5	J19	
	5	J20, J26, J27, J37	L3, Q1, T1
4	4	B17, K2, V4	L1
4	3	B12	V3
4	2	D49	
2	4	J17	
	4		J50, J94
3	3		A5, A8, N7, N14, N15, V1
3	2	D10, D11, D30, D34	N2
3	1	D16	
2	3	J6, J11	N8, N9
	3	J5, J25, J35	A7, J52, J73, N10, N13
2	2	J1, J2, J21	N1, N5
2	1	D20	C13, C14, C15, C16
1	2	J15	N4
	2	J3, J10, J36	J66, J67, J68, J69, J72, J77, J83
1	1	D40, E4	C12, F4 (d), F5 (d), F6 (d), G5 (e)

Notes :—

    (a) When working class C and D (4 and 5) trains, classes A1, A1/1, A2, A2/1, A2/2, A2/3, A3, A4, V2 and W1 take Group 8 loads.

    (b) Class B16/1 take Group 6 loads when working freight trains other than class C and D (4 and 5).

    (c) Class B17/6 take Group 5 loads when working braked freight trains.

    (d) Classes F4, F5, F6 take five wagons less than normal Group 1 loads.

    (e) Class G5 take six wagons less than normal Group 1 loads.

    The above table shows the general position, but in certain instances local variations in usage occurred. For instance, for a time at least, class K3 was derated to 5F in the Scottish Region and the W.D. 2-8-0's to 7F on the G.E. Section, whilst class O4 was up-rated to 8F by the London Midland Region. Locomotive classes not shown in the above table and still existing in May 1953 (e.g. J63, J65, J70, J71, J88, U1, Y1, Y3, Y4, Y8, Y9, Y11, Z4 and Z5) were either classified 0F, "Dock Tank" or not classified at all. No loads were published for these.

THE LOCOMOTIVE WORKS

The principal locomotive works of the L.N.E.R. were at Doncaster, Darlington, Gorton, Stratford, Cowlairs and Inverurie. At Doncaster and Darlington most of the locomotive construction undertaken by the Company was carried out, though Doncaster eventually became the sole works responsible for design.

In recounting the history of the various classes of locomotive, particularly those of pre-Grouping designs, reference will be made not only to Doncaster and Darlington but to the other locomotive works. These, to a varying degree, continued to play their part in the decentralised organisation of the L.N.E.R. long after Grouping, and to perpetuate characteristic features.

Brief details are also given below of works numbers and/or orders used by the different works. The individual numbers and orders will be dealt with in the articles on the locomotive classes. In no instances will estimated works numbers be quoted where official ones do not exist.

Great Northern Railway

The DONCASTER Locomotive & Carriage Works were originally built in 1853 as repair shops for the G.N.R., replacing earlier works at Boston. Locomotive construction at Doncaster began in 1867. Popularly known as " The Plant," the total area covered, including the adjacent carriage works, was eighty-four acres.

In 1897 Ivatt introduced Engine Order numbers at Doncaster commencing with E.O. 201 for a series of ten 4-4-0's Nos. 1071-80 (L.N.E.R. class D4). At first these order numbers applied also to Stores Orders, being used to cover orders for spare boilers as well as complete engines. Thus Stores Order 202 was for ten spare boilers whilst Engine Order 203 was for ten complete engines, 0-6-0ST's Nos. 1201-10 (L.N.E.R. class J52). This meant that there was no Engine Order 202 and this number remained a blank in the E.O. series. Thereupon it was decided to issue separate E.O.'s and S.O.'s for engines and boilers. This resulted in S.O. 204/5 being allocated to orders for spare boilers and S.O. 206 for the boilers associated with E.O. 204, 4-4-0's Nos. 1301-10 (L.N.E.R. class D4). To avoid further confusion caused by E.O. and S.O. series numbers being similar, all new boilers ordered after S.O. 206 were allocated order numbers in a new series commencing at S.O. 500 (these became Boiler Orders from 524 onwards, issued in May 1899), Engine Orders continuing from E.O. 205 upwards.

Engine Orders eventually terminated at E.O. 409 when the last steam engine order was completed in 1957. There were several gaps in the series, in addition to E.O. 202 already mentioned, and several cases of cancelled orders. In certain other cases of cancelled orders, the E.O. numbers were, however, reallocated. Certain outside-built engines received Doncaster E.O. numbers but not in every instance, whilst on the other hand a batch of Doncaster-built engines, 4-4-0 Nos. 1386-95 (L.N.E.R. class D2) did not receive an E.O. number but were allocated S.O. 1007 in the miscellaneous Stores Order series commencing at S.O. 1000.

From 1914 it became the practice with engines built at Doncaster to restrict individual Engine Orders to not more than ten engines each, and orders for more than ten engines were split up into more than one E.O.

Although the E.O. system was introduced for guidance in the works whilst the engines were under construction, this did not supersede the practice of fitting brass works plates bearing serial numbers which had commenced at No. 1 in 1867 and had reached 1000 by 1903. By 1952, when the practice of allocating works numbers was discontinued, only ten engines had been built at Doncaster without being given serial numbers. These were the L.M.S.-type 8F 2-8-0's of class O6 Nos. 3148-57 in 1945-46. This was deliberately done to balance ten works numbers not used in 1923, Nos. 1554-63, so that the 2,000th engine to be built at Doncaster, class A2/3 No. 500 then under construction, could be correctly given Doncaster works number 2000 of 1946.

Works plates sometimes went astray and often new ones were cast to replace them, but occasionally plates were fitted to the wrong engine and such errors were not always rectified.

Great Central Railway

The principal repairing shops of the Sheffield & Manchester Railway were at GORTON (Manchester), where they were established in 1848. These were retained as the main locomotive centre of the M.S. & L.R. and later G.C.R. During 1871-80, however, a number of new engines were built and existing engines renewed in the running shed shops at Sheffield, frames, boilers and cylinders being sent from Gorton. The Gorton works covered an area of fifty acres, the Carriage & Wagon Department having been moved to Dukinfield. Under British Railways, Gorton Works were closed on 31st May 1963.

The first locomotive was built at Gorton in 1858. The 500th was stated to be D6 class 4-4-0 L.N.E.R. No. 5858, turned out in 1898 and the 1,000th locomotive was ultimately officially estimated as B1 class 4-6-0 No. 61342, built in 1949.

In 1948, the Railway Correspondence & Travel Society drew the attention of British Railways, Eastern Region to the fact that B1's Nos. 61340-9 then building at Gorton included the 1,000th engine constructed there. As a result, when in 1950 Gorton commenced construction of a series of electric locomotives for the Manchester-Sheffield-Wath services, they appeared with plates bearing works numbers, the first from that works to do so. These works numbers were arrived at by estimation, none having previously been allotted. Nos. 26001-24/9/30 at first carried numbers 1004-27/32/3, but the Society suggested that the estimating had been done incorrectly and later these numbers were changed to 1008-31/6/7 respectively. The remaining electric locomotives built at Gorton have works numbers based on the revised calculations and the last engine to be built there was No. 27006 (works No. 1071) in 1954. In due course B1's 61340-9 were fitted with plates bearing works Nos. 998-1007.

The two companies absorbed by the G.C.R. both had small repair shops. Under the G.C.R., both of these were kept fully employed. They were at Tuxford (ex-L.D. & E.C.R.) and at Rhosddu, Wrexham (ex-W.M. & C.Q.R.). Tuxford was closed in May 1927 and Rhosddu about the same time. In addition, under the G.C.R., certain sheds had carried out heavy repairs; those known to have done this included Immingham, Mexborough, Sheffield, Woodford and Trafford Park (C.L.C.). This practice was discontinued by the L.N.E.R.

Great Eastern Railway

STRATFORD Locomotive & Carriage Works were constructed under " King " Hudson in 1847 for the Eastern Counties Railway, replacing the earlier works at Romford Factory which was later used by the Stores Department. With various enlargements the works ultimately covered an area of approximately sixty acres.

The earliest locomotive construction at Stratford was in 1851, and after 1882, with very limited exceptions, all locomotive construction for the G.E.R. was undertaken at Stratford. The 1,000th locomotive, J15 class 0-6-0 No. 7510, was built in 1899 and the last engine built there, an N7 class 0-6-2T completed in March 1924 as L.N.E.R. No. 999E, brought the total up to 1702.

Works numbers were never used at Stratford. Instead order numbers were issued which covered not only new engines but all jobs.

These order numbers were composed of letters of the alphabet, in order, suffixed by a number which progressed upwards by one each time the alphabet had been run through, e.g. A17 to Z17 would be followed by A18 to Z18, and so on.

No record has been traced of the earliest orders but it seems possible that Sinclair started the system when he came to Stratford in 1856. The first definite use of an order number for locomotives is of H7 for the Johnson 0-4-2T's Nos. 81/2/3 of 1872. The last order for new engines was K89 for N7 0-6-2T's Nos. 990-9E constructed in 1923-24. As far as new construction was concerned, each order was usually for ten engines. It was, of course, the Stratford order number for the first batch of engines of each class that was generally used by the G.E.R. to identify the class.

It is interesting to note that Adams took the Stratford order system to Nine Elms when he left the G.E.R. for the L. & S.W.R.

Heavy repairs were also carried out at Norwich and the use of the works there continued in the early years of Grouping.

North Eastern Railway

The North Road Engine Works at DARLINGTON were opened on 1st January 1863, replacing the earlier Stockton & Darlington Railway works at Shildon at which place but on a different site one of the principal wagon works of the N.E.R. and later of the L.N.E.R. was situated. After the Act for the Stockton & Darlington amalgamation became law in July 1863, Darlington continued to serve the Stockton & Darlington Section of the N.E.R. during its separate management until 1873. Thereafter it continued as a subsidiary works for the N.E.R. as a whole until, shortly after the transfer of the Headquarters of the Chief Mechanical Engineer of the N.E.R. from Gateshead to Darlington in 1910, all new engine and boiler building was concentrated at Darlington.

The first new engine was turned out from the works in 1864 and building ceased at Shildon in 1867. Some engines were built jointly by the two works in this period. The works numbers carried by certain of the new engines built between 1864 and 1885 are known but these numbers exceeded the number of new engines built and allowed for works numbers being given to substantially rebuilt engines. In 1886 a new series of works numbers was instituted and these continued to No. 555 in 1909 ; they included fifteen engines rebuilt in 1892-93 and allotted works numbers in 1893. No works numbers were used for the next 1054 engines built from 1910 to 1943 when, in an attempt to revert to the original list, class V2 No. 3675 was given Darlington Works No. 1903. This new series continued to be used for the remainder of the L.N.E.R. period and for a time by British Railways. Although Order Numbers were issued for new engines built at Darlington from 1886 onwards none appear to have been used before this date. The number was prefixed by the letter A and the same series of numbers appears to have been used for work other than new engine construction.

Including the Stooperdale Boiler Shops, Darlington Works covered an area of sixty-three acres.

GATESHEAD Locomotive Works dates from the Newcastle & Darlington Junction Railway opened in 1844 and the " new workshops" at Gateshead were established in 1853-54. Gateshead later became the headquarters of the Locomotive Department of the York Newcastle & Berwick Railway and afterwards of the N.E.R. After the transfer of the C.M.E.'s headquarters to Darlington in 1910, it continued as a main works, but the last new locomotives were constructed in 1910. In August 1932 the works were closed as an economy measure but were reopened during the 1939-45 War and continued in use afterwards for repair work until 1959.

The use of any works numbers by Gateshead before 1885 is not known but from this date until 1903 they were allotted on a yearly basis followed by the last two digits of the year in question, e.g. Nos. 1.86, 2.86 being the first numbers used in 1886. In some cases engines due to be built before the year end were given numbers for that year but, not being completed until the following year, were given new " works numbers" in the series for that year. From 1903 a new conventional numbering system was introduced and was used until new construction ceased in 1910.

YORK provided the works of the York & North Midland Railway. Locomotive assembly ceased in 1884 but the repair workshops continued, and rebuilding of certain of the J77 class 0-6-0T's was carried out at York in 1899-1904. York has also been the site of the principal carriage works of the N.E.R. and subsequently one of the main carriage works of the L.N.E.R. The works of the Leeds Northern Railway at Leeds ceased to operate as a principal locomotive works at an earlier date.

Hull & Barnsley Railway

The Locomotive Carriage & Wagon Works for this railway were at SPRINGHEAD, Hull. Including the adjacent locomotive running shed, an area of some forty acres was covered. The works as such were closed in 1924 though they continued to be used for repairs as part of the running depot. No locomotives were built at Springhead but a considerable amount of rebuilding was undertaken.

North British Railway

The Locomotive & Carriage Works at COWLAIRS, Glasgow were erected in 1841 by the Edinburgh & Glasgow Railway for the opening of the line from Glasgow to Edinburgh. In 1846 the North British Railway constructed St. Margaret's Works at Edinburgh for general work of all kinds connected with that line.

Under the Edinburgh & Glasgow Railway twenty-two locomotives were built at Cowlairs. After the amalgamation of the Edinburgh & Glasgow Railway with the N.B.R. in 1865, Cowlairs became the headquarters of the locomotive department of the enlarged railway and from 1869 all new locomotive work was done there.

Doubt exists as to the exact number of new locomotives built at Cowlairs ; it is not clear whether some engines of earlier years should be regarded as new engines or rebuilds, but down to the cessation of new construction in 1924 with N15 9227, the total built at Cowlairs was around 900 engines. Cowlairs never allotted works or order numbers though doubtless some internal system of references existed for shop and accountancy purposes during construction. After the Grouping, Cowlairs continued as the principal L.N.E.R. locomotive works in Scotland, but owing to lack of capacity a number of N.B.R. locomotives were repaired at Inverurie, Gateshead and Darlington.

There were also other locomotive works owned by the N.B.R. At Kipps, erected in 1837 and originally owned by the Ballochney Railway (later part of the Monkland system before absorption by the N.B.R.), repairs were carried out until May 1925. St. Margaret's, the original works of 1846 mentioned above, continued to do repair work until November 1925. At Burntisland, locomotive repair was carried out until September 1923 at the works erected in 1847 by the Edinburgh & Northern Railway. Occasional heavy repairs were also carried out at Dundee shed, the last example being in March 1926.

Great North of Scotland Railway

The original works were at KITTYBREWSTER, Aberdeen. Owing to the very cramped conditions there, the construction of new works at INVERURIE for locomotive, carriage and permanent way departments was begun in 1898, the total area covering twenty-four acres. The Locomotive Department moved to Inverurie in 1902.

Two engines were built in the small works at Kittybrewster and ten engines by the G.N.S.R. at Inverurie. Works numbers were not used by either works. After Grouping repair activities were extended to include engines of several N.B.R. classes.

Midland & Great Northern Joint Railway

Although after formation of the joint committee, primary responsibility in locomotive matters had devolved on the Midland Railway, the works at MELTON CONSTABLE continued to deal with all repairs to the M. & G.N. locomotive stock and in fact was responsible for virtually new construction with the 0-6-0T's and 4-4-2T's, later classified as J93 and C17 after being taken over by the L.N.E.R. Furthermore during the 1914-18 War, the works manufactured parts for J6 class 0-6-0's then under construction at Doncaster. Melton Constable ceased repairing engines almost immediately after the L.N.E.R. took over responsibility for operation of the joint line in October 1936.

London & North Eastern Railway

The normal practice of the L.N.E.R. was to continue to allocate pre-Grouping designs to their parent company's works for repair, with new designs to one or more works according to location or availability of accommodation. Pressure of work led from time to time to many exceptions to the normal allocation. For example, in the early years of Grouping, several N.B. and G.E. engines were overhauled at Gateshead and Darlington ; a few years later some G.E. engines were overhauled at Doncaster and also at Gorton.

Later a definite overall repair scheme was promulgated. From time to time changes were made in this, mainly concerning L.N.E.R. designs, such changes being usually to suit available capacity and as a consequence of additions and withdrawals of stock. Even so it was not until the later years of the L.N.E.R. that radical rationalisation took place and as an example the G.N. saddletanks in the London area for many years made the long journey to and from Doncaster before it was decided to save mileage by repairing them at Stratford.

The repairs allocation between works as in 1945 gave the approximate final position under the L.N.E.R., though this was, of course, amended with subsequent additions to stock. It was as under :—

Doncaster : Tender—A1, A3, A4, A10, C1, D1, D2, D3, J1, J2, J3, J4, J5, J6, K3, K5, O2, O3, O6, O7, V2, W1.

Tank—C12, J50, J52, J55, N1, N2, U1, Y3.

DES1, Sentinel Cars.

Gorton : Tender—B3, B4, B5, B6, B7, B8, B9, B18, B19, C4, C5, D6, D9, D10, D11, J10, J11, J39, O1, O4, Q4.

Tank—A5, C13, C14, F1, F2, J60, J62, J63, J67, J69, L3, M1, N4, N5, Q1, S1, Y3.

Sentinel Cars.

Stratford : Tender—B1, B2, B12/3, B17, D9, D15, D16, E4, J15, J17, J19, J20.

Tank—F3, F4, F5, F6, H2, J52, J65, J66, J67, J68, J69, J70, J93, L1, L2, M2, N7, V1, V3, Y3, Y4, Y6, Y10, Y11.

Darlington : Tender—A2/1, B1, B15, B16, C6, C7, D17, D20, D21, D49, J21, J24, J25, J26, J27, O6, O7, Q5, Q6, Q7, V2.

Tank—A5, A6, A7, A8, G5, J71, J72, J73, J75, J77, N8, N9, N10, N11, N12, N13, Q1, T1, V1, V3, Y1, Y3, Y7, Y8.

Sentinel Cars.

Cowlairs : Tender—A2/2, B1, D1, D11, D29, D30, D32, D33, D34, J35, J36, J37, J38, J39, K2, K3, K4, O7, V4.

Tank—C15, C16, F7, J72, J83, J88, N2, N14, N15, Q1, Y9.

Sentinel Cars.

Inverurie : Tender—B12, D31, D40, D41, D42, J36.

Tank—G10, J67, J69, Y9, Z4, Z5.

97

LIST OF NAMED ENGINES

NOTE.—The punctuation, or lack of it, in the list below is believed to be **correct.**

Gresley A1 (later A10) and A3 4-6-2 Classes

2500	35	Windsor Lad	2561	62	Minoru	2598	87	Blenheim
2501	36	Colombo	2562	63	Isinglass	2599	88	Book Law
2502	37	Hyperion	2563	64	William Whitelaw	2743	89	Felstead
2503	38	Firdaussi			(8/41)Tagalie	2744	90	Grand Parade
2504	39	Sandwich	2564	65	Knight of the	2745	91	Captain Cuttle
2505	40	Cameronian			Thistle	2746	92	Fairway
2506	41	Salmon Trout			(12/32) Knight of	2747	93	Coronach
2507	42	Singapore			Thistle	2748	94	Colorado
2508	43	Brown Jack	2565	66	Merry Hampton	2749	95	Flamingo
2543	44	Melton	2566	67	Ladas	2750	96	Papyrus
2544	45	Lemberg	2567	68	Sir Visto	2751	97	Humorist
2545	46	Diamond Jubilee	2568	69	Sceptre	2752	98	Spion Kop
2546	47	Donovan	2569	70	Gladiateur	2795	99	Call Boy
2547	48	Doncaster	2570	71	Tranquil	2796	100	Spearmint
2548	49	Galtee More	2571	72	Sunstar	2797	101	Cicero
2549	50	Persimmon	2572	73	St Gatien	4471	102	Sir Frederick
2550	51	Blink Bonny	2573	74	Harvester			Banbury
2551	52	Prince Palatine	2574	75	St Frusquin	4472	103	Flying Scotsman
2552	53	Sansovino	2575	76	Galopin	4473	104	Solario
2553	54	Manna	2576	77	The White Knight	4474	105	Victor Wild
		(11/26) Prince of	2577	78	Night Hawk	4475	106	Flying Fox
		Wales	2578	79	Bayardo	4476	107	Royal Lancer
2554	55	Woolwinder	2579	80	Dick Turpin	4477	108	Gay Crusader
2555	56	Centenary	2580	81	Shotover	4478	109	Hermit
2556	57	Ormonde	2581	82	Neil Gow	4479	110	Robert the Devil
2557	58	Blair Athol	2582	83	Sir Hugo	4480	111	Enterprise
2558	59	Tracery	2595	84	Trigo	4481	112	St Simon
2559	60	The Tetrarch	2596	85	Manna	4470	113	*Great Northern
2560	61	Pretty Polly	2597	86	Gainsborough			

*Later rebuilt to class A1/1 (Thompson).

Peppercorn A1 Class 4-6-2

60114	W. P. Allen	60131	Osprey	60147	North Eastern
60115	Meg Merrilies	60132	Marmion	60148	Aboyeur
60116	Hal o' the Wynd	60133	Pommern	60149	Amadis
60117	Bois Roussel	60134	Foxhunter	60150	Willbrook
60118	Archibald Sturrock	60135	Madge Wildfire	60151	Midlothian
60119	Patrick Stirling	60136	Alcazar	60152	Holyrood
60120	Kittiwake	60137	Redgauntlet	60153	Flamboyant
60121	Silurian	60138	Boswell	60154	Bon Accord
60122	Curlew	60139	Sea Eagle	60155	Borderer
60123	H. A. Ivatt	60140	Balmoral	60156	Great Central
60124	Kenilworth	60141	Abbotsford	60157	Great Eastern
60125	Scottish Union	60142	Edward Fletcher	60158	Aberdonian
60126	Sir Vincent Raven	60143	Sir Walter Scott	60159	Bonnie Dundee
60127	Wilson Worsdell	60144	King's Courier	60160	Auld Reekie
60128	Bongrace	60145	Saint Mungo	60161	North British
60129	Guy Mannering	60146	Peregrine	60162	Saint Johnstoun
60130	Kestrel				

Peppercorn A2 Class 4-6-2

525	A. H. Peppercorn	E530	Sayajirao	60535	Hornets Beauty
526	Sugar Palm	E531	Bahram	60536	Trimbush
E527	Sun Chariot	60532	Blue Peter	60537	Bachelors Button
E528	Tudor Minstrel	60533	Happy Knight	60538	Velocity
E529	Pearl Diver	60534	Irish Elegance	60539	Bronzino

Raven A2 Class 4-6-2

2400	City of Newcastle	2402	City of York	2403	City of Durham
2401	City of Kingston upon Hull			2404	City of Ripon

Thompson A2/I Class 4-6-2

3696	507	Highland Chieftain	3698	509	Waverley	3699	510 Robert the Bruce
3697	508	Duke of Rothesay					

Thompson A2/3 Class 4-6-2

500	Edward Thompson	515	Sun Stream	520	Owen Tudor
511	Airborne	516	Hycilla	521	Watling Street
512	Steady Aim	517	Ocean Swell	522	Straight Deal
513	Dante	518	Tehran	523	Sun Castle
514	Chamossaire	519	Honeyway	524	Herringbone

Gresley Streamlined A4 Class 4-6-2

4500	1	Garganey	2512	17	Silver Fox
		(3/39) Sir Ronald Matthews	4463	18	Sparrow Hawk
4499	2	Pochard	4464	19	Bittern
		(4/39) Sir Murrough Wilson	4465	20	Guillemot
4494	3	Osprey	4467	21	Wild Swan
		(10/42) Andrew K. McCosh	4468	22	Mallard
4462	4	Great Snipe	4469	—	Gadwall
		(7/41) William Whitelaw			(3/39) Sir Ralph Wedgwood
4901	5	Capercaillie	4482	23	Golden Eagle
		(9/42) Charles H. Newton	4483	24	Kingfisher
		(6/43) Sir Charles Newton	4484	25	Falcon
4466	6	Herring Gull	4485	26	Kestrel
		(1/44) Sir Ralph Wedgwood			(11/47) Miles Beevor
4498	7	Sir Nigel Gresley	4486	27	Merlin
4496	8	Golden Shuttle	4487	28	Sea Eagle
		(9/45) Dwight D. Eisenhower			(10/47) Walter K. Whigham
4488	9	Union of South Africa	4493	29	Woodcock
4489	10	Woodcock	4495	30	Great Snipe
		(6/37) Dominion of Canada			(9/37) Golden Fleece
4490	11	Empire of India	4497	31	Golden Plover
4491	12	Commonwealth of Australia	4900	32	Gannet
4492	13	Dominion of New Zealand	4902	33	Seagull
2509	14	Silver Link	4903	34	Peregrine
2510	15	Quicksilver			(3/48) Lord Faringdon
2511	16	Silver King			

" Antelope " BI Class 4-6-0

8301	1000	Springbok	1021	Reitbok	1215	William Henton	
8302	1001	Eland	1022	Sassaby		Carver	
8303	1002	Impala	1023	Hirola	1221	Sir Alexander	
8304	1003	Gazelle	1024	Addax		Erskine-Hill	
8305	1004	Oryx	1025	Pallah	1237	Geoffrey H Kitson	
8306	1005	Bongo	1026	Ourebi	1238	Leslie Runciman	
8307	1006	Blackbuck	1027	Madoqua	1240	Harry Hinchliffe	
8308	1007	Klipspringer	1028	Umseke	1241	Viscount Ridley	
8309	1008	Kudu	1029	Chamois	1242	Alexander Reith	
8310	1009	Hartebeeste	1030	Nyala		Gray	
	1010	Wildebeeste	1031	Reedbuck	1243	Sir Harold Mitchell	
	1011	Waterbuck	1032	Stembok	1244	Strang Steel	
	1012	Puku	1033	Dibatag	1245	Murray of Elibank	
	1013	Topi	1034	Chiru	1246	Lord Balfour of	
	1014	Oribi	1035	Pronghorn		Burleigh	
	1015	Duiker	1036	Ralph Assheton	1247	Lord Burghley	
	1016	Inyala	1037	Jairou	1248	Geoffrey Gibbs	
	1017	Bushbuck	1038	Blacktail	1249	Fitzherbert Wright	
	1018	Gnu	1039	Steinbok	1250	A Harold Bibby	
	1019	Nilghai	1040	Roedeer	1251	Oliver Bury	
	1020	Gemsbok	1189	Sir William Gray	61379	Mayflower (from 7/51)	

Great Central "Sir Sam Fay" B2 (later B19) Class 4-6-0

5423 1490 Sir Sam Fay
5424 — City of Lincoln
5425 1491 City of Manchester

5426 — City of Chester
5427 1492 City of London (removed 9/37)
5428 1493 City of Liverpool

Great Central "Lord Faringdon" B3 Class 4-6-0

6169 1494 Lord Faringdon
6164 1495 Earl Beatty
6165 1496 Valour

6166 1497 Earl Haig (removed 10/43)
6167 1498 Lloyd George (removed 8/23)
6168 — Lord Stuart of Wortley

Great Central "Immingham" B4 Class 4-6-0

6097 1482 Immingham

Great Central "Glenalmond" B8 Class 4-6-0

5004 1349 Glenalmond
5439 1350 Sutton Nelthorpe

5446 1357 Earl Roberts of
  Kandahar

5279 1358 Earl Kitchener of
  Khartoum

"Sandringham" B17 and B2 4-6-0 Classes

2800 1600 Sandringham
2801 1601 Holkham
2802 1602 Walsingham
2803 1603 Framlingham
2804 1604 Elveden
2805 1605 Burnham Thorpe
  (4/38) Lincolnshire
  Regiment
2806 1606 Audley End
2807 1607 Blickling
2808 1608 Gunton
2809 1609 Quidenham
2810 1610 Honingham Hall
2811 1611 Raynham Hall
2812 1612 Houghton Hall
2813 1613 Woodbastwick Hall
2814 1614 Castle Hedingham
2815 1615 Culford Hall
2816 1616 Fallodon
2817 1617 Ford Castle
2818 1618 Wynyard Park
2819 1619 Welbeck Abbey
2820 1620 Clumber
2821 1621 Hatfield House
2822 1622 Alnwick Castle
2823 1623 Lambton Castle
2824 1624 Lumley Castle
2825 1625 Raby Castle
2826 1626 Brancepeth Castle
2827 1627 Aske Hall
2828 1628 Harewood House

2829 1629 Naworth Castle
2830 1630 Thoresby Park
  (1/38) Tottenham
  Hotspur
2831 1631 Serlby Hall
2832 1632 Belvoir Castle
  (10/58) Royal
  Sovereign
2833 1633 Kimbolton Castle
2834 1634 Hinchingbrooke
2835 1635 Milton
2836 1636 Harlaxton Manor
2837 1637 Thorpe Hall
2838 1638 Melton Hall
2839 1639 Rendlesham Hall
  (1/38) Norwich
  City
2840 1640 Somerleyton Hall
2841 1641 Gayton Hall
2842 1642 Kilverstone Hall
2843 1643 Champion Lodge
2844 1644 Earlham Hall
2845 1645 The Suffolk
  Regiment
2846 1646 Gilwell Park
2847 1647 Helmingham Hall
2848 1648 Arsenal
2849 1649 Sheffield United
2850 1650 Grimsby Town
2851 1651 Derby County
2852 1652 Darlington

2853 1653 Huddersfield Town
2854 1654 Sunderland
2855 1655 Middlesbrough
2856 1656 Leeds United
2857 1657 Doncaster Rovers
2858 1658 Newcastle United
  (6/36) The Essex
  Regiment
2859 1659 Norwich City
  (9/37) East
  Anglian
2860 1660 Hull City
2861 1661 Sheffield Wednesday
2862 1662 Manchester United
2863 1663 Everton
2864 1664 Liverpool
2865 1665 Leicester City
2866 1666 Nottingham Forest
2867 1667 Bradford
2868 1668 Bradford City
2869 1669 Barnsley
2870 1670 Manchester City
  (5/37) Tottenham
  Hotspur
  (9/37) City of
  London
2871 1671 Manchester City
  (4/46) Royal
  Sovereign
2872 1672 West Ham United

Great Northern C2 Class 4-4-2

3990 Henry Oakley

Great Central C5 Class 4-4-2

5258 2895 The Rt. Hon. Viscount Cross
  G.C.B. G.C.S.I.
5259 2896 King Edward VII

5364 2897 Lady Faringdon
5365 2898 Sir William Pollitt

North British C10 and C11 4-4-2 Classes

9868 Aberdonian	9876 Waverley	9903 Cock o' the North
9869 Bonnie Dundee	9877 Liddesdale	(5/34) Aberdonian
9870 Bon-Accord	9878 Hazeldean	9904 Holyrood
9871 Thane of Fife	9879 Abbotsford	9905 Buccleuch
9872 Auld Reekie	9880 Tweeddale	9906 Teribus
9873 Saint Mungo	9881 Borderer	9509 Duke of Rothesay
9874 Dunedin	9901 St. Johnstoun	9510 The Lord Provost
9875 Midlothian	9902 Highland Chief	

Great Central D9 Class 4-4-0

6021 2307 Queen Mary	5104 — Queen Alexandra	5110 — King George V

Great Central " Director " D10 Class 4-4-0

5429 2650 Prince Henry	5433 2654 Walter Burgh Gair	5436 2657 Sir Berkeley
5430 2651 Purdon Viccars	5434 2655 The Earl of Kerry	Sheffield
5431 2652 Edwin A. Beazley	5435 2656 Sir Clement Royds	5437 2658 Prince George
5432 2653 Sir Edward Fraser		5438 2659 Worsley Taylor

Great Central " Director " D11 Class 4-4-0

5506 2660 Butler-Henderson	6385 2678 Luckie Mucklebackit
5507 2661 Gerard Powys Dewhurst	6386 2679 Lord Glenallan
5508 2662 Prince of Wales	6387 2680 Lucy Ashton
5509 2663 Prince Albert	6388 2681 Captain Craigengelt
5510 2664 Princess Mary	6389 2682 Haystoun of Bucklaw
5501 2665 Mons	6390 2683 Hobbie Elliott
5502 2666 Zeebrugge	6391 2684 Wizard of the Moor
5503 2667 Somme	6392 2685 Malcolm Graeme
5504 2668 Jutland	6393 2686 The Fiery Cross
5505 2669 Ypres	6394 2687 Lord James of Douglas
5511 2670 Marne	6395 2688 Ellen Douglas
6378 2671 Bailie Macwheeble	6396 2689 Maid of Lorn
6379 2672 Baron of Bradwardine	6397 2690 The Lady of the Lake
6380 2673 Evan Dhu	6398 2691 Laird of Balmawhapple
6381 2674 Flora MacIvor	6399 2692 Allan-Bane
6382 2675 Colonel Gardiner	6400 2693 Roderick Dhu
6383 2676 Jonathan Oldbuck	6401 2694 James Fitzjames
6384 2677 Edie Ochiltree	

Great Eastern " Claud " D14, D15 and D16 4-4-0 Classes

8900 2500 Claud Hamilton
2546 Claud Hamilton (from 8/47)

North British " Scott " D29 Class 4-4-0

9895 2400 Rob Roy	9243 2406 Meg Merrilies	9340 2411 Lady of Avenel
9896 2401 Dandie Dinmont	9244 2407 Madge Wildfire	9359 2412 Dirk Hatteraick
9897 2402 Redgauntlet	9245 2408 Bailie Nicol Jarvie	9360 2413 Guy Mannering
9898 2403 Sir Walter Scott	9338 2409 Helen Macgregor	9361 — Vich Ian Vohr
9899 2404 Jeanie Deans	9339 2410 Ivanhoe	9362 2415 Ravenswood
9900 2405 The Fair Maid		

North British " Scott " D30 Class 4-4-0

9400 — The Dougal Cratur	9416 2425 Ellangowan	9425 2434 Kettledrummle
9363 2417 Hal o' the Wynd	9417 2426 Cuddie Headrigg	9426 2435 Norna
9409 2418 The Pirate	9418 2427 Dumbiedykes	9427 2436 Lord Glenvarloch
9410 2419 Meg Dods	9419 2428 The Talisman	9428 2437 Adam Woodcock
9411 2420 Dominie Sampson	(Talisman for various periods)	9497 2438 Peter Poundtext
9412 2421 Laird o' Monk-	9420 2429 The Abbot	9498 2439 Father Ambrose
barns	9421 2430 Jingling Geordie	9499 2440 Wandering Willie
9413 2422 Caleb Balderstone	9422 2431 Kenilworth	9500 2441 Black Duncan
9414 2423 Dugald Dalgetty	9423 2432 Quentin Durward	9501 2442 Simon Glover
9415 2424 Claverhouse	9424 2433 Lady Rowena	

North British "Glen" D34 Class 4-4-0

9149	2467	Glenfinnan	9291	2478	Glen Quoich
9221	2468	Glen Orchy	9298	2479	Glen Sheil
9256	2469	Glen Douglas	9153	2480	Glen Fruin
9258	2470	Glen Roy	9241	2481	Glen Ogle
9266	2471	Glen Falloch	9242	2482	Glen Mamie
9307	2472	Glen Nevis	9270	2483	Glen Garry
9405	2473	Glen Spean	9278	2484	Glen Lyon
9406	2474	Glen Croe	9281	2485	Glen Murran
9407	2475	Glen Beasdale	9287	—	Glen Gyle
9408	2476	Glen Sloy	9503	2487	Glen Arklet
9100	2477	Glen Dochart	9504	2488	Glen Aladale

9490	2489	Glen Dessary
9502	2490	Glen Fintaig
9505	2491	Glen Cona
9034	2492	Glen Garvin
9035	2493	Glen Gloy
9492	2494	Glen Gau
	(7/25)	Glen Gour
9493	2495	Glen Luss
9494	2496	Glen Loy
9495	2497	Glen Mallie
9496	2498	Glen Moidart

Great North of Scotland D40 Class 4-4-0

6845	2273	George Davidson	6848	2276	Andrew Bain	6852	2279	Glen Grant
6846	2274	Benachie	6849	2277	Gordon Highlander	6854	2280	Southesk
6847	2275	Sir David Stewart	6850	2278	Hatton Castle			

"Shire" and "Hunt" D49 Class 4-4-0

234	2700	Yorkshire
251	2701	Derbyshire
253	2702	Oxfordshire
256	2703	Hertfordshire
264	2704	Stirlingshire
265	2705	Lanarkshire
266	2706	Forfarshire
236	2707	Lancashire
270	2708	Argyllshire
277	2709	Berwickshire
245	2710	Lincolnshire
281	2711	Dumbartonshire
246	2712	Morayshire
249	2713	Aberdeenshire
250	2714	Perthshire
306	2715	Roxburghshire
307	2716	Kincardineshire
309	2717	Banffshire
310	2718	Kinross-shire
311	2719	Peebles-shire
318	2720	Cambridgeshire
320	2721	Warwickshire
322	2722	Huntingdonshire
327	2723	Nottinghamshire
335	2724	Bedfordshire
329	2725	Inverness-shire

352	2726	Leicestershire
	(6/32)	The Meynell
336	2727	Buckinghamshire
	(5/32)	The Quorn
2753	2728	Cheshire
2754	2729	Rutlandshire
2755	2730	Berkshire
2756	2731	Selkirkshire
2757	2732	Dumfries-shire
2758	2733	Northumberland
2759	2734	Cumberland
2760	2735	Westmorland
201	2736	The Bramham Moor
211	2737	The York and Ainsty
220	2738	The Zetland
232	2739	The Badsworth
235	2740	The Bedale
247	2741	The Blankney
255	2742	The Braces of Derwent
269	2743	The Cleveland
273	2744	The Holderness
282	2745	The Hurworth
283	2746	The Middleton
288	2747	The Percy
292	2748	The Southwold
297	2749	The Cottesmore

*Later rebuilt to class D.

298	2750	The Pytchley
205	2751	The Albrighton
214	2752	The Atherstone
217	2753	The Belvoir
222	2754	The Berkeley
226	2755	The Bilsdale
230	2756	The Brocklesby
238	2757	The Burton
258	2758	The Cattistock
274	2759	The Craven
279	2760	The Cotswold
353	2761	The Derwent
357	2762	The Fernie
359	2763	The Fitzwilliam
361	2764	The Garth
362	2765	The Goathland
363	2766	The Grafton
364	2767	The Grove
365	2768	*The Morpeth
366	2769	The Oakley
368	2770	The Puckeridge
370	2771	The Rufford
374	2772	The Sinnington
375	2773	The South Durham
376	2774	The Staintondale
377	2775	The Tynedale

North British J36 Class 0-6-0

9605	—	St. Quentin
9608	—	Foch
9615	—	Verdun
9620	—	Rawlinson
9621	—	Monro
9627	—	Petain
9628	5216	Byng
9176	5217	French
9631	—	Aisne

9643	5219	Arras
9646	5222	Somme
9647	5223	Albert
9648	5224	Mons
9650	5226	Haig
9657	5233	Plumer
9659	5235	Gough
9660	5236	Horne
9661	—	Ole Bill

9662	—	Birdwood
9666	—	Marne
9673	5243	Maude
9676	—	Reims*
9682	5253	Joffre
9611	5268	Allenby
9612	5269	Ypres
65311		Haig (from 1953)

*Or Rheims—see page 56.

Great Northern K2 Class 2-6-0

4674 1764 Loch Arkaig	4692 1782 Loch Eil	4699 1789 Loch Laidon
4682 1772 Loch Lochy	4693 1783 Loch Sheil	4700 1790 Loch Lomond
4684 1774 Loch Garry	4697 1787 Loch Quoich	4701 1791 Loch Laggan
4685 1775 Loch Treig	4698 1788 Loch Rannoch	4704 1794 Loch Oich
4691 1781 Loch Morar		

K4 Class 2-6-0

3441 1993 Loch Long	3444 1996 Lord of the Isles
3442 1994 MacCailein Mór	3445 1997*MacCailin Mór
(7/38) The Great Marquess	3446 1998 Lord of Dunvegan
3443 1995 Cameron of Lochiel	(3/39) MacLeod of MacLeod

*Later rebuilt to class K1/1.

Metropolitan M2 Class 0-6-4T

6154 — Lord Aberconway	6156 9077 Charles Jones
6155 9076 Robert H Selbie	6157 — Brill

P2 Class 2-8-2 (later rebuilt to Class A2/2 4-6-2)

2001 501 Cock o' the North	2003 503 Lord President	2005 505 Thane of Fife
2002 502 Earl Marischal	2004 504 Mons Meg	2006 506 Wolf of Badenoch

" Green Arrow " V2 Class 2-6-2

4771 800 Green Arrow	4831 860 Durham School
4780 809 The Snapper	4843 872 King's Own Yorkshire Light
The East Yorkshire Regiment— The Duke of York's Own	Infantry
4806 835 The Green Howard	4844 873 Coldstreamer
Alexandra, Princess of Wales's Own Yorkshire Regiment	60964 The Durham Light Infantry (from 4/58)
4818 847 St. Peter's School York A.D. 627	

" Bantam Cock " V4 Class 2-6-2

3401 1700 Bantam Cock

North Eastern XI Class 2-2-4T

66 Aerolite

Clayton Steam Railcars§

285 Rapid	2101 Union	43303 Railway
287 Royal Sailor	2110 Comet	43304 Bang Up
289 Wellington	2121 Pilot	43305 Transit
296 Wonder	43302 Chevy Chase	

Sentinel Steam Railcars (100 h.p. 2-cylinder)§

21 Valliant	226 Ebor	263 North Star
22 Brilliant	237 Rodney	265 Neptune
26 Tally-Ho	238 Yorkshire Huzzar	267 Liberty
29 Rockingham	244 True Briton	272 Hero
210 Highflyer	250 Rob Roy	273 Trafalgar
212 Eclipse	253 Red Rover	283 Teazle
220 Waterwitch	254 Phoenix	2135 Integrity
225 True Blue	255 Perseverance	

Sentinel Steam Railcars (200 h.p. twin-engine)

220 Defence	248 Tantivy	2283 Old Blue
246 Royal Sovereign	2281 Old John Bull	

§The final numbers of these railcars have been used throughout.

Sentinel Steam Railcars (100 h.p, 6-cylinder)§

31 Flower of Yarrow	2144 Traveller	2257 Defiance
32 Fair Maid	2145 Ruby	2261 Diligence
33 Highland Chieftain	2147 Woodpecker	2267 Recovery
34 Tweedside	2151 Umpire	2268 Emerald
35 Nettle	2152 Courrier	2270 Independent
36 Royal Eagle	2198 Times	2271 Industry
37 Clydesdale	2200 Surprise	2276 North Briton
38 Pearl	2217 Royal Charlotte	2279 Norfolk
39 Protector	2218 Telegraph	31073 Quicksilver
310 Prince Regent	2219 New Fly	51908 Expedition
312 Retaliator	2231 Swift	51909 Waterloo
313 Banks of Don	2232 Alexander	51912 Rising Sun
314 Queen of Beauty	2235 Britannia	51913 Rival
2133 Cleveland	2236 British Queen	51914 Royal Forester
2136 Hope	2238 Celerity	43301 Commerce
2139 Hark Forward	2242 Cornwallis	
2140 Eagle	2245 Criterion	

§The final numbers of these railcars have been used throughout.

Sentinel Steam Twin Articulated Railcar

2291 Phenomena

Armstrong-Whitworth Diesel-Electric Railcars

25 Tyneside Venturer	224 Lady Hamilton	232 Northumbrian

Electric Locomotives named by British Railways
Class EM1

6701 26000 Tommy (from 6/52)

26046 Archimedes	26050 Stentor	26054 Pluto
26047 Diomedes	26051 Mentor	26055 Prometheus
26048 Hector	26052 Nestor	26056 Triton
26049 Jason	26053 Perseus	26057 Ulysses

Class EM2

27000 Electra	27003 Diana	27005 Minerva
27001 Ariadne	27004 Juno	27006 Pandora
27002 Aurora		

L.N.E.R. LOCOMOTIVE CLASSES AND PARTS

The list that follows features every locomotive class and subdivision (Part) used officially by the L.N.E.R. and its successors. The following explanatory notes on the column headings will be found helpful :—

(i) Column 3—Pre- and post-Grouping classifications are included in this column, as appropriate.

(ii) Column 4—Where more than one designer is shown, the original designer's name is the last one, the other(s) being responsible for the modifications.

(iii) Column 5—(a) The dates shown are when the class (or part) designation was introduced generally, except that where the class (or part) existed at Grouping, then the date is that of the oldest locomotive which became L.N.E.R. stock.
(b) These dates are not necessarily when the actual change was made ; frequently changes were not recognised by reclassification until some time afterwards.

(iv) Column 6—Only the briefest mention is made in this column of the differences causing the separate classification. Full details of these variations, and the dates they were applicable to individual engines, are included in the respective class articles.

104

1	2	3	4	5	6	7	8
Class	Section	Former Class	Designer	Date Class'n Introduced	Notes	Date Class'n Extinct	Disposal
4-6-2							
A	LNE	P2	Thompson/Gresley	1/43	Rebuilt from P2 class 2-8-2	5/43	Reclassified A2
A	LNE	—	Thompson/Gresley	5/44	Modification of V2 class 2-6-2	6/44	Reclassified A2/1
A1	GN	A1	Gresley	4/22	20" cyls., 180lb. pressure	12/24	Class divided into Parts 1 & 2
A1	GN & LNE	A1/1					Remaining 18 reclassified A10
A1	LNE	A1/2	Gresley	12/34	Parts 1 & 2 combined (alike from 9/33)	5/45	Remaining 18 reclassified A10
A1	LNE	A1	Gresley	9/45	Rebuild of engine 4470—250lb. pressure, separate valve gear	1/48	Reclassified A1/1
A1/1	BR	A1	Peppercorn	8/48	G.N. gauge (13' 4" max. height)	—	43 in stock at 31st Dec. 1962
A1/1	GN	A1	Gresley	12/24	A1 reclassified	9/33	Last (4477) altered to L.N.E. gauge
A1/2	LNE	4.6.2.	Thompson/Gresley	1/48	L.N.E. gauge (13' 2" max. height)	11/62	Only engine (60113) withdrawn
A2	LNE	A	Gresley	12/22	—	12/34	Reclassified A1
A2	NE	—	Raven	5/43	A reclassified	12/31	Reclassified A2/1
A2/1	LNE	A2	Thompson/Gresley	5/46	Standard design with 6' 2" coupled wheels	10/45	Reclassified A2/2
A2/1	LNE	A2	Peppercorn	12/47	Rebuild with G.N.-design boiler	4/47	Reclassified A2/3
A2/1	NE	A2/1	Gresley/Raven	9/29	A2 reclassified	—	7 in stock at 31st Dec., 1962
A2/2	LNE	A	Raven	12/31	A reclassified	12/31	Reclassified A2/2
A2/2	LNE	A2/1	Thompson/Gresley	6/44	A2/1 reclassified	5/37	Last engine (2403) withdrawn
A2/3	LNE	A2/2	Gresley/Raven	12/31	A2 reclassified	2/61	Last engine (60508) withdrawn
A3	LNE	A1	Thompson/Gresley	10/45	A1 reboilered with 220lb. pressure	2/37	Only engine (2404) withdrawn
A3/1	LNE	A1	Thompson	4/47	Parts 1, 2 & 3 combined (alike from 8/34)	7/61	Last engine (60502) withdrawn
A3/2	LNE	A1	Gresley	7/27	Engines retaining 20" cyls.	—	7 in stock at 31st Dec., 1962
A3/3	LNE	A1	Gresley	12/36	Cyls. lined to 18¼"	8/28	Class divided into Parts 1 & 2
A4	LNE	—	Gresley	8/28	Built with, or altered to, 19" cyls.	—	59 in stock at 31st Dec. 1962
A4/1	LNE	A4	Gresley	9/35	Middle cyl. lined to 17" from 18½"	8/34	Only engine (4480) altered to 19" cyls.
A10	LNE	A1	Gresley	5/45	250lb. pressure, streamlined	4/32	Only engine (2544) altered to 19" cyls.
						12/36	Reclassified A3
							27 in stock at 31st Dec., 1962
							2 in stock at 31st Dec. 1962
							Last engine (60068) rebuilt to A3
4-6-2T							
A5	GC	9N	Robinson	3/11	G.C. gauge, R.H. drive	12/48	Reclassified A5/1
A5 (LNE)	LNE	A5	Gresley/Robinson	9/25	L.N.E. gauge, L.H. drive	12/48	Reclassified A5/2
A5/1	GC	A5	Robinson	12/48	A5 reclassified	11/60	Last engine (69820) withdrawn
A5/2	LNE	A5 (LNE)			A5 reclassified		
A6	NE	W	Gresley/Robinson	12/48	Rebuilds of 4-6-0T's, first built 12/07	12/58	Last engine (69837) withdrawn
A7	NE	Y	Raven/W. Worsdell	1915	With 5' 6" boiler	3/53	Last engines (69796) withdrawn
A7/1	NE	A7	Raven	10/10	Rebuild with 4' 9" diag. 63B boiler	12/57	Last engines (69772/82) withdrawn
A8	LNE	H1	Thompson/Raven	9/43	Rebuilds from H1 class 4-4-4T's	6/60	Last engine (69786) withdrawn
A9	—	—	Gresley/Raven	7/31	Never used		Last engines (69870/8) withdrawn
			—				—
4-6-0							
B	LNE	—	Thompson	12/42	Standard general utility type	4/43	Reclassified B1
B1	GC	8C	Robinson	12/03	Built to compare with 4-4-2 (L.N.E.R. C4)	4/43	Reclassified B18
B1	LNE	B	Thompson	4/43	B reclassified	—	288 in stock at 31st Dec., 1962
B2	GC	1	Robinson	12/12	6' 9" coupled wheels and two inside cyls.	12/37	Class divided into Parts 1 & 2
B2	LNE	B17	Thompson/Gresley	8/45	2 cyl. rebuilds with 225lb. pressure	12/59	Last engine (61607) withdrawn

4-6-0 (contd.)

Class	Section	Former Class	Designer	Date Class'n Introduced	Notes	Date Class'n Extinct	Disposal
B2/1	GC	B2	Robinson	12/37	Retaining original 21¾" cyls.	8/45	Reclassified B19/1
B2/2	GC	B2	Robinson	12/37	With cyls. lined to 20⅞"	8/45	Reclassified B19/2
B3	GC	9P	Robinson	11/17	6' 9" coupled wheels and four cyls.	12/29	Class divided into Parts 1 & 2
B3/1	GC	B3	Robinson	12/29	Retaining orig. Stephenson valve gear	12/47	Last engine (1496) withdrawn
B3/2	GC	B3	Gresley/Robinson	12/29	Rebuilt from 9/29 with Caprotti valve gear	12/47	Last engine (1498) withdrawn
B3/3	GC	B3/2	Thompson/Robinson	10/43	Rebuild of engine 6166—2 cyls., Walschaert gear and 225lb. pressure	4/47	Only engine (61497) withdrawn
B4	GC	8F	Robinson	5/06	6' 7" coupled wheels and two outside cyls.	12/27	Class divided into Parts 1 & 2
B4/1	GC	B4	Robinson	12/27	Original saturated engines	10/28	Last engine (6098) superheated, to Part 2
B4/1	GC	B4/2	Robinson	12/28	Over 13' 0", sup., piston valves, 21" cyls.	8/40	Last engine (6100) cut down, to Part 3
B4/2	GC	B4	Robinson	12/27	Original dimensions but superheated	12/28	Engines reclassified by cyls. and valves
B4/2	GC	B4/2	Robinson	12/28	Over 13' 0", slide valves, 19" cyls.	8/40	Last engine (6097) cut down, to Part 4
B4/3	GC	B4/1	Robinson	8/34	Under 13' 0", piston valves, 21" cyls.	9/49	Last engine (1483) withdrawn
B4/4	GC	B4/2	Robinson	2/36	Under 13' 0", slide valves, 19" cyls.	11/50	Last engine (1482) withdrawn
B5	GC	8	Robinson	11/02	6' 1" coupled wheels and two outside cyls.	12/25	Class divided into Parts 1 & 2
B5	GC	B5	Robinson	12/25	Parts combined, but diff. cyls. marked	6/50	Last engine (1686) withdrawn
B5/1	GC	B5/1	Robinson	12/25	Original saturated engines	1/34	Last engine (6070) cut down below 13' 0"
B5/1	GC	B5	Robinson	1/34	Saturated engines, under 13' 0"	5/36	Last engine (6070) superheated, to B5/3
B5/2	GC	B5	Robinson	12/25	Rebuild (6/23) with 5' 0" superheated boiler	12/27	Only engine (5184) reverted to 4' 9" boiler
B5/3	GC	B5/1	Robinson	1/26	Superheated, under 13' 0", both 19" and 21" cyls.	12/37	Reclassified B5, all now sup. and under 13' 0"
B6	GC	8N	Robinson	7/18	5' 8" coupled wheels and two outside cyls.	12/47	Last engines (1347/8) withdrawn
B7/1	GC	9Q	Robinson	5/21	5' 7" coupled wheels, 4 cyls., over 13' 0"	2/50	Last engine (61705) withdrawn
B7/2	LNE	9Q	Robinson	8/23	As B7/1 but max. height under 13' 0"	7/50	Last engine (61711) withdrawn
B8	GC	1A	Robinson	6/13	5' 7" coupled wheels and two inside cyls.	12/38	Class divided into Parts 1 & 2
B8/1	GC	B8	Robinson	12/38	Retaining original 21¾" cyls.	4/49	Last engine (1357) withdrawn
B8/2	GC	B8	Robinson	12/38	With cyls. lined to 20⅞" from 6/27	11/47	Last engine (1349) withdrawn
B9	GC	8G	Robinson	9/06	5' 3" coupled wheels and two outside cyls.	12/24	Class divided into Parts 1 & 2
B9	GC	B9/2	Robinson	12/24	Part 2 reclassified (all same boiler from 4/29)	5/49	Last engine (1475) withdrawn
B9/1	GC	B9	Robinson	12/24	Retaining saturated 5' 0" boiler	4/29	Last engine (6114) superheated
B9/2	GC	B9	Robinson	12/24	With sup. 4' 9" boiler at higher pitch, from 10/24	12/37	Reclassified B9, but cyl. diam. marked
B10-B11	—	—	—	—	Never used	—	—
B12	GE	S69	S. D. Holden	12/11	5' 1¾" boiler with Belpaire firebox	11/54	Last engine (61539) withdrawn
B12 (LNE)	—	—	Gresley/S. D. Holden	9/28	With diag. 99 boiler and Lentz poppet valves	12/31	Reclassified B12/2
B12/1	LNE	B12 (LNE)	—	—	Never used officially—always B12	—	—
B12/2	LNE	B12 (LNE)	Gresley/S. D. Holden	12/31	B12 (LNE) reclassified	1/34	Last engine (8577) reboilered to Part 3
B12/3	LNE	B12	Gresley/S. D. Holden	5/32	Rebuilds with long travel valves, 5' 6" boiler, R.T. firebox	9/61	Last engine (61572) withdrawn
B12 (25A)	LNE	B12	Thompson/S. D. Holden	7/43	Rebuilds with 5' 1¾" diag. 25A boilers with R.T. firebox	12/48	Reclassified B12/4
B12/4	LNE	B12 (25A)	Thompson/S. D. Holden	12/48	B12 with diag. 25A boiler reclassified	11/53	Last engine (61524) withdrawn

Fig. 144   Class B12 No. 8547 passing Romford on a down Norfolk Coast express,
August 1933

Fig. 145   Class J15 No. 7925 ascending Belstead Bank, Ipswich, 1937

Fig. 146   Class F5 No. 7786 near Romford with an up local, August 1931

Fig. 147   Class D54 No. 053 at South Lynn, May 1938

Fig. 148   Class J93 No. 099 at Melton Constable, May 1937

Fig. 149   Class B15 No. 817 leaving Malton with an L.M.S. excursion to
Scarborough, August 1935

Fig. 150   Class C8 No. 731 leaving York on a down East Coast express, about 1932

Fig. 151   Class B16 No. 2381 approaching Scarborough

ig. 152   Class F8 No. 1582 on a local train in Northumberland

ig. 153   Class X3 No. 190 leaving York with G.E. inspection saloon. Number
              on rear bufferbeam, customary on N.E. Area tank engines

Fig. 154   Class D20 No. 1672 on a Newcastle express near York, about 1932

Fig. 155   Class J25 No. 5705 on trip work at Hull, April 1947

Fig. 156   Class G5 No. 1745 near Durham, 1936

Fig. 157   Class Q6 No. 2271 on a down mineral train near Durham, 1936

Fig. 158   Class C7 No. 2202 on an Edinburgh-Newcastle express near Burnmouth,
July 1938

Fig. 159   Class Q10 No. 3127, about 1923
Interim renumbering of H. & B. locomotives

Fig. 160   Class J23 No. 2460 leaving Malton on a Leeds-Whitby excursion, August 1935

Fig. 161   Class D34 No. 9278 *Glen Lyon* crossing the Forth Bridge with an up fast goods, 1929

Fig. 162 .Class Y9 No. 9146 at Portobello Yard, about 1933. With truck tender

Fig. 163 Class D30 No. 9501 *Simon Glover* ascending Cowlairs Bank on a train to Anstruther, about 1929. Painted black with number on tender—interim livery of 1928-29. A D11, D49 and N14 going down the bank light

4-6-0 (contd.)

Class	Section	Former Class	Designer	Class'n Introduced	Notes	Class'n Extinct	Disposal
B13	NE	S	W. Worsdell	6/99	6'1¼" coupled wheels and two outside cyls.	5/51	Last engine (1699) withdrawn
B14	NE	S1	W. Worsdell	12/00	6'8¼" coupled wheels and two outside cyls.	4/31	Last engine (2112) withdrawn
B15	NE	S2	Raven	12/11	5'6" boiler and two outside cyls.	12/47	Last engine (1696) withdrawn
B16	NE	S3	Raven	12/19	5'8" coupled wheels and three cyls.	6/37	Class divided into Parts 1 & 2
B16/1	NE	B16	Raven	6/37	Retaining Stephenson valve gear	9/61	Last engines (nineteen) withdrawn
B16/2	LNE	B16	Gresley/Raven	6/37	Rebuilt with Walschaert-Gresley gear	—	7 in stock at 31st Dec., 1962
B16/3	LNE	B16	Thompson/Raven	5/44	Rebuilt with 3 sets of Walschaert gear	—	15 in stock at 31st Dec., 1962
B17	LNE	B16/1	Gresley	12/28	'Sandringham', 3-cyl. type	12/33	Class divided into Parts 1 & 2
B17/1	LNE	B17	Gresley	12/33	Orig. batch with 9-plate coupled wheel springs	12/37	Combined with Parts 2 & 3—now 15 plates
B17/1	LNE	—	Gresley	12/37	Parts 1, 2 & 3 combined—all now 15 plates	12/52	Part 1 dropped and "3700" galls. substituted
B17 (3700)	LNE	B17/1	Gresley	12/52	Diag. 100 boiler and 3700-gall. tenders	12/59	Last engine (61625) withdrawn
B17/2	LNE	B17	Gresley	12/33	Engines built from 8/30 with 13-plate coupled wheel springs	12/37	Combined with Parts 1 & 3—now 15 plates
B17/3	LNE	—	Gresley	5/35	Engines built with 15-plate springs	12/37	Reclassified Part 1
B17/4	LNE	—	Gresley	3/36	Engines with 4200-gall. Gp. Std. tender	12/52	Part 4 dropped and "4200 galls." substituted
B17 (4200)	LNE	B17/4	Gresley	12/52	Diag. 100 boiler and 4200-gall. tender	6/60	Last engine (61660) withdrawn
B17/5	LNE	B17/4	Gresley	9/37	B17/4 fitted with streamlined casing	4/51	Last engine (61670) to Part 6
B17/6	LNE	—	Thompson/Gresley	12/46	Parts 1, 4 & 5 reboilered from 10/43 with diag. 100A boiler	8/60	Last engine (61668) withdrawn
B18	GC	B1	Robinson	4/43	B1 reclassified	12/47	Both engines (1479/80) withdrawn
B19/1	GC	B2/1	Robinson	8/45	B2/1 reclassified	7/47	Last engine (1491) withdrawn
B19/2	GC	B2/2	Robinson	8/45	B2/2 reclassified	11/47	Last engine (1492) withdrawn

4-4-2

Class	Section	Former Class	Designer	Class'n Introduced	Notes	Class'n Extinct	Disposal
C1	GN	C1	Ivatt	12/02	Large-boilered Atlantics—all varieties	11/50	Last engine (62822) withdrawn
C2	GN	C1	Ivatt	5/98	Small-boilered Atlantics—all varieties	7/45	Last engine (3252) withdrawn
C3	GC	8B & 8J	—	—	Never used	—	
C4	GC	C4	Robinson	12/03	Two outside cyls., simple	6/29	Class divided into Parts 1, 2 & 3
C4/1	GC	C4	Robinson	6/29	Saturated, 19" cyls., slide valves	1/36	Last engine (6094) superheated
C4/2	GC	C4	Robinson	6/29	As Part 1 but superheated, under 13'0" later	12/50	Last engine (2918) withdrawn
C4/3	GC	C4	Robinson	6/29	Superheated, 21" cyls., piston valves	3/39	Last engine (5267) cut down to Part 4
C4/4	GC	C4/3	Robinson	3/32	As Part 3 but max. height under 13'0"	11/50	Last engine (2901) withdrawn
C5	GC	8D & 8E	Robinson	12/05	Three-cyl. compound	12/47	Last engine (2897) withdrawn
C6	NE	V & V1	Raven	11/03	Two outside cyls.	3/48	Last engine (2937) withdrawn
C7	NE	Z	Raven	7/11	Three cyls.	12/33	Class divided into Parts 1 & 2
C7/1	NE	C7	Gresley/Raven	12/33	As originally built with piston valves	12/48	Last engine (2970) withdrawn
C7/2	NE	C7	W. Worsdell	12/33	Rebuilt with rotary cam Lentz valves	12/46	Last engine (2963) withdrawn
C8	NE	4CC	—	4/06	Four-cyl. compound	1/35	Last engine (730) withdrawn
C9	LNE	C7	Gresley/Raven	11/31	Not used until 11/31. Rebuilds from C7 with articulated tender and booster	—	
C10	NB	I	Reid	7/11	As built without superheater	1/43	Last engine (727) withdrawn
						6/25	Last engine (9901) superheated, to C11
C11	NB	H	Reid	5/15	With superheater	11/39	Last engine (9875) withdrawn

Class	Section	Former Class	Designer	Date Class'n Introduced	Notes	Date Class'n Extinct	Disposal
4-4-2T							
C12	GN	C2	Ivatt	2/98	All varieties	12/58	Last engine (67397) withdrawn
C13	GC	9K	Robinson	3/03	Saturated and superheated, over 13' 0"	12/27	Class divided into Parts 1 & 2
C13	GC	—	Robinson	12/27	Parts 1, 2 & 3 combined, all sup. and under 13' 0"	1/60	Last engine (67417) withdrawn
C13/1	GC	C13	Robinson	12/27	Both sat. and sup. engines, over 13' 0"	12/28	Reclassified to include saturated only
C13/1	GC	C13/1	Robinson	12/28	Saturated only, over 13' 0"	4/35	Last engine (5453) sup., to Part 2
C13/2	GC	C13	Robinson	12/27	Under 13' 0"—all were superheated	12/28	Reclassified to sup. engines over 13' 0"
C13/2	GC	C13/1	Robinson	12/28	Over 13' 0" and superheated	5/37	Last engine (5453) cut down, to Part 3
C13/3	GC	C13/2	Robinson	12/28	Under 13' 0" and superheated	12/38	Reclassified C13—all alike from 5/37
C14	GC	9L	Robinson	5/07	Similar to C13 but more water capacity	12/27	Class divided into Parts 1 & 2
C14	GC	—	Robinson	12/38	Parts combined, all sup. and under 13' 0"	1/60	Last engine (67450) withdrawn
C14/1	GC	C14	Robinson	12/27	Both sat. and sup. engines, over 13' 0"	12/28	Reclassified to include saturated only
C14/1	GC	C14/1	Robinson	12/28	Saturated only and over 13' 0"	1/35	Last engine (6125) superheated
C14/2	GC	C14	Robinson	12/27	Under 13' 0"—all were superheated	12/28	Reclassified to sup. engines over 13' 0"
C14/2	GC	C14/1	Robinson	12/28	Over 13' 0" and superheated	6/37	Last engine (6123) cut down, to Part 3
C14/3	GC	C14/2	Robinson	12/28	Under 13' 0" and superheated	12/38	Reclassified C14—all alike from 6/37
C15	NB	M	Reid	12/11	All saturated	4/60	Last engine (67474) withdrawn
C16	NB	L	Reid	12/15	Similar to C15 but superheated	4/61	Last engine (67485) withdrawn
C17	MGN	A	Marriott	7/42	First built 1904, taken over 10/36	7/44	Last engine (09) withdrawn
4-4-0							
D	LNE	D49/2	Thompson/Gresley	8/42	Rebuilt with two inside cyls. from D49/2	11/52	Only engine (62768) withdrawn
D1	GN	D1	Ivatt	3/11	Superheated and with piston valves	11/50	Last engine (2209) withdrawn
D2	GN	D1	Ivatt	6/98	Slide valves, long firebox, both sat. and sup.	6/51	Last engine (62172) withdrawn
D3	GN	D3	Gresley/Ivatt	11/12	Short firebox, 4' 8" boiler, rebuilt from D4	6/51	Last engine (62000) withdrawn
D4	GN	D2	Ivatt	12/96	As D3 but retaining orig. 4' 5" boiler	6/28	Last engine (4358) reboilered to D3
D5	GC	D11	Parker	7/95	7' 0" coupled wheels, slide valve, saturated	12/27	Class divided into Parts 1 & 2
D5/1	GC	D5	Parker	12/27	Saturated only	3/33	Last engine (5699) withdrawn
D5/2	GC	D5	Parker	12/27	Engines with superheater	10/32	Last engine (5694) withdrawn
D6	GC	D11A	Pollitt	9/97	7' 0" coupled wheels, piston valve, both sat. and sup.	12/27	Class divided into Parts 1 & 2
D6	GC	—	Pollitt	12/38	Superheated, under 13' 0"	12/47	Last engine (2106) withdrawn
D6/1	GC	D6	Pollitt	12/27	Both sat. and sup., over 13' 0"	8/35	Last engine (5856) cut down, to Part 2
D6/2	GC	D6	Pollitt	12/27	Superheated, under 13' 0"	12/38	Reclassified D6—all alike from 8/35
D7	GC	2 & 2A	Parker	11/87	6' 9" coupled wheels, slide valve, saturated	12/39	Last engine (5704) withdrawn
D8	GC	6DB, 11B, C & D	Parker	7/88	Double framed	3/26	Last engine (6415) withdrawn
D9	GC	D9/2	Robinson	10/01	Piston valve, 5' 0" boiler, both sat. and sup.	12/28	Class divided into Parts 1 & 2
D9	GC	—	Robinson	12/39	D9/2 reclassified	7/50	Last engine (62305) withdrawn
D9/1	GC	D9	Robinson	12/28	Superheated but still over 13' 0"	1/39	Last engine (6032) cut down to Part 2
D9/2	GC	D9	Robinson	12/28	Max. height under 13' 0" (from 8/28)	12/39	Reclassified D9—all alike from 1/39.

Class	Rly	Ref	Designer	Intro	Description	Withdrawn	Notes
D10	GC	11E	Robinson	8/13	—	10/55	Last engine (62653) withdrawn
D11	GC	11F	Robinson	12/19	As D10 but heavier and higher pitched boiler	12/24	Class altered to Part 1
D11/1	LNE	D11	Robinson	12/24	Engines over 13' 0" max. height	12/60	Last engine (62666) withdrawn
D11/2	LNE	6B	Gresley/Robinson	7/24	Reduced boiler mountings for N.B. gauge	1/62	Last engine (62685) withdrawn
D12	GC	T19	Sacré	5/77	Outside frames	3/30	Last engine (6464) withdrawn
D13	GE	Rbt.	J. Holden	1/05	Rebuilds from 2-4-0, both sat. and sup.	3/44	Last engine (8039) withdrawn
D14	GE	S46	J. Holden	3/00	4' 9" sat. boiler, R.T. firebox, short smokebox	3/31	Last engine (8875) rebuilt to D15/2
D14/1		D14	—	—	Never used		
D14/2		D56	Gresley/J. Holden	2/33	5' 1" boilers, R.T. firebox on orig. D14-type frames	5/36	Reclassified and merged into D16/3
D15	GE	D15/2	J. Holden	12/03	4' 9" boiler, sat. and sup. Belpaire, short smokebox	12/27	Class divided into Parts 1 & 2
D15/1	GE	D15	J. Holden	12/38	D15/2 reclassified	9/52	Last engine (62509) withdrawn
D15/2	GE	D15	Gresley/J. Holden	12/27	D15 reclassified, both sat. and sup.	3/35	Last engine (8899) altered to D15/2
D15/2	LNE		Gresley/Holden	12/27	Superheated, with extended smokebox	12/38	Reclassified D15—all alike from 3/35
D16	LNE	H88	Hill	3/23	5' 1" sup. boiler, Belpaire, both ext. and short smokeboxes	12/27	Class divided into Parts 1 & 2
D16/1	LNE	D16	Hill	12/27	Short smokebox type reclassified	3/34	Last engine (8846) to extended smokebox (D16/2)
D16/2	LNE	D16/2,	Gresley/Hill & Holden	12/27	As D16/1 but with extended smokebox (from 4/26)	1/52	Last engine (62590) withdrawn
D16/3	LNE	D16/2; & D16/2	Gresley/Hill & Holden	1/33	5' 1" boiler but round top firebox	10/60	Last engine (62613) withdrawn
D17/1	NE	M	W. Worsdell	12/92	7' 1¼ coupled wheels	9/45	Last engine (1629) withdrawn
D17/2	NE	Q	W. Worsdell	6/96	2t. 8c. lighter than D17/1, clerestory cab roof	2/48	Last engines (2111/2) withdrawn
D18	NE	Q1	W. Worsdell	5/96	7' 7¼ coupled wheels	10/30	Both engines (1869/70) withdrawn
D19	NE	3CC	W. Worsdell/Smith	5/93	As rebuilt 1898 to 3 cyl. compound	10/30	Only one engine (1619) withdrawn
D20	NE	R	W. Worsdell	8/99	6' 10" coupled wheels, 4' 9" boiler both sat. and sup.	12/42	Class divided into Parts 1 & 2
D20/1	NE	D20	Gresley/W. Worsdell	12/42	D20 reclassified, but all superheated	11/57	Last engine (62395) withdrawn
D21	NE	D20	W. Worsdell	12/42	Rebuilt with long travel piston valves (from 10/36)	5/57	Last engine (62375) withdrawn
D22	NE	R1	W. Worsdell/T. W. Worsdell	11/08	6' 10" coupled wheels, 5' 6" boiler	2/46	Last engine (1245) withdrawn
D23	NE	F	T. W. Worsdell	11/86	6' 8¼" coupled wheels, some rebuilt from compounds and 2-4-0	11/35	Last engine (1537) withdrawn
D24	NE	G	McDonnell	11/87	6' 1¼" coupled wheels, rebuilt from 2-4-0	5/35	Last engine (1120) withdrawn
—	NE	38	M. Stirling	12/84	Did not survive to get L.N.E.R. class	2/23	Last engine (281) withdrawn
D25	HB	J	Holmes	12/10	Both domeless and domed (from 9/29)	9/34	Last engine (2429) withdrawn
D26	NB	N	Holmes	4/86	7' 0" coupled wheels, as rebuilt by Reid from 3/11	7/33	Last engine (9596) withdrawn
D27	NB	K	Holmes	5/03	6' 6" coupled wheels	7/26	Last engine (9325) withdrawn
D28	NB	M	Holmes/D. Drummond	8/76	Rebuilds from N.B. '476' class with round cab (from 6/02)	11/24	Last engine (NB1321) withdrawn
D29	NB	M	Reid/D. Drummond	8/76	Rebuilds from N.B. '476' class with square cab, heavier than D27 (from 7/04)	9/26	Last engine (10387) withdrawn
D29	NB	J	Reid	7/09	6' 6" coupled wheels, 19" cyls., saturated	12/26	Class divided into Parts 1 & 2
D29/1	NB	D29/2	Reid	12/26	Part 2 reclassified, all sup. from 7/36	11/52	Last engine (62411) withdrawn
D29/2	NB	D29	Reid	12/26	D29 saturated reclassified	7/36	Last engine (9361) superheated
D30/1	NB	J	Reid	9/12	D29 as superheated (from 4/25)	12/38	Reclassified D29—alike from 7/36
D30/2	NB	J	Reid	4/14	6' 6" coupled wheels, superheated, 20" cyls. with 8" piston valves	1/51	Last engine (62417) withdrawn
D31	NB	M	Reid	6/84	As Part 1 but heavier and with 10" piston valves	6/60	Last engines (62421/6) withdrawn
D31/1	NB	D31/1	Reid & Chalmers/Holmes	12/38	Rebuilds of N.B. classes '574', '633' & '729'	12/27	Class divided into Parts 1 & 2
D31/2	NB	D31	Reid & Chalmers/Holmes	12/27	Part 1 reclassified, all now same springs	12/52	Last engine (62281) withdrawn
	NB	D31	Reid & Chalmers/Holmes	12/27	Laminated springs on bogie and driving axle	11/35	Reclassified D31—all now same
	NB		Chalmers/Holmes		With helical springs to all axles	By 11/35	Last engine to Part 1 springing

4-4-0 (contd.)

Class	Section	Former Class	Designer	Date Class'n Introduced	Notes	Date Class'n Extinct	Disposal
D32	NB	K	Reid	10/06	6'0" coupled wheels, saturated, 19" cyls.	12/24	Class divided into Parts 1 & 2
D32	NB	D32/2	Reid	12/38	D32/2 reclassified—all sup. from 2/26	3/51	Last engine (62451) withdrawn
D32/1	NB	D32	Reid	12/24	D32 saturated reclassified	2/26	Last engine (9891) superheated, to D32/2
D32/2	NB	D32	Reid	12/24	D32 as superheated (from 8/23)	12/38	Reclassified D32—alike from 2/26
D33	NB	K	Reid	10/09	As D32, but higher pitched boiler, heavier	12/26	Class divided into Parts 1 & 2
D33	NB	D33/2	Reid	12/38	D33/2 reclassified—all sup. from 4/36	11/52	Last engine (62462) withdrawn
D33/1	NB	D33	Reid	12/26	D33 saturated reclassified	4/36	Last engine (9866) superheated, to D33/2
D33/2	NB	D33	Reid	12/26	D33 as superheated (from 11/25)	12/38	Reclassified D33—alike from 4/36
D34	NB	K	Holmes	9/13	6'0" coupled wheels, superheated, 20" cyls.	11/61	Last engine (62496) withdrawn
D35	NB	L	Reid/Holmes	1/94	5'7" coupled wheels, saturated	11/24	Last engine (NB1439) withdrawn
D36	NB			2/19	Rebuild of D35, superheated	5/43	Only engine (9695) withdrawn
D37					Never used		—
D38	GNS	Q	Manson	8/90	6'6¼" coupled wheels, both sat. and sup.	1/38	Last engine (6875) withdrawn
D39	GNS		Cowan	1/79	6'1" coupled wheels, two out. cyls.	2/27	Last engine (6803) withdrawn
D40	GNS	V & F	Pickersgill & Heywood	9/99	6'1" coupled wheels, class V sat., F sup., window cab	6/58	Last engine (62277) withdrawn
D41	GNS	S & T	Johnson	12/93	Like D40 sat., but ordinary cab	2/53	Last engines (6241/2) withdrawn
D42	GNS	O	Manson	4/88	6'0¼" coupled wheels, both sat. and sup., 2100-gall. tenders	2/46	Last engine (6817) withdrawn
D43	GNS	P	Manson	5/90	Similar to D42, both sat. and sup, 3000-gall. tenders	1/38	Last engine (6812) withdrawn
D44	GNS	A	Manson	8/84	Similar to D42 sat., but shorter firebox and smaller cyls.	10/32	Last engine (6867) withdrawn
D45	GNS	M	Cowan	6/78	5'7" coupled wheels, two 17½" outside cyls.	6/32	Last engine (6840) withdrawn
D46	GNS	N	Manson	2/87	5'6¼" coupled wheels, sat., 165lb. press.	4/36	Last engine (6805) withdrawn
D47	GNS	L	Cowan	3/76	5'6¼" coupled wheels, two 16" out. cyls.	12/24	Reclassified D47/2
D47/1	GNS	K	Cowan	12/24	5'6¼" coupled wheels, two 16" out. cyls.	12/24	Allocated Class D47/2
D47/2	GNS	K	Cowan	12/24	D47 reclassified	1/26	Last engine (GNS 52A) withdrawn
D48	GNS	G	Manson	5/85	Previously unclassified by L.N.E.R.	7/25	Last engine (GNS 45A) withdrawn
D49/1	LNE		Gresley	11/27	6'8" coupled wheels, sat., 180lb. press.	11/34	Last engine (6869) withdrawn
D49/2	LNE		Gresley	3/29	'Shire' type, piston valve engines	7/61	Last engine (62712) withdrawn
D49/3	LNE		Gresley	5/28	'Hunt' type, rotary cam Lentz valves	3/61	Last engine (62747) withdrawn
D49/4	LNE		Gresley		With oscillating cam Lentz valves	11/38	Last engine (322) rebuilt to Part 1
D52	MGN	C	Johnson & Marriott	7/42	Engine 2768 remained officially class D. First built 1894, taken over 10/36, 4'2" boiler with R.T. firebox	9/43	Last engine (038) withdrawn
D53	MGN	C	Marriott	7/42	As rebuilt from 1929 with Belpaire firebox	1/45	Last engine (050) withdrawn
D54	MGN	CR bt.	Marriott	7/42	As rebuilt from 1909 with 4'9" Belpaire boiler	11/43	Last engine (056) withdrawn
—	MGN	A	Beyer, Peacock	3/82	Outside cyls. taken over 10/36, did not survive to get L.N.E.R. class	5/41	Last engine (025) withdrawn

4-4-0T

Class	Section	Former Class	Designer	Date Class'n Introduced	Notes	Date Class'n Extinct	Disposal
D50	NB	P	D. Drummond	5/79	6'0" coupled wheels	3/26	Last engine (10390) withdrawn
D51	NB	R	D. Drummond	6/80	5'0" coupled wheels	8/33	Last engine (10462) withdrawn

Locomotive classes — continued

Class	Rly	Class code	Designer	Built	Notes	Withdrawn	Last engine
E1	GN	E1	Stirling & Ivatt	3/84	As rebuilt (or built) with domed boiler	11/27	Last engine (3814) withdrawn
E2	GC	6D	Parker	4/87	Double frames	3/24	Last engine (GC506B) withdrawn
E3	GC	12A	Sacré	12/85	Outside frames, did not survive to get L.N.E.R. class	6/23	Last engine (GC169B) withdrawn
—	—	—	—		Never used		
E4	GE	T26	J. Holden	2/91		12/59	Last engine (62785) withdrawn
E5	NE	1463	Tennant	5/85		2/25	Last engine (1474) withdrawn
E6	NE	901	Fletcher	4/75	7'1¼" coupled wheels. No L.N.E.R. class allocated	7/25	Last engine (367) withdrawn
—	NE	1440	Fletcher	11/76	6'1¼" coupled wheels. No L.N.E.R. class allocated	2/25	Last engine (220) withdrawn
—	—	—	—		Never used		
E7	NB	P	Reid/Holmes/Wheatley	7/73		10/27	Last engine (10247) withdrawn

2-4-0T

Class	Rly	Class code	Designer	Built	Notes	Withdrawn	Last engine
E8	GC	12AM	Sacré	3/81	Outside frames	1/25	Last engine (GC450B) withdrawn

2-4-2T

Class	Rly	Class code	Designer	Built	Notes	Withdrawn	Last engine
F1/1	GC	3	Parker	6/89	Both saturated and superheated	12/27	Class part split into Parts 1 & 2
F1/1	GC	F1/1	Parker	12/27	Over 13'0", both sat. and sup.	12/34	Last engine (5596) cut down to Part 2
F1/2	GC	3alt	Parker	4/92	As Part 1 but greater coal and water capacity	12/27	Class part split into Parts 3 & 4
F1/2	GC	F1/1	Parker	12/27	Under 13'0", saturated	1/49	Last engines (7099 & 7100) withdrawn
F1/3	GC	F1/2	Parker	12/27	Over 13'0", both sat. and sup.	6/33	Last engine (5728) withdrawn
F1/4	GC	F1/2	Parker	12/27	Under 13'0", saturated (from 8/25)	4/45	Last engine (5732) withdrawn
F2	GC	9G	Pollitt	3/98	Similar to F1, but Stephenson valve gear instead of Joy		Last engine (7111) withdrawn
F3	GE	C32	J. Holden	4/93		12/50	Last engine (67127) withdrawn
F4	GE	M15	T.W. Worsdell	7/84		4/53	Last engine (67157) withdrawn
F5	GE	M15	T.W. Worsdell/S.D. Holden		With 160lb. pressure	6/56	Last engine (67195) withdrawn
F6	GE	Rbt.	S.D. Holden	10/11	Rebuilt from F4 with 180lb. press. (from 1911)	5/58	Last engine (67230) withdrawn
F7	GE	G69	S.D. Holden	4/11	5'4" coupled wheels	5/58	Last engines (7093/4) withdrawn
F8	NE	Y65	T.W. Worsdell	6/09	4'10" coupled wheels	11/48	Last engines (40 & 420) withdrawn
F9	CVH	A	Copus	3/86 / 7/23	First built 1887, taken over 7/23	4/38 / 1/30	Last engine (8312) withdrawn

0-4-4T

Class	Rly	Class code	Designer	Built	Notes	Withdrawn	Last engine
G1	GN	G1	P. Stirling	12/89	5'8" coupled wheels, with both domeless and domed boilers	2/27	Last engine (3766) withdrawn
G2	GN	G3	P. Stirling	11/81	5'2" coupled wheels, all as rebuilt with domed boiler	4/26	Last engine (696N) withdrawn
—	GN	G2	Ivatt/P. Stirling	4/76	Service loco. as rebuilt with crane. No L.N.E.R. class allocated	11/28	Only engine (No. 3 loco. crane) withdrawn
G3	GC	C	Kitson & Co.	11/97		11/35	Last engine (6402) withdrawn
G4	GE	S44	J. Holden	12/98		12/38	Last engine (8139) withdrawn
G5	NE	O	W. Worsdell	5/94		12/58	Last engine (67280) withdrawn
G6	NE	BTP	Fletcher	4/74		11/29	Last engine (9091) withdrawn
G7	NB	P	Holmes	4/86	All varieties	1/36	Last engine (1436) withdrawn
G8	NB	P	D. Drummond	1877		5/32	Last engine (NB1320) withdrawn
G9	NB	M	Reid	10/09		9/25	Last engine (9475) withdrawn
G10	GNS	R	Johnson	11/93	Originally 0-4-2T	11/40 / 8/47	Last engine (7505) withdrawn

4-4-4T

Class	Rly	Class code	Designer	Built	Notes	Withdrawn	Last engine
H1	NE	D	Raven	10/13		8/36	Last engine (1517) rebuilt to A8
H2	LPTB	H	Jones	11/37	First built 1920, taken over 11/37	11/47	Last engine (7511) withdrawn

0-6-0

Class	Section	Former Class	Designer	Date Class'n Introduced	Notes	Date Class'n Extinct	Disposal
J1	GN	J21	Ivatt	8/08	5' 8" wheels, sat., slide valves	11/54	Last engine (65013) withdrawn
J2	GN	J21	Ivatt	8/12	5' 8" wheels, sup., piston valves	7/54	Last engine (65020) withdrawn
J3	GN	J4	Gresley/P. Stirling, & Ivatt	5/12	5' 2" wheels, rebuilds of J4 type with 4' 8" boiler	12/54	Last engine (64140) withdrawn
J4	GN	J5	P. Stirling & Ivatt	12/73	With 4' 5" boiler, 17¼" cyls.	12/51	Last engine (64112) withdrawn
J5	GN	J22	Ivatt	10/09	5' 2" wheels, both sat. and sup., 18" cyls.	12/55	Last engine (65483) withdrawn
J6	GN	J22	Ivatt & Gresley	8/11	5' 2" wheels, piston valves	6/62	Last engines (64226/77) withdrawn
J7	GN	J9	P. Stirling	8/83	4' 8" wheels, with 4' 5" and also 4' 8" boiler	9/36	Last engine (4027) withdrawn
J8/309B	GC	18	Sacre	3/73	Works loco, inside framed	10/24	Only engine (GC309B) withdrawn
J8/1	GC	6A1	Parker	11/87	Double framed, with orig. 2500-gall. tender	5/30	Last engine (5551) withdrawn
J8/2	GC	6A1	Parker	pre-1921	With 3000-gall. tender substituted	5/28	Last engine (5555) withdrawn
J9	GC	9B &	Parker	2/91	Joy valve gear	12/27	Class divided into Parts 1 & 2
J9/1	GC	9E	Parker	12/27	Engines over 13' 0" max. height	7/33	Last engine (5740) withdrawn
J9/2	GC	J9	Parker	12/27	Under 13' 0" max. height (from 12/25)	12/36	Last engine (5743) withdrawn
J10/1	GC	9D	Parker	7/92	Similar to J9 but Steph. valve gear. With 7½" journals and 3080-gall. tender	7/34	Reclassified on height basis
J10/1	GC	J10/1	Parker	12/27	Now only including engines over 13' 0"	12/27	Last engine (5680) cut down to Part 2
J10/2	GC	9H	Pollitt	2/96	With 8" journals and 4000-gall. tender	12/27	Those over 13' 0" reclassified to Part 3
J10/3	GC	J10/1	Parker	12/27	Orig. Part 1 cut down below 13' 0" (from 8/25)	12/52	Last engine (65126) withdrawn
J10/3	GC	9H	Robinson	2/01	With 8" journals and 3080-gall. tender	12/27	Those over 13' 0" reclassified to Part 5
J10/3	GC	J10/2	Pollitt	12/27	Orig. Part 2 still over 13' 0" high	9/35	Last engine (5788) cut down to Part 4
J10/4	GC	J10/2	Pollitt	12/27	8" journals, 4000-gall. tender, under 13' 0" (from 7/25)	8/61	Last engine (65157) withdrawn
J10/5	GC	J10/3	Robinson	12/27	Orig. Part 3 still over 13' 0"	3/35	Last engine (5131) cut down to Part 6
J10/6	GC	J10/3	Robinson	12/27	8" journals, 3080-gall. tender, under 13' 0" (from 4/25)	8/61	Last engine (65198) withdrawn
J11	GC	—	Robinson	12/52	Parts 1, 2, 4 & 5 combined, all sup. and under 13' 0"	8/62	Last engines (64329 and 64445) withdrawn
J11/1	GC	9J	Robinson	9/01	Over 13' 0", sat. and sup., 3250-gall. tender	12/25	Combined with orig. Part 2
J11/1	GC	J11/1 & J11/1	Robinson	12/25	As before but now also incl. 4000-gall. tender	12/27	Divided again into Parts 1 & 2
J11/1	GC	J11/1	Robinson	12/27	Over 13' 0", sat. and sup., 3250-gall. tender	11/52	Part dropped—under 13' 0" since 1941
J11/2	GC	9J	Robinson	6/06	Over 13' 0", sat. and sup., 4000-gall. tender	12/25	All transferred to Part 1
J11/2	GC	J11/1	Robinson	12/27	Orig. Part 2 classification restored	11/52	Part dropped—under 13' 0" since 1941
J11/Eng. 16	GC	9J	Robinson	4/09	With Schmidt superheater and piston valves	12/25	Reclassified to Part 3
J11/3	GC	Eng. 16	Robinson	12/25	Engine 5016 with Schmidt sup. and piston valves	9/27	Piston valves removed; rebuilt to Part 2
J11/3	LNE	—	Thompson/Robinson	7/42	Rebuilds with long travel piston valves	10/62	Last engine (64354) withdrawn
J11/4	GC	J11/1	Robinson	12/27	Superheated, under 13' 0" (from 4/25), 3250-gall. tender	11/52	Part dropped—combined into J11
J11/5	GC	J11/2	Robinson	4/27	As Part 4 but 4000-gall. tender	11/52	Part dropped—combined into J11
J12	GC	6C	Sacré	8/80	Double frames	2/30	Last engine (6428) withdrawn

J13	GC	9	Parker	1/89	Similar to J9 but 4″ smaller wheels	12/27	Class divided into Parts 1 & 2
J13/1	GC	J13	Parker	12/27	Engines still over 13′ 0″	3/30	Last engine (5572) cut down to Part 2
J13/2	GC	J13	Parker	12/27	With max. height under 13′ 0″ (from 3/25)	11/35	Last engine (5572) withdrawn
J14	GE	N31	J. Holden	10/93	Similar to J15 but steam chests below cyls.	4/25	Last engines (GE981/7) withdrawn
J15	GE	Y14	T. W. Worsdell	7/83	—	9/62	Last engines (65361, 65462/4/5) withdrawn
J16	GE	F48	J. Holden	9/00	All saturated and round top firebox	1/32	Last engine (8200) reboilered to J17
J17	GE	G58	J. Holden	2/02	Belpaire firebox and all sup. by 7/32	9/62	Last engines (65541/76/82) withdrawn
J18	GE	E72	Hill	11/12	4′ 9″ boiler, long front overhang and with tail rods	10/36	Last engine (8241) rebuilt to J19/2
J19	GE	T77	Hill	8/16	As J18 but short front overhang and no tail rods	12/34	Reclassified to Part 1
J19	LNE	J19/2	Gresley/Hill	12/47	Part 2 reclassified—alike from 2/39	9/62	Last engines (64657/64) withdrawn
J19/1	GE	J19	Hill	12/34	J19 with Belpaire firebox reclassified	2/39	Last engine (8264) rebuilt to J19/2
J19/2	LNE	J18 & J19	Gresley/Hill	12/34	J18 and J19 rebuilds with R.T. firebox (from 10/34)	12/47	Part number no longer used
J20	GE	D81	Hill	4/20	5′ 1⅛″ boiler, with Belpaire firebox	1/56	Last engine (64676) reboilered to J20/1
J20/1	LNE	J20	Thompson/Hill	10/43	Reboilered with round top firebox	9/62	Last engines (64687/90/1/9) withdrawn
—	NE	1001	Bouch	5/74	Did not survive to get L.N.E.R. class	2/23	Last engine (1275) withdrawn
—	NE	398	Fletcher	10/74	No L.N.E.R. class allocated	3/28	Last engine (1412) withdrawn
J21	NE	C	W. Worsdell/ T. W. Worsdell	8/86	5′ 1¼″ wheels, all varieties	4/62	Last engine (65033) withdrawn
J22	NE	59	McDonnell	9/83	—	12/30	Last engine (131) withdrawn
J23	HB	B	M. Stirling	3/89	18″ cyls., domeless and domed, both sat. and sup.	12/28	Class divided into Parts 1, 2 & 3
J23/1	HB	J23	M. Stirling	12/28	Engines still domeless—all saturated	10/37	Last engine (2469) withdrawn
J23/2	HB	J23	Gresley/M. Stirling	12/28	With domed superheated boiler (from 7/23)	11/37	Last engine (2518) withdrawn
J23/3	HB	J23	Gresley/M. Stirling	12/28	With domed saturated boiler (from 3/28)	11/38	Last engine (2460) withdrawn
J24	NE	P	W. Worsdell	12/94	4′ 7¼″ wheels, 24″ stroke, all varieties	12/51	Last engine (65617) withdrawn
J25	NE	P1	W. Worsdell	5/98	4′ 7¼″ wheels, 26″ stroke, all varieties	6/62	Last engine (65726) withdrawn
J26	NE	P2	W. Worsdell	6/04	5′ 6″ boiler, all saturated	6/62	Last engines (six) withdrawn
J27	NE	P3	W. Worsdell	4/06	5′ 6″ boiler, both sat. and sup., heavier	—	79 in stock at 31st Dec., 1962
J28	HB	L, L1 & LS	M. Stirling	12/11	19″ cyls., domeless, both sat. and sup.	6/37	Last engine (2538) withdrawn
J28/1	HB	J28	Gresley/M. Stirling	6/28	Domed reboilering of L and LS classes	10/38	Last engine (2413) withdrawn
J28/2	HB	J28	Gresley/M. Stirling	6/28	Domed reboilering of L1 class	10/38	Last engines (2416/22) withdrawn
J28/3	HB	J28	M. Stirling	12/30	Domeless and superheated from J28	6/37	Last engine (2418) withdrawn
J29-J30	—	—	—	—	Never used	—	—
J31	NB	E	Reid/Holmes/Wheatley	12/67	—	4/37	Last engine (10206) withdrawn
J32	NB	C	Holmes/D. Drummond	1876	18″ cyls.	4/25	Last engine (NB1337) withdrawn
J33	NB	D	Holmes	11/83	Similar to J34 but longer wheelbase	12/38	Last engine (9169) withdrawn
J34	NB	D	D. Drummond	1879	17″ cyls.	1/28	Last engines (9138 & 9550) withdrawn
J35/1	NB	B	Reid	6/06	18½″ cyls., sat. and with piston valves	8/37	Last engine (9185) sup. to Part 5
J35/2	NB	B	Reid	7/06	As Part 1 but different boiler	6/25	Last engine (9330) altered to Part 1
J35/3	NB	B	Reid	12/08	Saturated and with slide valves	7/42	Last engine (9337) sup. to Part 4
J35/4	NB	B	Reid	4/23	Slide valves and superheated	12/62	Last engine (64491) withdrawn
J35/5	NB	J35/1	Reid	12/37	Piston valves and superheated (from 1/25)	3/62	Last engine (64472) withdrawn
J36	NB	C	Reid & Chalmers/Holmes	8/88	18″ cyls.	12/27	Class divided into Parts 1 & 2
J36	NB	J36/1	Reid/Holmes	12/38	Part 1 reclassified—all now same springs	—	32 in stock at 31st Dec., 1962
J36/1	NB	J36	Reid & Chalmers/Holmes	12/27	Laminated springs—leading and driving	11/35	Reclassified J36—all now alike
J36/2	NB	J36	Chalmers/Holmes	12/27	With helical springs to all axles	by 11/35	Last engine to Part 1 springing
J37	NB	B & S	Reid	7/14	19½″ cyls., all superheated	—	67 in stock at 31st Dec., 1962

Class	Section	Former Class	Designer	Date Class'n Introduced	Notes	Date Class'n Extinct	Disposal
0-6-0 (contd.)							
J38	LNE	—	Gresley	1/26	4' 8" wheels, with 4200-gall. Group Std. tender	12/31	Class divided into Parts 1 & 2
J38	LNE	J38/2	Gresley	12/38	J38/2 reclassified—tenders alike from 11/33	12/41	Divided into different Parts 1 & 2
J38/1	LNE	J38	Gresley	12/31	With tender fitted originally	11/33	Last engine (1428) got 3500-gall. tender
J38/1	LNE	J38	Gresley	12/41	With original diag. 97A boiler	—	3 in stock at 31st Dec., 1962
J38/2	LNE	J38	Gresley	12/31	With 3500-gall. Group Std. tender	12/38	Reclassified J38—alike from 11/33
J38/2	LNE	J38	Gresley	12/41	As reboilered with diag. 97 boiler (from 12/32)	—	30 in stock at 31st Dec., 1962
J39	LNE	—	Gresley	9/26	5' 2" wheels, as first built with 3500-gall. G.S. tender	12/30	Class divided into Parts 1 & 2
J39	LNE	—	Gresley	12/52	Parts 1, 2 & 3 combined	12/62	Last engines (eight) withdrawn
J39/1	LNE	J39	Gresley	12/30	With 3500-gall. Group Std. tender	12/52	Part classification discontinued
J39/2	LNE	J39	Gresley	12/30	With 4200-gall. Group Std. tender (from 5/29)	12/52	Part classification discontinued
J39/3	LNE	—	Gresley	10/34	With second-hand ex-N.E. tender	12/52	Part classification discontinued
J40	MGN	D	Johnson	7/42	First built 1896, taken over 10/36. 4' 2" boiler with R.T. firebox	6/44	Last engine (059) withdrawn
J41	MGN	D Rbt.	Marriott/Johnson	7/42	As rebuilt from 1921 with 4' 9" Belpaire boiler	7/43	Last engine (071) withdrawn
J42-J44	—	—	—	—	Never used	—	—
0-6-0DE							
J45	LNE	—	Thompson	5/45	Diesel-electric shunter	10/45	Classification altered to DES1
J46-J49	—	—	—	—	Never used	—	—
0-6-0T							
J50	GN	J23	Gresley	10/22	All varieties	12/39	Class divided into Parts 1, 2, 3 & 4
J50/1	GN	J50	Gresley	12/39	Rebuilds from J51/1	—	1 only in stock at 31st Dec., 1962
J50/2	GN	J50	Gresley	12/39	Rebuilds from J51/2, and first J50 batch	—	11 in stock at 31st Dec., 1962
J50/3	GN	J50	Gresley	12/39	As Part 2 but heavier and 4" longer	—	7 in stock at 31st Dec., 1962
J50/4	LNE	J50	Gresley	12/39	As Part 3 but vac. brakes and heater fitted	11/52	Combined with Part 3
J51/1	GN	J23	Gresley	1/14	With 2 tons coal and 1500 galls. water	3/35	Last engine (3158) reboilered to J50
J51/2	GN	J23	Gresley	12/14	With 3½ tons coal and 1520 galls. water	4/34	Last engine (3178) reboilered to J50
J52	GN	J13	P. Stirling & Ivatt	8/97	4' 5" domed boiler as built and as rebuilt from J53	12/40	Class divided into Parts 1 & 2
J52/1	GN	J52	P. Stirling & Ivatt	12/40	Rebuilds from orig. domeless J53	7/58	Last engine (68800) withdrawn
J52/2	GN	J52	Ivatt	12/40	As built with domed boiler	3/61	Last engines (68869/75) withdrawn
J53	GN	J14	P. Stirling	12/92	18" x 26" cyls., 4' 0½" domeless boiler, also 4' 2½" domed (from 4/25)	11/35	Last engine (3928) withdrawn
J54/1	GN	J15	P. Stirling	6/74	17½" x 26" cyls., with open cab, 4' 0½" and 4' 2½" domeless and domed boilers	10/32	Last engine (3801) withdrawn
J54/2	GN	J16	Ivatt/P. Stirling	10/91	Built with full cab	9/33	Last engine (3920) rebuilt to J55
J55	GN	J16	P. Stirling	9/97	Rebuilds from J54/1 & J54/2 with 4' 5" domed and domeless boilers	7/50	Last engine (68319) withdrawn
J56	GN	J17	P. Stirling	2/77	As J54/1, but shorter wheelbase	12/32	Last engine (3608A) withdrawn
J57	GN	J18	P. Stirling	12/82	17½" x 24" cyls., 6" smaller wheels, both domeless and domed	6/38	Last engine (3685) withdrawn
—	GN	J19 conv.	P. Stirling	9/02	16" x 22" cyls., no L.N.E.R. class allotted	4/27	Last engine (3470A) withdrawn
J58	GC	18	Robinson/Sacré	12/02	Saddletank, 5' 3" wheels, originally 0-6-0	8/30	Last engine (6483) withdrawn
J59	GC	18T	Sacré	10/71	4' 9" wheels, saddletank	1/29	Last engines (6451/75) withdrawn
J60	GC	B	Kitson & Co.	2/97	Saddletank	8/48	Last engine (8368) withdrawn
J61	GC	4	Contractors	6/76		12/27	Class divided into Parts 1 & 2
J61/1	GC	J61	Manning, Wardle	12/27	With open cab	3/29	Only engine (6469) withdrawn
J61/2	GC	J61	Hudswell, Clarke	12/27	With full cab	4/31	Only engine (5278) withdrawn

J62	GC	5	Pollitt	1/97	Saddletank	11/51	Last engine (68200) withdrawn
J63	GC	5A	Robinson	8/06	Sidetank version of J62	2/57	Last engine (68210) withdrawn
—	GC	7	Parker	2/85	Did not survive to get L.N.E.R. class	7/23	Last engine (GC11B) withdrawn
J64	MSL	—	Hudswell, Clarke	7/24	First built 1904, taken over 7/24, with both 13" and 14" cyls.	12/29	Last engine (8317) withdrawn
J65	GE	E22	J. Holden	2/89	14" x 20" cyls., 160lb. press. and 600-gall. tanks	10/56	Last engine (68214) withdrawn
J66	GE	T18	J. Holden	6/86	16½" x 22" cyls., 160lb. press. and 1000-gall. tanks	9/62	Last engine (Dept'l 32) withdrawn
J67	GE	R24	J. Holden	3/90	Similar to J66 but longer wheelbase	12/38	Reclassified to Part 1
J67/1	GE	J67	J. Holden	12/38	J67 reclassified	11/58	Last engine (68616) withdrawn
J67/2	GE	J69	J. Holden	3/38	Rebuilds to 160lb. from J69 and J68 (one engine only) class retaining larger tanks	2/58	Last engine (68628) withdrawn
J68	GE	C72	Hill	6/12	1200-gall. tanks, 180lb., side window cab	9/61	Last engines (68642/6/9) withdrawn
J69	GE	R24 Rbt. & S56	J. Holden	8/02	180lb. press., both rebuilt (from J67) and newly built	12/52	Class divided into Parts 1 & 2
J69/1	GE	J69	J. Holden	12/52	Engines with 1140 to 1200-gall. tanks	9/62	Last engine (Dept'l 45) withdrawn
J69/2	GE	J69	J. Holden	12/52	Later rebuilds from J67 retaining 1000-gall. tanks (from 6/46)	9/62	Last engine (Dept'l 44) withdrawn
J70	GE	C53	J. Holden	10/03	Tram engines	8/55	Last engine (68226) withdrawn
—	NE	44	W. Worsdell/Fletcher	12/98	No L.N.E.R. class allocated	9/26	Last engine (106) withdrawn
J71	NE	E	T. W. Worsdell	11/86	4' 7¼" wheels	2/61	Last engine (68233) withdrawn
J72	NE	E1	W. Worsdell	12/98	Similar to J71, but 4' 1¼" wheels	—	18 in stock at 31st Dec., 1962
J73	NE	L	W. Worsdell	12/91	4' 7¼" wheels, larger than J71	11/60	Last engine (68361) withdrawn
J74	NE	8	Tennant/McDonnell	8/85	—	9/31	Last engines (20, 461/7) withdrawn
J75	HB	G3	M. Stirling	12/01	4' 6" wheels, both domeless and domed	1/49	Last engine (8365) withdrawn
J76	NE	124	Fletcher	8/81	With both 4' 7¼" and 4' 10¼" wheels	1/29	Last engine (602) withdrawn
J77	NE	290	W. Worsdell/Fletcher	6/99	With both round and square top cab, originally 0-4-4T	2/61	Last engine (68408) withdrawn
J78	NE	H1	T. W. Worsdell	12/88	Fitted with crane	4/37	Last engine (590) withdrawn
J79	NE	H2	W. Worsdell	3/97	As J78 but without crane	8/37	Last engine (1662) withdrawn
J80	HB	G2	M. Stirling	8/92	5' 1" wheels, both domeless and domed	9/31	Last engine (2450) withdrawn
J81	NB	E	Holmes/Wheatley	2/72	Saddletank with 5' 0" wheels	2/24	Last engine (NB1216) withdrawn
J82	NB	R	D. Drummond	1875	—	11/26	Last engine (NB1328) withdrawn
J83	NB	D	Holmes	8/00	—	12/62	Last engine (68477) withdrawn
J84	NB	E	Holmes/Wheatley	10/73	Saddletank with 4' 0" wheels	6/24	Last engine (NB1259) withdrawn
J84	E & WYU	—	Manning, Wardle	7/23	Saddletank, first built 6/95, taken over 7/23	6/30	Last engine (3112) withdrawn
J85	NB	E	Holmes/Whealtey	6/70	Saddletank with 4' 3" wheels	9/24	Last engine (NB1168) withdrawn
J85	E & WYU	—	Manning, Wardle	7/23	Saddletank, as rebuilt from 0-6-2T 8/19, taken over 7/23	2/33	Last engine (3114) withdrawn
J86	NB	E	Holmes/Wheatley	10/70	Classified in error—only engine was identical with J81	10/24	Only engine (NB1173) withdrawn
J87	—	—	—	—	Never used	—	—
J88	NB	F	Reid	12/04	Outside cyls.	12/62	Last engine (68345) withdrawn
J89	—	—	—	—	Never used	—	—
J90	GNS	D	Manson	5/84	16" cyls.	3/36	Last engine (6842) withdrawn
J91	GNS	E	Manson	6/85	18" cyls.	6/34	Last engine (6841) withdrawn
J92	GE	204	Johnson	4/27	Crane tanks—reclassified from Z4	11/52	Last engine (Dept'l 35) withdrawn
J93	MGN	M.R.	Marriott	7/42	Outside cyls., first built 1897, taken over 10/36	8/49	Last engine (0489) withdrawn
—	MGN	—	Fox, Walker	1877	Outside cyl. saddletank, taken over 10/36, did not survive to get L.N.E.R. class	10/37	Only engine (MGN16A) withdrawn
J94	LNE	WD	Hunslet Eng. Co.	6/46	Saddletank built from 1/44 for War Dept.	—	45 in stock at 31st Dec., 1962

2-6-0

Class	Section	Former Class	Designer	Date Class'n Introduced	Notes	Date Class'n Extinct	Disposal
K1	GN	H2	Gresley	8/12	With 4' 8" boiler	7/37	Last engine (4636) reboilered to K2
K1	LNE	K4	Thompson/Gresley	12/45	2 cyl. rebuild from 3 cyl. K4 class	12/46	Only engine (1997) reclassified Part 1
K1	BR	—	Peppercorn	5/49	2 cyl. based on Thompson design	—	67 in stock at 31st Dec., 1962
K1/1	GN	K1	Thompson/Gresley	12/46	Thompson K1 reclassified	6/61	Only engine (61997) withdrawn
K2	GN	—	Gresley	12/29	All three varieties combined	12/38	Class divided into different Parts 1 & 2
K2/1	GN	H3	Gresley	5/14	5' 6" boiler, journals 8¼" x 9, including rebuilds from K1	12/29	Class part discontinued
K2/1	GN	K2	Gresley	12/38	K1 engines reboilered from 4' 8" to 5' 6" (from 6/20)	12/60	Last engine (61728) withdrawn
K2/2	GN	H3	Gresley	2/16	5' 6" boiler, journals 9" x 11"	12/29	Class part discontinued
K2/2	GN	K2	Gresley	12/38	With both journal sizes but not K1 rebuilds	6/62	Last engine (61756) withdrawn
K3	GN & LNE	—	Gresley	3/20	3 cyls, 6' 0" boiler and built to G.N. gauge	12/24	Reclassified to Part 1
K3/1	LNE	K3/2 & K3/3	Gresley	12/47	Engines now similar but 7 with G.N. tender	12/62	Last engine (61985) withdrawn
K3/2	LNE	K3	Gresley	8/24	K3 reclassified	10/40	Last engine (4004) altered to Part 2
K3/3	LNE	—	Gresley	4/29	Built to L.N.E. gauge	12/47	Class part discontinued
K3/4	LNE	—	Gresley	7/30	West. and vac. brake and 6" shorter coupled springs	12/35	Reclassified to Part 2
K3/5	LNE	—	Gresley	3/31	As Part 2 but reduced weights	12/35	Reclassified to Part 2
K3/6	LNE	—	Gresley	7/34	As Part 2 but slightly heavier engine; As Part 2 but different coupled springs	12/35	Reclassified to Part 2
K4	LNE	—	Gresley	1/37	3 cyl., 5' 6" boiler	12/61	Last engine (61994) withdrawn
K5	LNE	K3/2	Thompson/Gresley	6/45	2 cyl. rebuilt from K3/2 and with 225lb. pressure	6/60	Only engine (61863) withdrawn

2-6-4T

Class	Section	Former Class	Designer	Date Class'n Introduced	Notes	Date Class'n Extinct	Disposal
L1	GC	1B	Robinson	12/14	—	12/38	Class divided into Parts 1 & 2
L1	LNE	L1	Thompson	5/45	—	12/62	Last engines (sixteen) withdrawn
L1/1	GC	L1	Robinson	12/38	Retaining 21" cyls.	5/45	All reclassified to L3
L1/2	LPTB	K	Jones/Maunsell	11/37	With cylinders lined to 20" (from 7/27). First built 1925, taken over 11/37	5/45	Only engine (5342) reclassified L3
L3	GC	L1/1 & L1/2	Robinson	5/45	L1 Parts combined and reclassified	10/48	Last engine (9070) withdrawn

0-6-4T

Class	Section	Former Class	Designer	Date Class'n Introduced	Notes	Date Class'n Extinct	Disposal
M1	GC	D	Thom	5/04	First built 1915, taken over 11/37	7/47	Last engine (9082) withdrawn
M2	LPTB	G	Jones	11/37	—	10/48	Last engines (9076/7) withdrawn

0-6-2T

Class	Section	Former Class	Designer	Date Class'n Introduced	Notes	Date Class'n Extinct	Disposal
N1	GN	N1	Ivatt	4/07	All varieties	4/59	Last engine (69462) withdrawn
N2	GN	N2	Gresley	12/20	Condensing, 12' 7" to chimney, R.H. drive	12/40	Merged into Part 2 but retaining R.H. drive
N2/1	—	—	—	—	Never used	—	—
N2/2	LNE	—	Gresley	5/25	L.H. drive and 4" higher chimney, but incl. N2 engines from 12/40	9/62	Last engines (69504/20/9/46) withdrawn
N2/3	LNE	—	Gresley	11/25	As orig. N2/2 but 8¼" journals against 7¼"	6/61	Last engine (69564) withdrawn
N2/4	LNE	—	Gresley	9/28	As N2/3 but condensing and 12' 7" to chimney, heavier	9/62	Last engines (69568/75/9/83/93) withdrawn
N				—	Never used	—	—

Class	Rly	Orig. class	Builder	Date	Details	W'drawn	Notes
N4/1	GC	N4/1	Parker	12/8?	…JOY valve gear	12/27	Class Part divided into Parts 1 & 2
N4/2	GC	9Aalt.	Parker	12/27	Orig. Part 1 still over 13' 0" high	8/39	Last engine (5623) altered to part 2
N4/2	GC	N4/1	Parker	12/27	As Part 1 but 5 cwt. coal and 60 galls. water extra	12/92	Reclassified to Parts 3 & 4
N4/3	GC	N4/2	Parker	12/27	Orig. Part 1 cut down below 13' 0" (from 10/2)	12/54	Last engines (69225/8/30/2) withdrawn
N4/4	GC	N4/2	Parker	12/27	Orig. Part 2 still over 13' 0" high	3/35	Last engine (5715) altered to Part 4
N5	GC	9C, 9F, & 9O	Parker	9/91	As Part 3 but cut down below 13' 0" (from 5/25)	4/52	Last engine (69246) withdrawn
N5/1	GC	N5/2	Parker	12/47	Similar to N4 but Steph. valve gear, both saturated and superheated	12/27	Class divided into Parts 1 & 2
N5/2	GC	N5	Parker	12/27	All sat. and under 13' 0" with 1360-gall. tanks	12/60	Last engine (69307) withdrawn
N5/2	GC	N5	Parker	12/27	Both sat. and sup. still over 13' 0" high	10/38	Last engine (5770) altered to Part 2
N5/3	GC	N5/2	Robinson/Parker	12/38	Both sat. and sup. cut down below 13' 0" (from 3/25)	12/47	Class part discontinued
N6	GC	A	Kitson & Co.	9/95	One engine with 1840-gall. tanks (from 11/15)	2/52	Only engine (69311) withdrawn
N7	GE	L77	Hill	12/14	Belpaire firebox, incl. sat. and both 12 and 18 el. superheater	10/38	Last engine (6414) withdrawn
N7/1	LNE	—	Gresley	8/25	Similar to N7 (18 el. sup.), but detail variations, heavier	6/49	Last engine (9602) reboilered to Part 4
N7/2	LNE	—	Gresley	6/27	As Part 1 but with longer valve travel	9/56	Last engine (69627) reboilered to Part 5
N7/3	LNE	—	Gresley	1/27	As Part 2 but round top firebox	12/58	Last engine (69695) withdrawn
N7/4	LNE	N7	Thompson	2/40	Orig. N7 rebuilt with R.T. firebox	9/62	Last engines (69632/40/6) withdrawn
N7/5	LNE	N7/1	Thompson	5/43	Orig. N7/1 rebuilt with R.T. firebox	9/62	Last engine (69621) withdrawn
N8	NE	B	W. Worsdell	6/86	5' 1¼" coupled wheels, both sat. and sup.	9/62	Last engine (69671/92/7, 69725) withdrawn
N9	NE	Z	T. W. Worsdell	5/93	Similar to N8 sat., lighter	10/56	Last engine (69390) withdrawn
N10	NE	U	W. Worsdell	10/02	4' 7¼" coupled wheels	7/55	Last engines (69429) withdrawn
N11	HB	F1	M. Stirling	2/01	4' 9" coupled wheels	4/62	Last engines (69097, 69101/9) withdrawn
N12	HB	F2	M. Stirling	11/01	4' 6" wheels, both domeless and domed	5/46	Last engine (2480) withdrawn
N13	HB	F3	M. Stirling	11/13	4' 6" wheels, both domeless and domed, heavier	8/48	Last engine (9089) withdrawn
N14	NB	A	Reid	9/09	Short cab, max. axle load 17t. 4c.	10/56	Last engines (69114) withdrawn
N15/1	NB	A	Reid	6/10	Similar to N14 but long cab, max. axle load 18t. 18c.	3/54	Last engines (69120/5) withdrawn
N15/2	NB	—	Reid	6/10	As Part 1 but larger water capacity	12/62	Last engine (69178) withdrawn
N16-N17	NB	A	Reid	—	Never used	10/62	Last engine (69128) withdrawn
N18	CVH E&	—	Hudswell, Clarke	7/23	First built 8/08, taken over 7/23	7/28	Only engine (8314) withdrawn
N19	WYU	—	Manning, Wardle	7/23	First built 5/99, taken over 7/23	3/28	Last engine (3115) withdrawn
2-8-0							
O1	GN	O1	Gresley	12/13	2 outside cyls.	2/44	Reclassified to O3
O1	LNE	O4	Thompson/Robinson	2/44	Rebuilds from O4 with new cyls. and diag. 100A boiler	—	30 in stock at 31st Dec., 1962
O2	GN	O2	Gresley	5/18	3 inclined cyls. and orig. Gresley gear	5/48	Only engine (3921) withdrawn
O2/1	GN	O2	Gresley	5/21	3 horiz. cyls. and std. Gresley gear, 9" x 51" crankpins, orig. over 13' 0" high	—	1 only in stock at 31st Dec., 1962
O2/2	LNE	—	Gresley	10/32	8¼" x 6" crankpins, under 13' 0"	—	8 in stock at 31st Dec., 1962
O2/3	LNE	—	Gresley	4/32	As Part 2 but window cab and Group Std. tender	—	14 in stock at 31st Dec., 1962
O2/4	LNE	—	Thompson/Gresley	10/43	Parts 1, 2 & 3 with diag. 100A boiler	—	17 in stock at 31st Dec., 1962
O3	GN	O1	Gresley	2/44	Original O1 reclassified	12/52	Last engine (63484) withdrawn

2-8-0 (contd.)

Class	Section	Former Class	Designer	Date Class'n Introduced	Notes	Date Class'n Extinct	Disposal
O4/1	GC	8K	Robinson	9/11	4000-gall. tender orig. with scoop, without from 12/40	—	29 in stock at 31st Dec., 1962
O4/2	GC	8K	Robinson	11/20	As Part 1 but with 3250-gall. tender	12/24	Engines transferred to Part 1
O4/2	GC	O4/1	Robinson	12/25	With boiler mountings to suit N.B. gauge (from 5/23)	12/46	Engines transferred to Part 1
O4/3	LNE	—	Robinson	12/27	Ex-R.O.D. (from 12/23) with 4000-gall. tender, no scoop	12/40	Engines merged with Part 1
O4/4	ENE	O4/3	Gresley/Robinson	7/29	Rebuilt with O2-type boiler from O4/3	8/47	Last engine (3882) reboilered to Part 8
O4/5	LNE	O4/1 & O4/3	Gresley/Robinson	6/32	Rebuilds with modified O2 boiler	4/59	Last two engines (63745 & 63851) withdrawn
O4/6	LNE	O5	Robinson	12/38	Rebuilds from O5 but retaining wide cab (from 7/22)	—	5 in stock at 31st Dec., 1962
O4/7	LNE	—	Gresley/Robinson	11/39	Rebuilds from Parts 1, 2 & 3 with diag. 15D boiler	—	7 in stock at 31st Dec., 1962
O4/8	LNE	—	Thompson/Robinson	12/46	Rebuilds with diag. 100A boiler (from 4/44)	—	75 in stock at 31st Dec., 1962
O5	GC	8M	Robinson	1/18	As O4 but 5' 6" boiler	1/43	Last engine (5422) reboilered to O4/6
O6	LNE	8F	Stanier	12/46	L.M.S. type built from 6/44 under War emergency	1/48	Last engine (3554) sent to L.M. Region
O7	—	W.D.	Riddles	12/46	'Austerity' engines bought from War Dept.	12/48	Class reverted to "W.D."

2-8-2

Class	Section	Former Class	Designer	Date Class'n Introduced	Notes	Date Class'n Extinct	Disposal
P1	LNE	—	Gresley	6/25	3 cyl., 5' 2" coupled wheels, with and without booster and both 180 and 220 lb.	7/45	Last engine (2393) withdrawn
P2	LNE	—	Gresley	5/34	3 cyl., 6' 2" coupled wheels, with rotary cam operated poppet valves	10/34	Reclassified Part 1
P2/1	LNE	P2	Gresley	10/34	P2 reclassified	4/38	Only engine (2001) rebuilt to Part 2
P2/2	LNE	—	Gresley	10/34	Walschaert/Gresley gear and piston valves	12/44	Last engine (2003) rebuilt to Class A2
P2/3	LNE	—	Gresley	9/36	As Part 2 but boiler with combustion chamber	4/44	Only engine (2006) rebuilt to Class A2

0-8-0

Class	Section	Former Class	Designer	Date Class'n Introduced	Notes	Date Class'n Extinct	Disposal
Q1	GN	K1	Ivatt	2/01	With slide valves, both sup, and sat.	10/35	Last engine (3447) withdrawn
Q2	GN	K1	Ivatt	12/08	Q1 rebuilt with piston valves—all sup.	12/35	Last two engines (3416/7) withdrawn
Q3	GN	K2	Gresley/Ivatt	2/14	Q2 rebuilt with larger boiler	2/37	Only engine (3420) withdrawn
Q4/1	GC	8A & Q4/2	Robinson	11/02	Both sat. and sup. with 3250-gall. tender	12/24	Part re-used to differentiate heights
Q4/1	GC	Q4/1	Robinson	12/24	Over 13' 0", both sat. and sup., both tenders	12/28	Part re-used for 4000-gall. tenders only
Q4/1	GC	Q4/1	Robinson	12/28	Over 13' 0", both sat. and sup., 4000-gall. tender	12/43	Part re-used for saturated only
Q4/2	GC	Q4/1	Robinson	12/43	Under 13' 0" but still saturated	6/51	Last engine (63204) withdrawn
Q4/2	GC	8A & Q4/2	Robinson	7/05	Both sat. and sup. with 4000-gall. tender	12/24	Part re-used to mean under 13' 0"
Q4/2	GC	Q4/2	Robinson	12/24	Under 13' 0", both sat. and sup., both tenders	12/28	Part re-used for 4000-gall. tenders only
Q4/2	GC	—	Robinson	12/28	Under 13' 0", sup. only, 4000-gall. tender	9/51	Last engines (63202/25) withdrawn
Q4/3	GC	—	Robinson	12/28	Over 13' 0", sat. and sup., with 3250-gall. tender	10/30	Last engine (6074) altered to Part 1
Q4/4	GC	—	Robinson	12/28	Under 13' 0" (from 12/25), sup. only, with 3250-gall. tender	5/30	Last engine (6141) altered to Part 2

Class	Rly	Code	Designer	Built	Details	W/D	Remarks
Q5	NE	T & T1	W. Worsdell	8/01	2 outs cyls, 4' 9" sat. boiler, both slide and piston valves	12/32	Class divided into Parts 1 & 2
Q5/1	NE	Q5	W. Worsdell	12/32	Q5 retaining 4' 9" boilers	10/51	Last engine (3326) withdrawn
Q5/2	LNE	Q5	Gresley/W. Worsdell	12/32	Rebuilt with 5' 6" boiler (from 10/32)	5/49	Last engine (3305) withdrawn
Q6	NE	T2	Raven	2/13	2 outs. cyls, 5' 6" boiler	12/62	118 in stock at 31st Dec., 1962
Q7	NE	T3	Raven	10/19	3 cyls.	—	Last engines (63471/3/4) withdrawn
Q8-Q9	—	—	—		Never used		—
Q10	HB	A	M. Stirling	2/07	Domeless Belpaire boilers	2/24	Class divided into Parts 1 & 2
Q10/1	HB	Q10	M. Stirling	12/24	Q10 retaining domeless boilers	3/28	Last engine (2512) reboilered to Part 2
Q10/2	HB	Q10	Gresley/M. Stirling	12/24	Rebuilds with domed R.T. boiler (from 10/24)	11/31	Last engine (2502) withdrawn
0-8-0T							
—	GC	WMCQ	Willans	1903	Did not survive to get L.N.E.R. class	8/23	Only engine (GC400B) withdrawn
Q1	LNE	—	Thompson/Robinson	6/42	Rebuilds from Q4 class 0-8-0	12/46	Class divided into Parts 1 & 2
Q1/1	LNE	Q1	Thompson/Robinson	12/46	With 1500-gall. tanks and 4½ tons coal (from 6/42)	8/59	Last engine (69928) withdrawn
Q1/2	LNE	Q1	Thompson/Robinson	12/46	With 2000-gall. tanks and 4 tons coal (from 11/43)	9/59	Last engine (69936) withdrawn
0-8-2T							
R1	GN	L1	Ivatt	7/03	4' 2" and 4' 8" boilers, both sat. and sup.	2/34	Last engine (3154) withdrawn
0-8-4T							
S1	GC	8H	Robinson	12/07	3 cyls, saturated	12/32	Class divided into Parts 1 & 2
S1/1	GC	S1	Robinson	12/32	S1 saturated and (from 7/40) superheated	1/56	Last engine (69902) withdrawn
S1/2	LNE	S1	Gresley/Robinson	12/32	Rebuilt 1/32 with booster on bogie, and sup.	1/57	Only engine (69901) withdrawn
S1/3	LNE	—	Gresley	12/32	Built 5/32, like Part 2 but less water and more coal	1/57	Last engine (69905) withdrawn
4-8-0T							
T1	NE	X	W. Worsdell	9/09	3 cyls, both sat. and sup.	6/61	Last engine (69921) withdrawn
2-8-0+0-8-2							
U1	LNE	—	Gresley	6/25	—	12/55	Only engine (69999) withdrawn
2-6-2T							
V1	LNE	—	Gresley	9/30	3 cyl., with 180lb. pressure	12/62	Last engines (67630/64/80) withdrawn
V3	LNE	—	Gresley	9/39	As V1 but 200lb. pressure	—	26 in stock at 31st Dec., 1962
2-6-2							
V2	LNE	—	Gresley	6/36	3 cyl., 6' 2" coupled wheels	—	115 in. stock at 31st Dec., 1962
V4	LNE	—	Gresley	2/41	3 cyl., 5' 8" coupled wheels	11/57	Last engine (61701) withdrawn
4-6-4							
W1	LNE	—	Gresley	6/30	Both as built and as rebuilt	6/59	Only engine (60700) withdrawn
2-2-4T							
X1	NE	66	W. Worsdell	4/02	2 cyl. compound, 5' 7½" driving wheels	5/34	Only engine (66) withdrawn
X2	NE	957	W. Worsdell	4/03	6' 1½" driving wheels, rebuild from G6 class	4/37	Only engine (957) withdrawn
X3	NE	190	W. Worsdell	6/94	6' 6¼" driving wheels	12/36	Last engine (190) withdrawn

Class	Section	Former Class	Designer	Date Class'n Introduced	Notes	Date Class'n Extinct	Disposal
4-2-2							
X4	GC	13	Pollitt	1/00	Both saturated and superheated	8/27	Last engine (5972) withdrawn
0-4-0T							
Y1	LNE	—	Sentinel	9/25	Single speed engines	12/28	Reclassified to Part 1
Y1/1	LNE	Y1	Sentinel	12/28	Original Y1 reclassified	—	1 only in stock at 31st Dec., 1962
Y1/2	LNE	—	Sentinel	12/28	As Part 1 but 3½ cwt. more coal	6/61	Last engine (Dept'l 54) withdrawn
Y1/3	LNE	—	Sentinel	12/30	As Part 2 but only 14t. 0c. total weight	9/51	Only engine (8139) withdrawn
Y1/4	LNE	—	Sentinel	12/31	As Part 2 but smaller grate and boiler	10/56	Only engine (Dept'l 51) withdrawn
Y2	GC	4	Manning, Wardle	3/83	Saddletanks	7/31	Both engines (6430/1) withdrawn
Y3	LNE	—	Sentinel	12/27	As Y1 but bigger boiler and two-speed gearbox	—	3 in stock at 31st Dec., 1962
Y4	GE	B74	Hill	7/13	—	4/48	Last engine (8081) withdrawn
Y5	GE	209	Neilson & Co.	5/74	Saddletanks	11/52	Last engine (68083) withdrawn
Y6	GE	G15	T. W. Worsdell	8/83	Tram engines	11/52	Last engine (68088) withdrawn
Y7	NE	H	T. W. Worsdell	12/88	3' 5" wheels	11/56	Last engine (Dept'l 55) withdrawn
Y8	NE	K	T. W. Worsdell	6/90	3' 0" wheels	12/56	Last engine (68095) withdrawn
Y9	NB	G	Neilson & Co.	12/82	Saddletanks	12/62	Last engine (68186) withdrawn
Y10	LNE	—	Sentinel	7/30	Double-ended tram engines	2/52	
Y11	GE & NB	—	Motor Rail & Tram Co.	12/43	First built 12/19, previously unclassified, both with and without cab	11/56	Last engine (15099) withdrawn
0-6-0							
Y10	NB	—	Holmes/Wheatley	5/68	As rebuilt in 7/02	12/25	Only engine (NB1011) withdrawn
0-4-2T							
Z1-Z3	GE	—	Johnson	5/68	Never used	—	Reclassified to J92
Z4	GNS	204	Manning, Wardle	4/27	Crane tanks—these engines were 0-6-0 type. Smaller engines reclassified from Z5	4/60	Last engine (68190) withdrawn
Z5	GNS	X & Y	Manning, Wardle	1/15	Both 3' 6" (X) and 4' 0" (Y) coupled wheels	4/27	Class divided into Z4 and Z5
Z5	GNS	—	Manning, Wardle	4/27	Engines with 4' 0" coupled wheels only	4/60	Last engine (68192) withdrawn
—	CVH	—	Neilson & Co.	7/23	First built 1877, taken over 7/23, did not survive to get L.N.E.R. class	8/23	Only engine (C.V.H.1) withdrawn

ILLUSTRATIONS

Acknowledgment of illustrations :—

Drummond Young (Fig. 1), Elliott & Fry (Fig. 2), C. Smith (Figs. 3, 47, 66), British Railways (Figs. 4, 5, 6, 7, 8, 9, 31, 44, 56, 57, 63, 75, 79, 84, 87, 88), G. R. Grigs (Figs. 10, 14, 96, 97, 103, 104, 105, 118, 124, 142, 143, 145, 146, 161), C. Stevens (Figs. 11, 12, 169), Colling Turner (Figs. 13, 15, 16, 70, 78, 99, 110, 111, 116, 156, 157), W. Clark (Figs. 17, 62, 67, 68, 72, 73, 77), W. Leslie Good (Figs. 19, 98, 127, 136), Locomotive Publishing Co. (Figs. 20, 43, 45, 46, 50, 119, 121, 129, 151, 152), H. C. Casserley (Figs. 22, 26, 30, 34, 53, 140, 147, 148, 155, 170, 171), R. D. Stephen (Fig. 23), W. H. Whitworth (Figs. 24, 25, 29, 35, 131), R. H. Inness (Figs. 27, 28, 32, 33, 90), E. V. Fry (Figs. 36, 37, 39, 91, 120, 132), N. Fields (Figs. 38, 55, 138), J. H. Platts (Figs. 40, 81), T. G. Hepburn (Figs. 41, 42), W. J. Reynolds (Fig. 49), Mrs. A. Yeadon (Fig. 51), J. J. Cunningham (Fig. 52), L. & G.R.P. (Fig. 54), E. Neve (Figs. 58, 65, 69, 82), L. Hanson (Figs. 59, 64), K. Risdon Prentice (Fig. 60), Real Photographs (Figs. 61, 165), R. F. Orpwood (Fig. 71), J. Robertson (Figs. 74, 86), M. G. Boddy (Fig. 76), J. L. Stevenson (Fig. 80), K. Hoole (Fig. 83), J. R. Paterson (Figs. 85, 92, 93), J. T. Rutherford (Figs. 89, 100), C. Ord (Figs. 94, 150, 154), M. W. Earley (Figs. 95, 101, 107, 109, 137, 144, 158), H. Gordon Tidey (Figs. 102, 106, 114, 115, 153, 167, 168), Dr. I. C. Allen (Figs. 108, 141), R. D. Pollard (Figs. 112, 113), J. M. Craig (Figs. 117, 163, 164), A. R. Goult (Fig. 130), R. C. Nelson (Fig. 133), A. G. Ellis (Fig. 134), T. M. S. Findlater (Fig. 135), J. P. Wilson (Fig. 139), Lance Brown (Figs. 149, 160), C. J. L. Romanes (Figs. 159, 162, 166). Figs. 8, 48, 126 and 134 are by courtesy of George Dow, and figs. 112 and 113 by N. Fields.

NEW INFORMATION AND REVISIONS

Fig. 164   Class C16 No. 9447 on an evening train to Helensburgh, near Partick
in 1929

Fig. 165   Class C11 No. 9874 *Dunedin* on an Aberdeen to Edinburgh express
near North Queensferry, about 1927

Fig. 166   Class J37 No. 9139 on an East Coast goods passing Drem, about 1925.
N.B.R. 3500-gallon tender

Fig. 167   Class G10 No. 6885 leaving Aberdeen on a suburban train

Fig. 168   Class D42 No. 6872 on a Ballater train leaving Aberdeen

Fig. 169   Class D29 No. 9340 *Lady of Avenel* leaving Aberdeen on an up
fish train, 1928

Fig. 170   Class Z4 No. 8191 shunting in Aberdeen docks, October 1947.
Wartime lettering " N E "

Fig. 171   Class J83 No. 8477 at Waverley station, April 1948.   Post-war green
livery, with number in centre of bunker rear.   N.B.R. power class plate
still on bunker side above L.N.E.R. number plate

re-entered works on 27/10/44.

The Complete Renumbering of 1946. First paragraph, penultimate line. Renumbering date of 7773 to be amended to "by 5/51" from 8/51.

40   Column 1, paragraph 3, line 5. In order of age is wrong because 4488-92 preceded 2509-12.

Column 1, last paragraph. No. 2548 (not 4485) was the last to be renumbered, on 25th April 1946, to 517.

Column 2, lines 2 & 3. 20 V2's were renumbered (not 19), the additional engine being No. 709.

42   The 1952 Departmental Stock List. A more complete and up-to-date version of the table (i.e. with later additions to Departmental Stock, namely class J50 Nos. 13-16, B1 Nos. 17-32 and J72 Nos. 58/9) will be found in Part 10A at pages 24-27. The following amendments to Part 1 should be noted:-

Renumbering Dates – Nos. 12, 37/8, 40/1 received their new numbers by (not at) the dates shown. No. 100 was renumbered 1/59, not 2/59.

Normal Location – No. 7 was at Lowestoft from c.11/61, No. 32 was attached to Stratford Carriage Works from 10/52, and No. 39 went to Cambridge Chesterton Junction Engineers' Yard in 3/55.

Withdrawn – No. 37 was withdrawn 1/56, not 3/56. Dates subsequent to the publication of Part 1 were: 7 5/64, 10/1/2 5/65, 33 12/63, 40 5/64, 41 3/63, 100 4/64.

43   Column 1, end of paragraph 1. "Lettered" should read "relettered".

Column 1, paragraph 2, line 4: "Goods grey" livery was introduced in 1912 on the G.N.R. Line 18: The paint used by the G.E.R. was darker than Royal blue, being correctly Sissons Ultramarine in Oil, which had a purplish shade to it.

Column 2, line 4. Strictly speaking, the so-called engraved numberplates on N.B.R. engines were actually cast with sunken characters which were then filled with black wax. However, among the N.B.R. engines

which came into the L.N.E.R., the following did have cast numberplates with raised characters: (1) the 1921 batch of class J37 0-6-0's, (2) all the Duplicate List engines from No. 1070 upwards.

44   Column 2, paragraph 1. During the early months of 1924 Gorton Works turned out quite a number of repaired engines without repainting them because of an urgent need for them in traffic. Beginning in March 1924 the G.C.R. numberplates were generally replaced by new ones of similar style but carrying the L.N.E.R. number.

Column 2, paragraph 2. Add that class B13 No. 2006 was specially painted in L.N.E.R. green livery in 1925 in order to take part in the Stockton & Darlington Centenary celebrations.

Column 2, paragraph 3. Delete D23 and E1 from list.

45   Column 1, paragraph 3, line 7. .... many small tenders........ delete "small".

Column 2, line 9. Change 1938 to November 1937.

Column 2, paragraph 2. Add – When the "N E" lettering was introduced, Gorton Works changed from 7½ in. to 12 in. characters on tank engines and continued to use the latter size on some when the full "L N E R" lettering was reintroduced after the 1939-45 War.

In order to aid visibility in black out conditions during the War, many shunting engines had their bufferbeams painted white at that time.

Just before the proposed general application of green livery, class B1 4-6-0 Nos. 1040-93 were turned out new from N.B.L. Co. in 1946 painted black with red lining, instead of unlined black still normally in use at that time.

Column 2, penultimate paragraph, line 20. Add V3 to the list of classes painted green.

46   Paragraph 1, final line. Reference to Fig. 132 should more correctly read Fig. 54.

Column 2, line 5. 1944-46 should read 1943-46 (Darlington Works began showing the paint date on locomotives in May 1943).

47 Lined Black Livery – Class N2. The "No." and figures on the front bufferbeam were in 4½" transfers, not 4¼".

49 Column 1, paragraph 2, line 9. Although the name *Aerolite* was revived (see lines 11 & 12), new nameplates were fitted, which were not part of its original construction.

Column 2, paragraph 4, line 9. The name *Waverley* was also used again on a N.B.R. Atlantic.

50 Column 2, foot of page. The standard length of the long pattern of nameplate was 4' 2½", but *Flying Fox* received 3' 6" plates in place of the 2' 8" type.

52 First line. The reference to figure 71 should be 72.

Second line. May 1938 should read August 1938.

53 Final paragraph of A4 class. Add that Lord Faringdon was Deputy Chairman of the L.N.E.R. from 1923 until his death in March 1934.

B1 Class. It should be mentioned that the directors' names affixed to eighteen B1's were those not already borne by Class A4 locomotive. It is understood that Rupert E. Beckett declined to have his name included. As appears on page 99, the B1 engines named were Nos. 1036, 1189, 1215, 1221, plus the sequence 1237 to 1251, but with 1239 omitted which engine presumably had been ear-marked to be named Rupert E. Beckett.

54 Column 1, paragraph 2, line 8. "enamelled plates" should read "painted panels".

Column 2, end of paragraph 3. *Rendlesham Hall* should read *Rendelsham Hall*.

Paragraph 5. *Lincolnshire Regiment* was ceremonially named at Lincoln on 4th May 1938, not 30th April.

55 Column 1, paragraph 1, line 14. When the names were first painted on the D11's the letters were fully shaded. The same applied to the N.B.R. 4-4-0's (classes D29, D30 and D34), the change to Gill Sans lettering coinciding with the abolition of shading.

56 K4 Class. The events surrounding the naming of these engines are more fully (and more accurately) described in Part 6A, page 149.

57 Railcars, second paragraph. According to Armstrong Whitworth's employees, *Lady Hamilton* was intended for trial on the Southern Railway and was so named in allusion to *Lord Nelson*, the first engine of the Company's principal express passenger class of locomotive.

61 Column 1, paragraph 2, line 9. "In 1908" to read "In 1907..."

62 Column 1, table. Some engines of G.C. class 12A had tenders of 2000 gallons capacity.

Column 2, paragraph 3. It would appear that the G.E.R. so-called 3300-gallon tenders were identical to and had the same capacity as the 3450-gallon type. None of the later official records made any reference to the existence of 3300-gallon capacity tenders.

The table showing the position on the G.E.R. at Grouping should more correctly read as follows:-

Water Capacity	Coal Capacity	Water Pickup	Attached to Classes
2500 galls.	5 tons	No	J14
3066 galls.	5 tons	No	J14, J15
2755 galls.	5 tons	No	J15, D13
2640 galls.	5 tons	No	D13, E4, J14, J15, J16/17 (8150-69)
2790 galls.	5 tons	No	D13 (8020-9), D14/15 (8890-9), E4 (7407-16)
3450 galls.	5 tons	Yes	D14/15, D16 (from March 1923)
3500 galls.	5 tons	No	J16/17, J18, J19, J20
3700 galls.	4 tons	Yes	B12

64 Table in first column. The 1800-gallon/2½-ton tender type was also used on class E7.

66 Column 1, final paragraph, lines 14-16. The first straightsided tender came out in February 1929 from Darlington coupled to class D49 No. 2753, not K3 No. 1300.

Column 2, line 1. After "with the high front-end" add : Beginning with the N.B.L.-built class B1 1040 onwards, the front-end design was further modified. The large coal door was dispensed with and a large double-deck locker fitted in the centre of the coal plate. Access to fuel was through two small doors located beneath the locker, the doors opening outward into the cab.

67 Column 2, final paragraph, line 14. "in May 1941" to read "from February 1941".

69 Column 2, line 10. "12 Q4's" to read "12 O4's". Regarding removal of water pick-up gear, a general instruction had been issued in 1937 that water scoops were to be removed from the tenders of D17/1, D17/2, D20 and J21 engines. The reference to the removal of scoop gear from G.C. Section engines is not quite correct. Authority to remove it from classes J11, O4 and Q4 had been given early in 1939 but was rescinded on 29th June of that year. Agreement to remove the gear from a large number of classes as stated was given in March 1946.

75 Second table. Delete L.N.E.R. Diag. No. 17 from entry against Gorton Type 8G.

76 Table of L.N.E.R. Boiler Diagrams. The 15C type was carried by class S1 engines 6170-3 and not just by 6170.

77 Diagram 63A: add H1 and T1.

Diagram 63C: add T1.

Diagram 69: add N12.

Diagram 105: boiler also used on S1/1 (engine 69903/6173).

Diagram 118: fitted to A2/2 from March 1951, not February.

80 Column 1, paragraph 2, penultimate line. Class X4 should be added to the list of G.C.R. locomotives that ran with the later plain type of chimney.

83 Group 4: D43 should read D40.

84 Column 2, paragraph 4, line 1. Dinting should read Glossop.

95 Great Eastern Railway. Official G.E.R. records, supported by calculation, show that the 1000th engine built at Stratford was No. 7648, not 7510 (the 980th). The total number of engines built there was 1682, not 1702.

It has been confirmed that the first use of an order number for new locomotives was J2 for the five X class 2-4-0WT's of 1862.

96 Gateshead Works dealt only with the N.E. Northern Division engines until the end of May 1923. The first of a regular flow of Southern Division engines to go there was No. 1803 (York) at the beginning of June, followed by Nos. 1991 (Neville Hill), 2307 (York), 1173 and 575 (Dairycoates), then 1556 (Darlington).

Gateshead Works was closed at the end of January 1933 (not August 1932). The last engine to go into the works was class J72 2321 on 3rd January for a light repair, whilst the last engine ex-shops was class G5 1791 on the 30th after a general repair.

Springhead Works closed in August 1924.

98 Gresley A1 (later A10) and A3 4-6-2 Classes. No. 2574: There was a full point after the St of *St. Frusquin*.

99 "Antelope" B1 Class 4-6-0. *A Harold Bibby* had a full point after the initial A, i.e. *A. Harold Bibby*.

100 Sandringham B17 and B2 4-6-0 Classes. 2839/1639: *Rendlesham Hall* should read *Rendelsham Hall*.

101 Great Central "Director" D10 class 4-4-0. The nameplates on Worsley Taylor carried a hyphen between the words.

L.N.E.R. LOCOMOTIVE CLASSES AND PARTS

(pages 104-120)

A (ex-P2) Class
Classification extinct 4/43, not 5/43.

A2 (ex-A) Class
Classification introduced 4/43, not 5/43; extinct 8/45, not 10/45.

A2/2 (ex-A2) Class
Classification introduced 8/45, not 10/45.

B4 Class
Classification introduced 6/06, not 5/06.

B7/1 Class
5'8" coupled wheels, not 5'7".

B9 Class
5'4" coupled wheels, not 5'3".

B12 (LNE) Class
Classification extinct 12/29, not 12/31.

B12/2 Class
Classification introduced 12/29, not 12/31.

B16/3 Class
Classification introduced 4/44, not 5/44.

C6 Class
N.E.R. used the classification V/09, not V1.

C11 Class
Add after "with superheater" that the original saturated version dated from 7/06.

D9 (ex-GC 11B, C & D) Class
4'9" boiler as well as 5'0".

D23 Class
Coupled wheel diameter 6'1¼", not 6'1½".

D27 Class
Class introduced 5/77, not 8/76.

D28 Class
Rebuilds from N.B. 476 class from 6/04, not 7/04.

D29 (ex-D29/2) Class
All superheated from 8/36, not 7/36.

D29/1 Class
Classification extinct 8/36, not 7/36.

D29/2 Class
Alike from 8/36, not 7/36.

D34 Class
The restored engine, N.B.R. No. 256, was kept in B.R. running stock until 12/62, so technically No. 62496 was not the last survivor.

D39 Class
Class introduced 12/78, not 1/79.

D40 Class
Class introduced 10/99, not 9/99

D45 Class
Class introduced 8/78, not 6/78.

D48 Class
5'6" coupled wheels, not 5'6½".

J8/1 and J8/2 Class
Former class 6AI, not 6A1.

J9/2 Class
Under max. height from 1/25, not 12/25.

J11/2 (ex-9J) Class
Class introduced 8/05, not 6/06.

J13 Class
3" smaller wheels than J9, not 4".

J23/2 Class
Classification extinct 11/38 (engine 2476), not 11/37 (2518).

J35/2 Class
Classification extinct 1/26, not 6/25.

J37 Class
Class introduced 12/14, not 7/14.

J58 Class
Class introduced 10/02, not 12/02; 5'1¼" wheels, not 5'3".

G.C.7 Class
Designer Sacré, not Parker.

J66 Class
Class introduced 5/86, not 6/86.

J69 Class
Class introduced 7/02, not 8/02; extinct 3/50, not 12/52.

J69/1 & J69/2 Class
Classification introduced 3/50, not 12/52.

J80 Class
5'0" wheels, not 5'1"; classification extinct 8/31, not 9/31.

J82 Class
Class introduced 11/75.

J84 Class
4'3" wheels, not 4'0".

J86 Class
Delete "Classified in error – only engine was

identical with J81", insert "Saddletank with 5'0" wheels".

J91 Class
Delete "18" cylinders", insert "As J90, but boiler further forward".

J93 Class
Last engine was 8489, not 0489.

L2 Class
Designer was Hally (Maunsell), not Jones (Maunsell).

N4/1 Class
Last engine (5623) was altered to N4/2 in 8/36, not 8/39.

N4/2 Class
Second entry to read ".......13'0" (from 10/25)".

N4/4 Class
The date that the first engine was cut down in height was 3/28, not 5/25.

N7/GE Class
Introduced 1/15, not 12/14.

N7/2 Class
Introduced 7/27, not 6/27.

N7/3 Class
Introduced 11/27, not 1/27; the last engines withdrawn were 69692/7, 69725, not 69632/40/6.

N7/5 Class
The last engines withdrawn were 69632/40/6/71, not 69671/92/7, 69725.

N11 Class
Designer Kitson & Co., not M. Stirling.

N15/2 Class
To read "as part 1, but Westinghouse brake"; last engines 69128/88, not 69128.

R1 Class
Introduced 6/03, not 7/03.

X1 Class
56 withdrawn 6/34, not 5/34.

Y2 Class
Class extinct 6/31, not 7/31.

This table was compiled to 30/12/62, at which date 85 classifications were still in use. By April 1968 all had been rendered extinct by withdrawal of the engines concerned, except for the case of class J38/1 the last engine of which was reboilered to J38/2. For completeness, the dates that these classifications became extinct, together with the last engine(s), are given below. Where more than one engine number is quoted, all were withdrawn

from service on the same day. Of course, some locomotives (notably in class A4) still exist today in running order by virtue of preservation. Full details will be found in Part 10A of this series.

Class	Date extinct	Last engine(s)
A1 (Peppercorn)	6/66	60145
A2 (Peppercorn)	12/66	60532
A2/3	6/65	60512/22
A3	1/66	60052
A4	9/66	60019/24
A4/1	8/64	60012
B1	4/68	Deptl. 30/2
B16/2	7/64	61435
B16/3	6/64	61418/34/44/ 8/54/63
J27	9/67	65811/55/79/ 82/94
J36	6/67	65288, 65345
J37	4/67	64602/11/20
J38/1	11/63	65918 (reboilered to Part 2)
J38/2	4/67	65901/29
J50/1	9/63	68892
J50/2	5/65	Deptl. 10-13
J50/3	9/65	Deptl. 14
J72	10/67	Deptl. 58
J94	10/67	68012
K1	12/67	62005
O1	7/65	63589/90, 63630/46, 63725/68, 63868/79
O2/1	9/63	63927
O2/2	9/63	63936/9/40/3
O2/3	11/63	63969/81/4
O2/4	11/63	63924/75
O4/1	2/66	63764
O4/6	6/65	63913
O4/7	12/65	63770
O4/8	4/66	63653, 63781, 63818/58
Q6	9/67	63344/87/95
V2	12/66	60836
V3	11/64	67620/8/46/ 90/1
Y1/1	4/63	Deptl. 39
Y3	5/64	Deptl. 7, 40
Y4	12/63	Deptl. 33

ILLUSTRATIONS

Figure

12   King's Cross to Leeds train, not Edinburgh.

50   Photograph taken in 1929, not 1928.

99   The date that the photograph was taken
      must have been later than 1937 because
      "Class B17" appears on the locomotive's
      bufferbeam. (This feature was introduced in
      March 1938 and No. 2814 got it in June of
      that year).

114   The location is Ruislip.

Acknowledgements: Fig. 24 by P.F.Cooke, not
W.H. Whitworth; Fig. 92 by W.J. Reynolds, not
J.R. Paterson.

Map

By mistake, the line from Malton to Driffield
was omitted, as also was the Snape branch between
Wickham Market and Saxmundham.

SOME OTHER RCTS BOOKS

THE RAILWAYS OF KEYNSHAM
Featuring Fry's Chocolate Passenger and Freight Operations

Readers of this budget priced book will not merely find the facts and figures of Keynsham's railways, they will feel the atmosphere of the place through local personalities and staff. Imagine the heavy smells of smoke and fog mixing with chocolate. All the necessary detail is here, from the first coming of the railway, the arrival of Fry's, the creation of Fry's own railway infrastructure, the freight and passenger services provided for the factory, the growth years, decline, threat of closure and above all a happy ending with a buoyant present day scene (a new service to Filton Abbey Wood added recently). The Bristol-Bath route and Keynsham's four other industrial sidings are also comprehensively covered. Author Russell Leitch can claim fifty years of interest in Bristol area railways. Who better to take us on this fascinating trip to the past?
Laminated cover, 160 pages, 80 illustrations including 7 maps and drawings

SPECIAL OFFER!!!
GREAT NORTHERN LOCOMOTIVE HISTORY

This major four-volume work covers the complete story of the Great Northern Railway, Doncaster Works and its locomotives, from earliest days to The Grouping. Each class is covered from all six designers - Cubitt, Bury, Sturrock, Stirling, Ivatt and Gresley. 1,553 Doncaster built engines are covered, plus those bought in. Their robust design was demonstrated by almost half of the GN locomotives passed to the LNER at Grouping survived into British Railways ownership 25 years later. The set totals 804 pages with 738 illustrations. Buy the complete set now for a major 40% reduction!

SPECIAL OFFER FOR THE FOUR VOLUME CASEBOUND SET £40.95

The published price of these books totals £69.80.

So buy now and save almost £30.00!!

LMS LOCOMOTIVE DESIGN AND CONSTRUCTION
Locomotive Engineers, their Designs and Modifications

Author Arthur Cook interviewed many LMS locomotive engineers over the years to extract much new material and give a new insight into their designs' origins and performances for this book. It initiates the main part of the Society's Locomotives of the LMS series, dealing with the post-grouping era. The railway's design policies, origins and building programmes are meticulously traced with engine diagrams and modifications fully documented. An account of the development of piston valves and valve events on the LMS includes an appendix outlining the fundamentals of valve events, invaluable for preservationists.
Board covers, 175 pages, 110 illustrations.

BRITISH RAILWAYS STANDARD STEAM LOCOMOTIVES
Volume 1 Background to Standardisation and the Pacific Classes

Immediately British Railways was formed in January 1948, the railway Executive instructed Robert Riddles to design a series of standard locomotive designs. The intention was to gain material savings in running and maintenance costs by adopting as standard the best practices of the four independent companies. In this major new series, the Society presents for the fist time the complete story of British locomotive standardisation from the days of the Robinson ROD 2-8-0s to the twelve BR Standard designs totalling 999 locomotives. This book, by Paul Chancellor and Peter Gilbert, presents the Standards' design history and for each of the 66 locomotives in the popular Britannia, Duke and Clan classes its complete construction, modification, allocation and operating history.

Larger page size 212 x 272mm, Casebound, 184 pages, 151 illustrations including 17 in colour

LMS DIESELS
Locomotives and Railcars

Today's British motive power fleet is a tribute to the pioneering work of the LMS Classes 56, 58, 60 and HST power cars use AC generators based on the 10800 Hawk development and Class 77 electrics used LMS designed bogies. Classes 40, 50 and DP2 used LMS designed engines and Peak Classes 44-46 used cab design from the famous 10000 and 10001. Our first generation diesel multiple units owe much to the 1938 80000-2 LMS railcars. And, of course, our Classes 08 and 11 bear testimony to the quality of their LMS design 60 years ago! Author Edgar Richards takes readers through the fascinating history of LMS diesel development. From the first steam conversion in 1932 to the rugged 0-6-0 shunters built in large numbers for war service at home and abroad, the revolutionary main line 10000, 10001, 10100 and 10800, and the Michelin Coventry and LMS railcars, in total 208 locomotives, 15 railcars and 5 trolleys were operated by the LMS. Full details of their design, construction, modification, liveries allocation and use are included. This book includes much new material and is highly recommended.

Casebound, 219 pages, 125 illustrations

LMS LOCOMOTIVE NAMES
The Named Locomotives of the London, Midland and Scottish Railway and its Constituent Companies

The LNWR had a vigorous naming policy and the Midland Railway an equally determined anti-naming stance. The 1923 grouping set the stage for an absorbing battle within the management teams over naming policy with Derby's early policy success followed by Crewe's ultimate victory. Author John Goodman's absorbing read presents the full story of the LMS and its constituent companies' naming policies and the history of each named engine owned by the LMS, a total of 812. The LNWR contributed 668 of these and a complete presentation of its complex renaming system is an invaluable inclusion.

Casebound. 211 pages, 124 photographs, 25 drawings

RCTS Publications List

Title of Book	ISBN No.	*Price
The Railways of Keynsham	0901115827	£9.95
Special Offer Set of Great Northern Railway		£40.95
Gt Northern Locomotive History		
(individual books)		
1: 1847-1866	0901115614	£12.95
2: 1867-1895	0901115746	£19.95
3A: 1896-1911	090111569X	£19.95
3B: 1911-1923	0901115703	£16.95
BR Standard Steam Locomotives - Background		
to Standardisation and the Pacifics	0901115819	£19.95
LMS Diesels	0901115762	£19.95
LMS Locomotive Names	0901115797	£18.95
Western Change	0901115789	£15.95
LMS Locomotive Design and Construction	0901115711	£16.95
Locomotives of the LNER:		
Part 1 Preliminary Survey	0901115118	£12.95
Part 2A Tender Engines A1-A10	0901115258	£14.95
Part 2B Tender Engines B1-B19	0901115738	£13.95
Part 9A Tank Engines L1-L19	0901115401	£10.95
Part 9B Tank Engines Q1-Z5	090111541X	£10.95
Part 10A Departmental Stock, Engine Sheds,		
Boiler and Tender Numbering	0901115657	£10.95
Part 10B Railcars and Electrics	0901115665	£13.95
Highland Railway Locos 1855-1895	0901115649	£12.95
Highland Railway Locos 1895-1923	090111572X	£16.95
Shildon-Newport in Retrospect	0901115673	£10.95
Lord Carlisle's Railways	0901115436	£7.95

LOW STOCK TITLES - ORDER NOW WHILE STOCKS LAST

Locomotives of the LNER:		
Part 7 Tank Engines A5-H2	0901115134	£10.95
Part 11 Supplementary Information	0901115800	£10.95
Locomotives of the GWR:		
Part 11 Rail Motors	090111538X	£4.95

Available from: *Hon Assistant Publications Officer, Hazelhurst, Tiverton Road, Bampton, Devon*
EX16 9LJ, quoting ref: Books 2/97.

THE RAILWAY CORRESPONDENCE AND TRAVEL SOCIETY

(Founded 1928)

Joint Founders:	L. B. LAPPER and A. E. BROAD
President:	A. H. GOULD
Vice-Presidents:	F. K. DAVIES, E. V. FRY, G. R. GRIGS and J. B. SWEET

Hon. Chairman:	R. A. LISSENDEN
Hon. Secretary:	P. DAVIES
Hon. Treasurer:	J. REDGATE
Hon. Managing Editor, "The Railway Observer"	D. B. BIRD
Hon. Publications Officer:	A. R. WOOD, 11 Suffield Close, Long Stratton, Norfolk NR15 2JL, England

---

The objects of the Society are to extend interest in railways and to afford members every opportunity of studying all aspects of railway and locomotive working.

The Society's activities include visits throughout the year to motive power depots, works and other centres of railway interest, rail tours, lectures, film displays, etc., and many other facilities. There are branches throughout Great Britain.

Every member receives the Society's monthly illustrated magazine, *The Railway Observer* which, in addition to articles, has the latest locomotive news and notes.

The affiliated societies afford facilities to members, particularly to those visiting countries abroad.

The Hon. Publications Officer invites new volunteer authors and readers with interesting subjects for future books to contact him.

Applications for membership, accompanied by a stamped addressed envelope, should be sent to Mr. T. J. Edgington, 20 Baker Street, York, YO3 7AX.

Readers seeking copies of our out-of-print books are invited to contact our Hon. Librarian at 17 Raisins Hill, Pinner, Middlesex HA5 2BU for assistance.